# THE
# IMAGINATION
# CHALLENGE

## STRATEGIC FORESIGHT AND INNOVATION
## IN THE GLOBAL ECONOMY

ALEXANDER
MANU

The Imagination Challenge:
Points of Departure for Strategic Creativity and Innovation
Alexander Manu

New Riders
1249 Eighth Street
Berkeley, CA 94710
510/524-2178, 800/283-9444
510/524-2221 (fax)

Find us on the Web at: www.newriders.com
To report errors, please send a note to errata@peachpit.com

New Riders is an imprint of Peachpit, a division of Pearson Education

Senior Executive Editor: Marjorie Baer
Development Editor: Camille Peri
Production Editor: Andrei Pasternak
Indexer: Jack Lewis
Interior Design: Andrei Pasternak
Composition: Maureen Forys, Happenstance Type-O-Rama
Cover Design: Alexander Manu

ISBN 0-321-41365-2

9 8 7 6 5 4 3 2 1

Printed and bound in the United States of America

# Dedication

To Jens Bernsen, who had the foresight to see beyond the obvious at all times.

# Acknowledgements

This book began as an idea, growing more and more through the nourishment of people who generously offered their brilliant knowledge, vision, and insight—people to whom I would like to express my deep appreciation and gratitude:

Marjorie Baer, who approached me after my South by Southwest keynote speech in Austin with the question "Can you write a book about this?" Her belief that these ideas would be of benefit to a larger audience, and her support and guidance in the writing and editing of this book have been invaluable.

Matthew Jones, whose elegant and articulate research perspectives were the basis for this book's articulation of the action research method in action. Matthew has been a traveler on a shared journey, and an invaluable collaborator.

Vanessa Harden, for being the trigger that initiated research into data transfer with her work on cyborgs, sexuality, and data storage. Kelly Seagram, for contributing her precise and thought-provoking analysis on data signals and business intelligence in emerging signals. Shay Steinberg, for her insights into imagination and play, her interview with Mitchel Resnick, and her warmth and contagious enthusiasm.

Joshua Brasse, for his gift as a storyteller, providing the scenarios "The Squared Sense of Touch," "Elephant Shoe," "Playing in the Sandbox," "Demo Quixotic: A Second Life Future Scenario," "University in a Pixel," and "Not What It Seems"; and for eloquently translating sketches of conversations into visual illustrations.

The case studies and ideas presented in Chapters 11, 12, and 13 were generated using adaptive inquiry research methods developed at the Beal Institute for Strategic Creativity at the Ontario College of Art and Design in Toronto, through the dedicated support and ingenuity of my colleagues, who were absolutely essential in shaping the paths we would take and the places we would discover. My thanks to Michelle DesGroseilliers for her strength and foresight, and ability to keep the road ahead clear, as she transformed obstacles into opportunities.

Mathew Lincez, a master of cultural translation, who tagged, linked, and hip-hopped—bridging the dark and the light, the good and the bad, and paving the way for new economic models of empowerment. I owe him my thanks for remaining true to his nature by informing it with lived experiences and for continually provoking and inspiring change.

Bob Logan, Karen King, Catharine MacIntosh, and Greg van Alstyne, for their knowledge, talent, experience, and awareness, and for their extraordinary capacity to share it and use it. Richard (Ricky) Thomas, who devours knowledge and tears up the data field with his mind, for his inspiring and acute analysis of the potentialities in human augmentation and networked behavior systems, and for his contributions to the final chapter. Dave Pollard and John Sutherland at Innova, for their collaboration and insights in developing the economic opportunity filters. My colleagues at the Ontario College of Art and Design: Lenore Richards, who in her tenure as dean of design over the past decade has created an environment in which individual voices, passion, and expertise are seen as a unique and enriching resource; and Ron Shuebrook, an artist and guide, for his wisdom informed by knowledge, compassion, and humanity.

Special thanks to Chris Matthews for contributing his savvy insight and astute observations as author of Chapter 14 of this book. His experience as global marketing manager at Specialized Bicycles in California, as well as our collaboration while Chris was an MBA candidate at the Joseph L. Rotman School of Management, provided valuable insights into the imaginative process.

Many thanks as well to Mitchel Resnick at the MIT Media Lab for generously giving his time and contributing his knowledge to the discussion of Lifelong Kindergarten. His well-articulated passion and dedication to emerging learning models have been exemplary in their consistency over the years and greatly clarified the direction of this book.

Bob Young's permission to remix his ideas and words made it unnecessary to conjure a hypothetical example of possibility engineered. Who better to provide an outstanding real-life example? My thanks to Bob for also seeing early on the potential embedded in the future of inquiry at the Beal Institute.

Any methodology is as great as the people who embrace it in everyday life, and my thanks go to Jaime Borras, senior fellow and senior vice president of advanced technology and innovation at iDEN Mobile Devices, Motorola; Eric Eaton, director of intellectual property strategy at Motorola Mobile Devices; and Katherine Henderson, director of brand marketing and business team leader for premium brands at Whirlpool Canada—for their continual dialogues and support as we pioneered the process of adaptive inquiry, and for their repeated and successful attempts to change the innovation ecology in their organizations.

The voice of this book would have been different without Michele Perras; we have both "spoken" every word written here, and her intelligent humanity, imagination, and creative brilliance allowed both of us to rise to the challenge of transforming ideas into meaningful tools. Whether in the domain of ideas or fine silver, she is a skilled artisan. Her commitment, dedication, and unique ability eased my part in this journey.

Camille Peri edited this book with openness, exuberance, and energy; her expertise in reshaping and polishing the voice of the story, extracting the underlying threads, and always encouraging more clarity and understanding are evident in the final material. Her outstanding ability to mediate between the desires of the writer and the needs of the reader brought clarity and focus to the critical ideas of the book, making her contribution an invaluable one.

Also invaluable were the contributions of Andrei Pasternak, Charlene Will, and Maureen Forys in bringing this book to life in record time and for designing an engaging and inspiring layout. Thanks to Doug Adrianson for his sharp eye and diligence with the text. And to Rebecca Ross and the family at Peachpit Press, many thanks for embracing the ideas in this book early on, and for guiding me through the process.

For their love, patience, and understanding of my absence while present—and even more for their stunning ability to teach, inspire, and allow me to imagine what could be possible—I thank my family: Booboo, Sasha, Sophie, and my father, Herman Manu, who has been a constant polisher of my ideas over time.

Finally, one last thanks, to Nancy Beal Young, whose vision, enthusiasm, and support were integral in creating a place where the collective potential of an exceptional team could flourish. This book is in many ways the result of her belief in that new energy. More than anything, my thanks for getting on the path and not getting off, even when we had to break new ground.

# Contents

# 1

# What if Your Mirror Could Speak?

The Mirror. The object that "sees" you every day—revealing every imperfection, every change in your skin tone, every bump. If you could ask your mirror anything, what would it be? What if the smart mirror of the future could diagnose health problems and keep you up on the latest news?

Imagination is about exploring answers to the question "What if...?" What if every person, place, and object could speak to one another? What would be the subject of their conversations? What if the capacity for transformation was present in each of us? Are you ready for the answers? If so, read on...

# How Did You Get Here?

At dawn on October 12, 1492, a fleet of three ships—the Niña, the Pinta, and the Santa María—reached land for the first time since leaving Spain two months earlier. It was an island in the Bahamas, close to San Salvador, and the people who greeted Columbus—the Taino—called it Guanahani. By all accounts, the Taino lived peacefully—farming, fishing, and trading with the people on nearby islands. To sustain local trade and community, the Taino shared a common language throughout the islands. Their villages were led by the *cacique*, the chief, and advised by the *bohique*, the village shaman.

When Columbus and his men landed, the Taino greeted them with gifts, food, and drink. They had never encountered white men before—fully clothed, bearded, and carrying the grandiose fanfare of the Spanish conquistadors. The two groups managed to establish a common ground for communication, but accounts mention one detail that perplexed the Taino.

"How did you get here?" they asked.

"Well, we traveled on those three big boats that you can see over there," the Spanish men answered.

"What boats do you mean? We can see no boats!"

While their culture was richly developed and articulated, the Taino had no frame of reference for boats of the style, size, and purpose that the Spanish used. The Taino built boats for trade and local travel, but were not competing for economic dominance or trying to establish colonial control over trade routes and territory. They were initially unable to "see" the Spanish ships because they simply had no relevance to what the Taino were accustomed to, and thus no meaning.

"The trickster was asking the Taino to 'see' with their minds in order to be able to see with their eyes. He knew that imagination creates a space for meaning and possibility; one cannot see what one cannot imagine."

The Taino *bohique*—the trickster shaman—contemplated the boats and the Spanish, and said to the villagers, "Close your eyes and I will describe the boats to you." He created a space in their imaginations for the possibility of a boat that big and what it meant. As a medium into hidden possibility, he was asking the Taino to "see" with their minds in order to be able to see with their eyes. He knew that imagination creates a space for meaning and possibility; one cannot see what one cannot imagine.

*The landing of Columbus.* ➜

The Niña, the Pinta, and the Santa María were a new variable in the Taino's environment. But they were unidentifiable "signals," meaningless until the trickster established a space for belief, where that meaning could be constructed and the impact of that possibility considered.

Like the Taino, organizations and people around the world are currently struggling to see and interpret what is in front of them. A fundamental transformation is occurring in the way we create, value, and exchange knowledge. This is fueled, in part, by our changing relationships with technology, as well as our rapidly shifting social values and economies. Our technology is becoming smaller, faster, and smarter, and its integration will soon be ubiquitous—determining different ways of living, learning, communicating, building, and destroying. And each development is rapidly succeeded by something faster or more powerful, receding as quickly as it emerged. As we consumers and designers struggle to keep up with the accelerated pace of change—discarding fax machines as quickly as we adopt Bluetooth—we also struggle with the implications of our actions.

### TECHNOLOGY

the sum of a society's or culture's practical knowledge, especially with reference to its material culture.

We know that these implications will affect everyone. What is more relevant, and more challenging to articulate, is *how*. What kinds of ideas will we choose to inform our current choices and future decisions, such as which technologies we use and which relationships we foster?

The terms of engagement are also changing. People no longer passively accept a new technology, idea, product, or service as it was originally intended. Rather, we increasingly encourage and empower each other to participate in the creation and exchange of knowledge, experience, skill, and ideas—our social capital. As this shift gains momentum around the world, businesses urgently need a new capability to identify the value in this social capital—mapping and extracting the benefit of ideas to billions of people—in order to remain relevant in an evolving social and economic climate.

This book is about imagination and exploring the "What if…?" that could provide those insights.

With more than 20 years of experience as a product development consultant, I have worked with brilliant hardware engineers, savvy marketing people, street-smart buyers for large retail chains, and clever corporate strategists, all uniquely competent in their fields of expertise—and because of that, all at times uniquely unable to see behavior, expectations, and responses to new technologies as components of their work. As a result, I have seen countless inventions shelved and many opportunities missed. This book is an attempt to change that.

Back in 1948, in *Mechanization Takes Command*, Swiss architecture critic Sigfried Giedion called for a new type of creativity in order to maximize the promise of mechanization. "To carry through the mechanizing of production," he wrote, "another class of inventors, another class of doers proved necessary." One may argue that we have now arrived at similar crossroads.

The platform of technologies currently on the threshold of emergence—artificial intelligence (AI), Radio Frequency Identification (RFID), nanotechnology, biotechnology, to name a few—require a different capability to carry through on their promises because the nature of the promises has changed. Rather than asking, "What can this do?" we must now ask, "What else can this be?"

To be clear, the focus of this new capability is not actually on what technology can do, but on what *we* can do with it. And in order to stretch to meet our ultimate capabilities, we must have the courage to be what we dream—as individuals, cultures, businesses, and organizations. While our social institutions may restrict and discourage the cultivation of courage or curiosity—as they are too invested in maintaining the status quo—our desire for it as people is real. Our passion for it is real. As further illustrated in the chapters ahead, we only need the tools and the understanding of how to use them. Like the Taino, we need a trickster—a medium into the possibilities of any experience.

## MODERN-DAY TRICKSTERS

One of the oldest archetypes in human history is the trickster—the catalytic shape-shifter. The trickster first emerged in the visual record more than 17,000 years ago as a shamanic bird-man in the caves at Lascaux, and has since appeared as a fundamental character in every culture around the world. As animals, deities, spirits, or cultural heroes, tricksters fuel our mythology, inspiring invention and innovation. Whether appearing as a raven on the Pacific coast or a gnome in Lower Saxony, the trickster's longevity as an archetype lies in its capability for adaptation and transformation, appearing when perceptions and values are outmoded, close-minded, or irrelevant.

"People such as George Lucas, Peter Jackson, and Steven Spielberg are Chief Possibility Officers whom we have elected to create extraordinary journeys. When we pay to see their films, we engage in an imaginative contract with them, agreeing to suspend our disbelief for the duration of the experience."

As the creators and narrators of stories, tricksters extend the possibilities of our imagination, often by rebelling against normal expectations and values to uncover new meaning and knowledge. The Taino *bohique* narrated a new story, with Spanish ships and a distant land, of men who had different values, ambitions, experiences, and knowledge. The role of the trickster is to tear down old frameworks in our imagination and the imagination of our society, and foster frameworks for new possibilities in experience and meaning.

> "As the creators and narrators of stories, tricksters extend the possibilities of our imagination, often by rebelling against normal expectations and values to uncover new meaning and knowledge."

The modern-day trickster tends to thrive in the social spaces that can fully support it—particular disciplines like the arts or professional sports. Hollywood is the best known of these, where the modern experts of fantasy and myth make their magic. In this sense, we could say that people such as George Lucas, Peter Jackson, and Steven Spielberg are Chief Possibility Officers whom we have elected to create extraordinary journeys. When we pay to see their films, we engage in an imaginative contract with them, agreeing to suspend our disbelief for the duration of the experience—and sometimes beyond it. Such a contract might read like this:

> *"This is a story about the lands of Middle Earth, where the Dark Lord Sauron forged the Ring of Power to control all the creatures of Middle Earth. Taken from him in an epic battle, The Ring fell into the hands of a Hobbit, Bilbo Baggins. Unable to resist his power, Bilbo passes The Ring on to Frodo Baggins, along with the only task available: to destroy the Ring of Power. Frodo begins a dangerous journey through the lands of Middle Earth with a Fellowship that will protect him on his mission to destroy The Ring in the only place it can be destroyed: the fires of Mount Doom."*

Once engaged in this contract, we expect both the promise of the story and a compelling delivery. The people who offer this promise have recognized the trickster capability within themselves, nurturing it to its fullest possibility. But they are simply a few of the best known tricksters in our midst. In reality, each one of us has the potential to discover and use the trickster capability as a medium into the creation of new and meaningful experiences. We are most inclined to recognize and use this capability when undergoing major changes and transitions in our lives; when things seem most uncertain, we are more likely to open ourselves up to imagining *what might be*. We are tricksters when we allow ourselves to imagine

*The trickster, one of the oldest archetypes in human history.* ➔

our possibility. What I propose in the pages that follow is a means to recognize this capability in ourselves and in our organizations, as something that can be cultivated, nurtured, and applied.

## FINDING OUR INNER TRICKSTERS

One of my earliest childhood recollections is of my grandmother ironing one day, softly humming a Yiddish song. My sister walked into the room and excitedly announced, "The Russians just sent the first cosmonaut into space. His name is Yuri Gagarin." Grandmother interrupted her humming and asked, "Is this good for the Jews?"

Grandmother imagined what this event could mean for the Russians and the space race, as well as to her community, her family, and herself. She established the relevant connections that included both the endless prospects for mankind and the intimate implications at her dinner table, or in her neighborhood. The potential of these connections gave meaning to Yuri Gagarin in my grandmother's eyes.

"To see possibility and create a space where possibility can emerge, we must become tricksters ourselves, engaging in the story that translates the information around us into imaginative potential."

Meaning is our fuel for being—we are meaning-making machines. Constantly forming schemas and structures around our experiences, we actively construct the ethical values that direct our goals, choices, and behaviors. The choices we make in assigning meaning and value define who we are. Like my grandmother, we ask, "What does this mean to me, to *my* life?"

However, sometimes our vision and capability are clouded by expectations, habits, or fears, and we are unable to comprehend or adapt to what something means. This "new thing" on the horizon is meaningless—we don't know how to see what it represents, what it could be, how it will affect us, or our friends or families. Like the Taino, we cannot see the boats even though they are right in front of our eyes.

To see possibility and create a space where possibility can emerge, we must become tricksters ourselves, engaging in the story that translates the information around us into imaginative potential. For example, when considering the headline "NASA Takes Google on Journey into Space," we must ask and be able to answer the questions "Is this good for our organization?" and "What could it mean for us?" Both the questions and their answers are a compass pointing to new possibilities.

How do we rediscover this capability in ourselves—as individuals, organizations, and societies? I propose that imagination is the key. Like the Taino, we must allow for the opportunity of new narrative, as stories create a space where anything is possible. When our mind is at play, we do not worry about the logical constraints of reality. Through our belief, we all become tricksters narrating the possibility of a person, a place, or a technology, participating and performing as the story unravels.

# Why Imagination?

Imagination is often mistakenly considered the same as creativity, but there is an important difference: Imagination suggests ideas resulting from freedom of thought, while creativity suggests some actual aspect of creation, even if only in concept. Likewise, there is a distinction between invention and innovation: The former is the creation of something new; the latter is getting further ahead because of it.

> **IMAGINATION**
>
> 1. the ability to form images and ideas in the mind, especially of things never seen or never experienced directly.
>
> 2. the part of the mind where ideas, thoughts, and images are formed.

The primary challenge of the Industrial Age was an example of the innovation: to simply mechanize everything that had once been handcrafted. Electricity was developed, structured, and integrated to speed things up or make them more powerful. Over the course of time, the product archetype changed very slowly—a blender was still a blender, whether it was hand-powered or electric. However, when we began to develop electronic and then digital technologies, and then add them to our electrified objects, the business model shifted toward greater product innovation. Users had greater opportunity to choose between multiple products offering the same function, with each product expressing a different aesthetic or demographic. This multiplicity of choice then pressured companies to deliver a competitive advantage.

The skill required to move the mechanical artifact into the electrical age was a learnable one, and so was the skill required to move electronic platforms into digital. This was pure product innovation, with direct cost reduction benefits on the side of the maker, and a modicum of functional or price benefits for the user.

The progression from one technology phase to the next required technical skill, creativity, and capability, but little imagination. Creativity drove the desire for innovation, but imagination was left to advertising agencies, which were charged with branding a product with core values—or, like the Taino trickster before them, creating a space in the user's imagination for the possibility of something never seen before, and what it meant.

"The status quo requires tactics, while the exploration of possibility requires a strategic vision. Strategic vision is more difficult to measure, and its rewards, however great, may lie beyond the horizon."

In the early 1920s, the question was simple: "What else can we use the electric motor for?" The answers: electric blenders, electric hair dryers, electric irons, electric waffle makers, and so on. This was the model of the innovation company, an entity built on advancing technology as it was being tactically applied to archetypes from the mechanical age. Keeping up with innovations in technology was all that was necessary.

Today a common question asked in research-and-development departments around the world is equally simple: "What else can we use RFID tags for?" However, the parameters of the dilemma are quite different: There are very few archetypes that express the potential capabilities of "smart tags." It isn't just a matter of speeding up an existing function. The answer requires a new model of innovation and a new type of corporation—one that is capable and ready to establish new archetypes.

This new capability requires strategic creativity—the ability to use imagination to develop new and original ideas for a strategic purpose—but most of all it requires the prerequisite for creativity: imagination, both as a capability to be learned and as an attitude to be nourished.

Why Imagination? Because creativity is no longer enough; creativity can only add value. Corporations need imagination to *create value* and answer the questions challenging them:

✦ What can we dream about?

✦ How far can we dream?

✦ How can we make these dreams a reality?

## WHAT DRIVES IMAGINATION?

In 1896, Guglielmo Marconi successfully completed the first point-to-point communication of a wireless signal, two kilometers across the Salisbury Plain in England. He followed the next year with a transmission over water to Flat Holm Island, from Lavernock Point in South Wales. These events were enough to ignite the imagination of the press, which erupted with a plethora of prophecies, each more outrageous than the last. Or were they?

In *Imagining Tomorrow: History, Technology, and the American Future,* edited by Joseph Corn, Susan Douglas summed up the predictions made in the early 1900s about the future of radio: "Love and life will be 'perfected' as wireless communication will ease loneliness and isolation." Douglas quotes a *New York Times* prediction that "wireless telegraphy will make a father on the old New England farm and his son in Seattle neighbors."

*Century Magazine* also made this stunning prediction in 1901:

> "If a person wanted to call to a friend he knew not where, he would call in a very loud electromagnetic voice, heard by him who had the electromagnetic ear, silent to him who had it not. 'Where are you?' he would say. A small reply would come 'I am at the bottom of a coal mine, or crossing the Andes, or in the middle of the Atlantic.'"

This was a vision of technological augmentation before nanotechnology, before the microchip. Before the technological capability was present, the desire emerged.

**"In case after case, we find that it is behavior—our latent need to fulfill our life's goals—that drives us to understand the far-reaching potential of new and otherwise 'disruptive' innovations."**

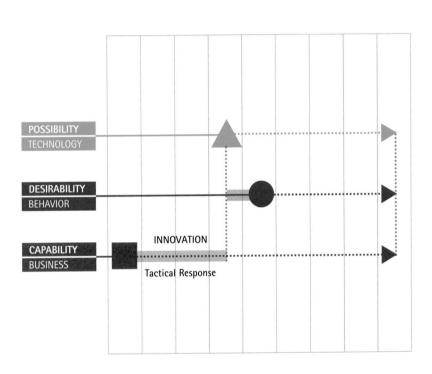

POSSIBILITY
TECHNOLOGY

DESIRABILITY
BEHAVIOR

CAPABILITY
BUSINESS

INNOVATION

Tactical Response

This raises the legitimate question: What comes first? Is it behavior—our desire for a better life triggered by the possibilities of current technology—that in turn triggers the development of new capabilities? Or does technology follow its own path, imposing itself on us and determining our lives?

The press's enthusiastic acceptance and fearless predictions about the new technology suggest that behavior was indeed the key motivator—that a better life with better possibilities was desired. However, business and government did not share this enthusiasm. Maintaining the status quo is a tempting proposition, especially in the face of the unknown. The status quo requires tactics—short-term solutions to an existing problem—while the exploration of possibility requires a strategic vision—the ability to develop long-term ideas and solutions to something completely new. Strategic vision is more difficult to measure, and its rewards, however great, may lie beyond the horizon.

> **LATENT NEED**
>
> the need to satisfy the latent goals of love, esteem, and self-actualization, which are accessible to the conscious mind but not consciously expressed. We permanently seek the conditions that will allow these needs to be realized.

A vision of the future may be seen as an escape from the problems we face every day, but is also a manifestation of hope and the formation of a new goal that then becomes a need. In case after case, we find that it is behavior—our latent need to fulfill our life's goals—that drives us to imagine and understand the far-reaching potential of new and otherwise "disruptive" innovations. Sometimes this drive is pursued with too much optimistic fervor, but at all times it leads business, government, and other capability-building entities by decades. The alignment of desire, possibility, and capability is rare, but it happens. It happened in 1961.

## SHOOTING FOR THE MOON

On May 25, 1961, in a Special Message to the Congress on Urgent National Needs, President John F. Kennedy declared the following ambitious goal: "I believe that this nation should commit itself to achieving the goal, before this decade is out, of landing a man on the moon and returning him safely to the earth."

His declaration was an expression of desire, both visionary and competitive, in an era of Cold War politics and Soviet space supremacy. Desire to believe in the possibility of technology was what would drive the technology itself and the United States' capability to deliver on this goal, as well

← *The limits of the tactical response.*

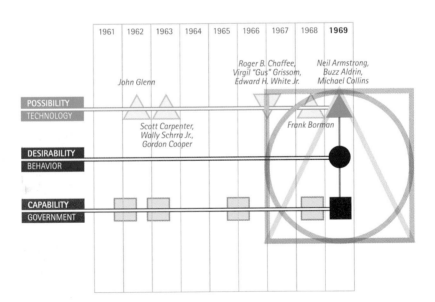

as enthralling the imagination of American culture. If we put the three elements required to meet this challenge—technology, desire, and capability—on a timeline, we would see that in 1961, desire far surpassed both the technology available and the capability of the infrastructure. Yet when President Kennedy defined this task as "urgent," he created a space for belief in the minds of those around him, and the goal suddenly became a priority need for the U.S. government.

"In 1961, desire far surpassed both the technology available and the capability of the infrastructure. Yet when President Kennedy defined this task as 'urgent,' he created a space for belief in the minds of those around him, and the goal suddenly became a priority need for the U.S. government."

Where did this desire emanate from? Was it to satisfy what psychologist Abraham Maslow defined as the universal need for love and esteem—to foster belonging and status in the eyes of the public? Or to satisfy what Maslow called the need for safety, to create and maintain security in the context of the geopolitical realities of the 1960s? Both.

In a memo to Vice President Lyndon Johnson the month before, Kennedy had posed this question: "Do we have a chance of beating the Soviets by putting a laboratory in space, or by a trip around the moon, or by a rocket to land on the moon, or by a rocket to go to the moon and back with a man? Is there any other space program which promises dramatic results in which we could win?" And so Kennedy's desire for esteem—for himself and what he represented—set in motion a goal that resulted in one of the most celebrated technological achievements in American history.

In 1961, the desire was all there was. The technology was sketchy; it had not been tested extensively, and numerous satellite launch failures had occurred at Cape Canaveral, Florida. The necessary governmental capability—NASA—was in its infancy, formed just a few years earlier. The gap between possibility, capability, and desire could not have been greater considering the time limit Kennedy imposed. And yet the goal gave the push, and the technological possibility followed, led by an infrastructure capability that grew through success as well as catastrophic failures.

NASA embraced Kennedy's challenge. Project Apollo became its consuming passion and, at a cost of $25.4 billion, one of the most significant expenditures ever undertaken by the American government. On July 20, 1969, it also became one of humanity's historic achievements. "That's one small step for man, one giant leap for mankind," said astronaut Neil

← *Aligning desire, technology, and capability: the timeline of the Project Apollo space program.*

Armstrong as he set foot on the moon. His statement signified the fulfillment of Kennedy's challenge and the temporary alignment of desire, possibility, and capability.

## THE IMAGINATION GAP

*Everyone takes the limits of his own vision for the limits of the world.*
—philosopher Arthur Schopenhauer

In the nearly four decades since Kennedy's challenge was met, the occasions have been rare when such alignments have had a similar scope of influence. Instead, emerging technologies have exposed a widening gap in many organizations, individuals, and cultures—a gap between what we are currently capable of and what is possible. We are adept at understanding our current capabilities, yet we do not often explore "What if...?" and guide our actions toward what we see. We are surrounded by advanced technologies and innovative practices, yet few of us see and pursue them beyond their immediate application.

"The Internet explosion and dot-com bubble, eBay, Amazon, RedHat, Google—what organizations saw their emerging potential? Who sees the possibilities of remix culture, MMORPGs, Web 2.0 technologies, and so on?"

I call this the *imagination gap*. In this book, I will define methods and behaviors for bridging this gap and aligning ourselves with capability and possibility.

> **IMAGINATION GAP**
> the gap between current capability and future possibility.

To recognize when the imagination gap exists is difficult, and to recognize, as well as admit, a missed opportunity that stems from it is even more so. However, in an October 2005 memo, Ray Ozzie, Microsoft's former chief technology officer (now chief software architect) did so in reference to his company's failure to lead in the development of Voice over Internet Protocol (VoIP), the technology that enables phone calls via broadband Internet connections.

> *"While we've led with great capabilities in Messenger & Communicator, it was Skype, not us, who made VoIP broadly popular and created a new category. We have long understood the importance of mobile messaging scenarios and have made significant investment in device software, yet only now are we surpassing the Blackberry."*

His was a courageous admission of both the existence of the imagination gap and Microsoft's failure to bridge it. Time and time again, we see this. The Internet explosion and dot-com bubble, eBay, Amazon, RedHat, Google—what other organizations saw beyond their emerging potential? Who sees beyond the obvious possibilities of RFID, remix culture, Massively Multiplayer Online Role Playing Games (MMORPGs), Web 2.0 technologies, and so on? What organizations are ready to pursue new capabilities in order to deliver on the possibilities that these technologies represent?

Author Arthur C. Clarke once suggested that the very people who invent technologies are often the ones to miss their full possibilities. Clarke calls it a "failure of nerve"—that even when given all the relevant facts, one cannot see that "they point to an inescapable conclusion." While JFK sought to align desire, possibility, and capability—addressing a single, visionary goal—Clarke suggested that we must understand the multiple meanings and implications of innovation. His words are both an intellectual challenge and a challenge to our courage, sensitivity, and imagination.

In *Profiles of the Future: An Inquiry Into the Limits of the Possible*, Clarke wrote:

> "Without going into technical details (of interest largely to those who can already think of the answers) the time will come when we will be able to call a person anywhere on Earth, merely by dialing a number. He will be located automatically, whether he is in mid ocean, in the heart of a great city, or crossing the Sahara. This device alone may change the patterns of society and commerce as greatly as the telephone, its primitive ancestor, has already done. Its perils and disadvantages are obvious; there are no wholly beneficial inventions. Yet think of the countless lives it would save, the tragedies and heartbreaks it would avert. No one need ever again be lost, for a simple position- and direction-finding device could be incorporated in the receiver on the principle of today's radar navigational aids. And in case of danger or accident, help could be summoned merely by pressing an 'Emergency' button."

Clarke has more or less described the current capabilities of a cell phone and a range of possible behaviors that it would affect and reveal. Given the seeming omnipresence of mobile phones today, we can relate quite easily to his ideas. But imagine reading this in 1961, a full 12 years before the first prototype of a cell phone was released, and the depth of vision is extraordinary. The desirability was expressed; once the technology and capability became aligned, we were given the cell phone.

# The Imagination Challenge

*If we learn to see, then there is no end to the new worlds of our vision.*
—Carlos Castaneda

As we discussed earlier, the challenge for product development and innovation in the Industrial Age was to extend the limits of technology—by improving how things were made, what they were made of, or the capabilities of the machine that made them. These were logical, technical limitations, and they were eventually transcended by technological innovation.

In the current cultural and technological paradigm, the development model calls for something different. It calls for understanding and mapping of behavior—understanding the current limits of knowledge and wisdom, as well as the limits of people and their environment. This is not a technical challenge, nor is it a tactical one; it is a strategic challenge to our limits as humans and to our desire to transform them into possibility. This is the Imagination Challenge.

Technology is a medium into the unseen possibilities of any experience. The Imagination Challenge, as detailed throughout this book, encourages individuals and corporations to create the indispensable condition required to deliver the promise of new technologies—the ecology of play. By generating a new network of concept makers and business leaders, the Imagination Challenge will redefine the role of technology—not as the cause for meaning and purpose, but as the method for how to achieve them.

## If Toothbrushes Could Talk

Imagine for a moment that your toothbrush could speak. What would you like to know? What sort of questions would you ask?

"Do I have any cavities?"

"Am I healthy?"

Suddenly one question leads to a stream of others, and a floodgate opens. And these questions are powerful—they do not ask us to consider how to make a better toothbrush, but to consider what else a toothbrush could be. As triggers directing us toward new outcomes, imaginative questions enable us to engage in seemingly trivial conversations with all seriousness. And the answers could lead to the most powerful frontline diagnostic tool in the home.

I propose that challenges to imagination are the keys to creativity, and the skill of retrieving imagination resides in the mastery of play. The search for a meaningful and relevant future starts by reclaiming play as an ageless and indispensable condition of every human being. The ecology of play and imagination is the ecology of possibility; a space free of the boundaries of day-to-day logic and constraints, where we can dream—embarking on a journey through Middle Earth with a couple of friends, or landing a human on the moon.

## RELEASED BY IMAGINATION

Visualize a chessboard. Eight rows of eight cells in alternating rank and file—sometimes wood, sometimes marble, sometimes a combination of pixels. Thirty-two pieces, 16 to a side, poised for the opening move. The game unfolds on the board, the movement of each piece limited by the type and range of motion it can perform: Rook moves horizontal and vertical, bishop moves diagonal, and so on. You seek to win using strategies and tactics that transcend these limits in movement.

You are bound by the architecture of the board and the rules of the game, and by your own ability to maximize future play. A good chess player can see 15 or more moves into the future with one strategy, which must then be tailored and adapted with each subsequent move by his opponent. Despite the constraints of the board and the range of motion for each piece, the opportunities are astounding; it has been estimated that there are more possible games of chess than there are atoms in the universe. The range of possibility is almost infinite when we understand the strategic relationship that develops between opponents.

"By aligning his rational thinking with intuition, feeling, continual learning, and adaptation, Garry Kasparov adjusted his play to maximize his own capability in the context of the game. This intentional flexibility creates a new mental space—a temporary play space."

In 1996, then World Chess Champion Garry Kasparov faced off in a match against IBM's Deep Blue. Over the six-game series, IBM programmers adapted Deep Blue's code in an attempt to match Kasparov's intuition, pattern recognition, responsiveness, learning capability, and passion during play—the key qualities that differentiated human and AI capabilities at that time. (Since then, AI advances have ensured an almost certain win for the computer.) But the programmers could not adapt the computer's behavior to secure a victory over Kasparov; although Deep Blue won the first game, Kasparov won the following three and drew two. Why? Strategic foresight.

By aligning his rational thinking with intuition, feeling, continual learning, and adaptation, Kasparov adjusted his play to maximize his own capability in the context of the game. It is the difference between *forecast* and *foresight*; the difference between estimating your adversary's next move and thinking, imagining, and shaping the future.

The formal architecture of the game is a platform, while the variable pieces are in a constant state of transition, and success depends on adapting behavior, intent, and expectation to each event. This intentional flexibility creates a new mental space—a temporary play space—that has structure and rules yet supports unlimited exploration and undiscovered potential. But this potential becomes apparent only to the player with strategic foresight.

### TEMPORARY PLAY SPACE

a mental construct formed when we engage in any kind of compelling narrative or play behavior; a flexible platform for the exploration of imaginative possibility. At times, the TPS framework is provided and we need only to engage—such as when watching a film or reading a novel. At other times, we must create the framework ourselves, such as when we play chess or create a castle from a refrigerator box.

The temporary play space is the trickster's domain—and the best chess players are tricksters in action. Problems become opportunities to ask imaginative questions that can unfold new strategies or capabilities. While there are contexts and codes that support the game, the only limits are the limits of their imaginations.

# Interpreting the Signals

While everyone is not a grand chess master, we all possess the potential to see the signals around us and explore the "What if...?" We naturally sense that there may be other possibilities in a particular context, and yet we have been effectively trained to ignore all but the most empirical and immediate signals, or new information. Why?

There seems to be a current cultural consensus that the signals present in emerging behaviors such as blogging or innovations such as VoIP are "weak," and so we will interpret their meaning after they have matured or ripened. (I discuss this and Igor Ansoff's Weak Signal Theory in more depth in Chapter 7.) This relationship assumes that we all have the capability to receive and contextualize information, as long as the signal is strong and clear.

## SIGNALS

the representation of an emerging behavior or technology that disrupts the status quo. Signals have four distinct attributes:

*precise:* the dimensions of the opportunity are exact, accurate, and detailed. The precise phase of a disruptive innovation usually aggregates and obsolesces predecessors. In benefits terms it is an enhancement.

*undeniable:* the opportunity is real, cannot be ignored or refused, and it shows the potential for high impact.

*intuitive:* the opportunity can be defined but it has multiple manifestation possibilities. In the course of time, these possibilities will change.

*sensed:* there is awareness of possibility in the signal. It has multiple, yet undefined strategic opportunity directions.

But what if something different is true—that our ability to receive and understand a signal is more significant than a signal's intensity? What is the relationship between a signal and the rest of the world, and what is our relationship with it? How do we constrain and direct our interpretation and understanding? Our success or failure to recognize the meaning and relevance of signals is contingent on how agile and insightful we strive to be. But most of all, it depends on strategic foresight: our capability to construct images of the future with the tools of the present.

Whenever we come across a new technology or service, it has the potential to change our behavior as we negotiate new interactions with it. This shift in our normal behavior may be subtle or explicit, such as using a mobile phone to create a short film. Depending on how receptive we are, however, we may overlook potential implications of the product or service beyond that moment.

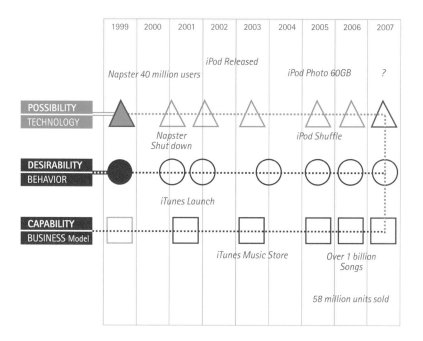

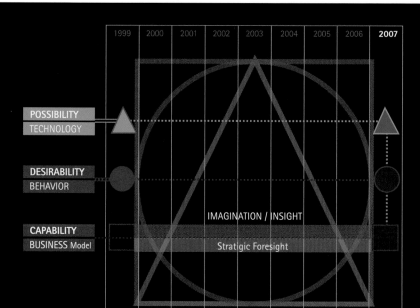

When Napster exploded into mainstream culture, most organizations and media sources initially saw it as a means to bypass the music industry's existing purchasing structure—a digital extension of the mix tape within an "underground" community. And at first, this was the precise extent of Napster's impact. But Napster also revealed a deeper desire among people to create and share a mobile digital music library. This desire then became a need, and the need required new technologies and social behaviors as sustenance, leading to massively accepted peer-to-peer (P2P) networks, iTunes, iPods, and the MP3 revolution—anything that would enable a user to create, maintain, and collaborate on an ever-evolving compendium of immediate, personalized content. Napster's format allowed for the fast, cheap, and accessible exchange of music, and this exchange quickly expanded to include all forms of digital content, from top-down organization to bottom-up emergence, remix to mashup. People established relationships and built communities based on the quality, type, and purpose of the content they were exchanging, and Internet-mediated platforms such as MySpace, Wikipedia, and Del.icio.us were born and continue to flourish.

"Napster revealed a deeper desire among people to create and share a mobile digital music library. This desire then became a need, and the need required new technologies and social behaviors."

In 1999, an astute observer probably would have sensed that the desire to download music would contribute to a social media explosion, Web 2.0 technologies, and a redefinition of social exchange and social capital. But it would have been extremely difficult to track its exact trajectory, unless he or she pursued the question "What if...?"

# Why We Need to Unlearn

As discussed earlier, our culture has systematically discouraged imaginative pursuits and play except in controlled circumstances such as professional sports or the arts. Our schools and governments teach the limits and rewards of rational behavior, encouraging tactics and logic rather than strategy and play. But without play, the imagination withers away. We can remedy this loss by recovering our imagination—a recovery that begins with unlearning what we have been taught.

← *Napster's impact: from music exchange to social media explosion.*

Unlearning allows for the discovery and framing of powerful questions, and the ability to explore our imagination without expectation or inhibition. These questions create a space where possibility can exist, where every signal that emerges is an opportunity to map possibility for the future of business, technology, or society.

"The need for unlearning is proportional to our new capacity for imaginative pursuits. We need to unlearn in order to believe in possibility, in order to explore unseen opportunities."

These maps already exist throughout our culture—as a space not bound by rationality but by imagination. Music, literature, theatre, and film are a few of the platforms that draw us in and engage us, allowing us to understand with our hearts as well as our minds. In any of these areas, we enter into an imaginative contract that is fulfilled when we find meaning in the experience that resonates in our own lives. The challenge is to extend this behavior beyond these areas and our comfortable limits, to see what else the contract could be.

The need for unlearning is proportional to our new capacity for imaginative pursuits. We need to unlearn in order to believe in possibility, in order to explore unseen opportunities. We see examples of this every day. Though we have learned that one cannot produce products before establishing a need, we all know 1,000 products and services that would have never been introduced if we had followed the classic value-chain process of need identification, starting with the inaccurate and misleading consumer focus group.

*"We don't need this."*

*"No one will use this."*

*"It is naïve to think people will walk and talk on the phone at the same time."*

*"No one needs more than 640K of memory."*

Learning is at times about limits, and limits prevent us from being imaginative about possibility. Unlearning opens us up to the new. We needed to unlearn that music is meant to be listened to while sitting in a chair or being in a group of people. We needed to unlearn that we need to be connected to the wall while talking on the phone. We needed to unlearn in order to see it as "normal" to have a camera and a cell phone as one and the same product.

What do we believe could be possible?

*"One day people will walk and listen to their own play list on a device hanging from their neck."*

*"One day a surgeon in Texas will operate on a patient in Alaska."*

We need to unlearn what we are told that people want.

# Mapping Possibility

Imagine three parallel timelines. On the first, place technology; on the second, user behavior; and on the third, the organization that can deliver the technology to the user. Technology represents possibility. Behavior holds the motivation and wish to use that possibility, and also represents desirability. Organization—government, business, and so on—holds the infrastructural capability to deliver and sustain possibility.

"Organizations attempt to 'monetize' new technology through tactical developments, patents, or copyright. However, technology cannot be monetized. It is the use of technology by people—behavior—that can be monetized."

As we have seen, the capabilities of organizations often lag behind both advances in technology and the latent needs that emerge from them. For convenience, some term new technologies as "disruptive" or "weak signals" because their immediate impact is seen as peripheral or their significance is misunderstood. But when the signals are seen as accelerators of profound transformation, organizations rush into a tactical frenzy to bridge the gap between desirability and capability. This is frequently reactive, perpetuating the too little, too late approach to innovative evolution.

Through this approach, organizations attempt to "monetize" new technology through tactical developments, patents, or copyright—catching the latest lucrative wave. However, this approach doesn't address the critical factor in innovation or invention: Technology itself cannot be monetized. It is the use of technology by people—behavior—that can be monetized.

## STRATEGIC CAPITAL

the excess of an organization's future possibility over its current capability; indicates the organization's ability to remain relevant in an evolving social and economic ecology. Strategic capital is defined by three measures:

*hindsight:* the ability to evaluate technologies within the context of associated behaviors.

*insight:* the ability to recognize these behaviors as signals of latent human needs.

*foresight:* the ability to translate this understanding into strategic opportunity.

A strategic approach calls for the mapping of each new possibility and its pending behavioral desirability. As JFK did with the space program, we must align corporate strategy and business models with the shifting landscapes of technology and behavior. This alignment itself is strategic foresight and its chief tool is the imagination. The outcome of this process is the creation of strategic capital. The art of discovering and maximizing strategic capital is called *strategic creativity.*

## STRATEGIC CREATIVITY

the art of discovering and amplifying the three key components of strategic capital—hindsight, insight, and foresight—in order to leverage specific core capabilities of an individual or organization; redefines and creates products, services, and systems that realign people's needs and desires with the possibilities of new technology and the capabilities of organizations.

Corporations need to cultivate imagination in their concept-making activities to ensure their prosperity and continued integration into the social, economic, and cultural landscape. Today very few corporations have objectives in imagination—in fostering environments that trigger the imaginative process and imaginative behaviors. However, effective business change is not accomplished by fitting strategic creativity to business, but by fitting business to strategic creativity.

The necessary intervention to accomplish this is our Imagination Challenge. We cannot go along simply improving existing technology. By now we have motorized, electrified, and digitized almost everything—our challenge today is to define new strategic directions for technology. This is purely a challenge of imagination.

We have no excuse to fail here.

The Imagination Challenge proposes a set of tools for strategic creativity, for strategically applying the benefits and value of imaginative pursuits. Illustrated as a string of research- and concept-generation activities, they aim at generating new economic models that create or reshape organizational strategy. Strategic creativity is both a capability to be learned—a "how to"—and a discipline—a "what." Its processes define the concerns, conceptualize the possibilities, and create the methodologies that can effectively manage the creation of future technology applications and products, systems, communications, services, and environments.

## WHO SHOULD READ THIS BOOK?

Is this book for managers or academics? Both. We believe that business managers and the academic audience will find value in an infusion of impetus, new ideas, and methods. The future will be shaped by the imaginative mind and a new ecology of learning—free of barriers, fears, and inhibitions. And that future is now.

# Engineering Possibility

*Creativity represents a miraculous coming together of the uninhibited energy of the child with its apparent opposite and enemy, the sense of order imposed on the disciplined adult intelligence.*

—author Norman Podhoretz

One would be hard pressed to describe as "work" the daily activities of Michael Faraday, the man who invented the electric motor in 1821. Few of his daily tasks fell under what we would consider the definition, behavior, or process of work. However, all fit within the characteristics of play and play behavior. Faraday spent his days building and experimenting with devices simply for the sake of exploring "What if...?"

Faraday's invention of the electric motor was the classical result of play: There was no obvious monetary or practical value immediately apparent, and yet it provided the curious and the contemplative with a platform for exploration. His discoveries and subsequent writings about them triggered the imagination of his colleagues and competitors, inspiring them to try to define the opportunities the device might yield.

I have proposed that most invention comes out of play. Play behavior and play ecology are necessities to invention, and the willingness to suspend reality—another characteristic of play—is necessary during the process of evaluation. For years after the invention of the electric light bulb, it was demonstrated as "entertainment" at country fairs, along with giant vegetables, prize-winning pigs, and other exhibits that were extraordinary and beyond the constraints of people's daily life. In many respects, the archaic county fair was the temporary play space for the popular acceptance of the electric light bulb.

"The Millenial Generation is play-wise and play-ready, and it will bring this expectation and capability to the workplace. Organizations have the unique opportunity to direct this generation's expertise toward strategies that will lead to massive innovation."

From this understanding of invention as play, we can deduce two important points. The first is the need for companies engaged in innovation to create an ecology of play. The second is related to the crucial role of the mastery of play.

The Millenial Generation—anyone born after 1980—has engaged in play patterns that far exceed those of other generations in their complexity and diversity. Computers and digital technologies have always been present in their lives, in multiple venues and multiple platforms. They invest endless hours in play—and play is the primary reward. They are play-wise and play-ready, and they will bring this expectation and capability to the workplaces of the future. However, many organizations are managed by people born long before 1980. Rather than looking at Millenials as a threat to established methods, organizations have the unique opportunity to direct their expertise toward strategies that will lead to massive innovation and permanently redraw the value chain.

The ecology of work is determined by outcomes and outputs; it contends that people must engage in a sequence of tasks directed toward a specific outcome in order to achieve it. I argue that work is ruled by process, and further, that process kills imagination. At every step in a process, the individual is less concerned with the value of the task and more concerned with accomplishing it within time and other constraints.

The ecology of play is free, separate from daily life, uncertain in its outcomes, unproductive in "productivity" benchmarks and terms of reference, and make-believe. We do not question its motives nor do we question its outcomes. While at play, we do not expect to gain status; satisfaction comes purely from participating in a flow of imaginative and insightful moments. In it, no activity feels like a task. Work tasks can be accomplished in mediocre ways, but play will never accept mediocrity because then it would no longer be satisfying.

The Imagination Challenge requires that we create a new ecology for possibility within organizations, an ecology that is not superficial—colorful furniture, funny toys, and the ubiquitous pool table—but deep, at the human level, affecting the way we think and discover meaning, purpose, and relevance. The imaginative ecology is populated by dreamers as well as builders of dreams—their complementary capabilities are both needed. We need to treat imagination as something that merits the full-time commitment of individuals and the corporation.

# Points of Departure

How do we construct such an ecology of possibility? How do we translate the concepts of strategic creativity into our work lives? Later chapters in this book provide a practical guide to doing so. Chapter 11 is a workbook of adaptive action research methods that guide the pursuit of possibility. This chapter shows how to develop a flexible perspective that cultivates and stimulates possibility through repeating cycles of inquiry, reflection, and analysis, followed by collaborative review. To accurately foster this perspective, the research methods themselves must exercise the same flexibility and acceptance toward ideas and signals generated during the research process.

One platform for this exploration is future scenarios, which can shift our perspectives toward the possibility of new behaviors and help us understand the new and unexplored meaning of signals. Untethered by the weights of logic, reason, and expectation, we can imagine anything in these stories. Much as Arthur Clarke's vision of cell phones didn't address technical details, future scenarios move our focus away from the practicality of tangible, mechanical devices, and toward the possibility of devices that are driven by behavior.

> **FUTURE SCENARIO**
>
> a story about people and how they interact with daily life, chores, and objects; describes interactions with technologies, products, and services that do not yet exist; describes *possibility.*

Most people do not understand the specific technical coding of VoIP—how it is structured or where it is flawed—yet they understand how it meets or does not meet their needs, and how it affects their behavior and relationships with others. Similarly, future scenarios focus on using a tool or a technology to fulfill a certain behavior, personal desire, or social need. When you think about a toothbrush speaking to you, you do not think about how this is possible. You do not question whether or technology is available and applicable, but rather you imagine how it will bring meaning into your life.

Future scenarios are an integral element in navigating the imagination gap. They allow us to shed the social constraints of rationality by creating a space where the imagination can run free. However, a scenario is a dead thing without a willing trickster and a curious audience. With both, we can maximize the full possibilities of the story, and the future.

Chapters 12 and 13 elaborate on these aspects of this journey to discovery. Applying action research to Dataspace, the preeminent new field of opportunity, these chapters provide a practical guide to using imagination as a method to amplify the signal of data, data transfer, and so on. They also provide a list of emerging signals that will, or could, inform the reality of corporate business decisions in the next few years.

# Big Questions

The future is a set of questions, some bigger than others. Every disruption in technology brings with it new sets of questions. This is what we are confronted with today: powerful questions, as powerful as the ones that followed the discovery of electricity.

We are entering an era of trial and error, experimentation, orientation, failure, and discovery. As values and needs shift, and as the Millenial Generation gains strength, we will enter into an era of play and imagination. These are times in which we need to take everything less seriously, open ourselves to possibility, and enjoy the journey. The rewards will come, but none will be more satisfying than our return to the children we once were.

Like the trickster, this book will be your interpreter and guide to reaping the rewards from this journey. We began with the story of the Taino's discovery of Columbus, a story from the past that illustrates our central belief for the future: that emerging possibilities are in our midst, right in front of our eyes. We just need new capabilities to see them and new tools to create meaning and wealth from them.

# 2
# The Flop to
# the Top

*Mr. McGuire:* "I just want to say one word to you—
just one word."

*Ben:* "Yes, sir."

*Mr. McGuire:* "Are you listening?"

*Ben:* "Yes, I am."

*Mr. McGuire:* "Plastics."

*Ben:* "Exactly how do you mean?"

*Mr. McGuire:* "There's a great future in plastics. Think
about it. Will you think about it?"

—Advice to recent college graduate Ben Braddock
  from the older generation in the 1967 film *The
  Graduate.*

# Dick Fosbury

This is Dick Fosbury. Does anybody remember him? He is the man who invented the Fosbury Flop, and with it became the first human being to look at the sky while high jumping. During a turbulent decade when most social and political traditions were wrenched painfully from their moorings, Fosbury simply jumped backward. His action set off a controversy among professional athletes at the 1968 Summer Olympics in Mexico City—and earned him an Olympic record and gold medal.

Before 1968, athletes used the straddle method—face down, clearing the bar with a leading arm and leg and then the stomach. But starting in 1962, the sand and wood shavings in the landing box were gradually replaced with foam rubber. Fosbury understood that foam is different from sand. It has no "material memory," so it can spring back, offering the jumper more protection and more possibility.

"Dick Fosbury saw something that anyone else could have seen— the foam in the landing box as a signal of opportunity, an open discovery available to everyone. But only he understood the possibility inherent in the new material."

However, traditions die hard. Even after his 7-foot, 4¼-inch gold-medal jump (his third attempt at those Games, by the way) was televised throughout North America, people could not believe that someone had jumped backward. Years later, Fosbury commented, "Most of the elite athletes had invested so much time in their technique and movements that they didn't want to give it up, so they stuck with what they knew." The other athletes saw foam rubber as having the same possibility as the sand and wood shavings, and matched their performance accordingly.

In 1969, Roy Blount Jr. wrote in *Sports Illustrated* that the "Fosbury Phenomenon" had given rise to two questions: "'Will the Flop revolutionize high jumping?' and 'Will it cause the cream of America's young manhood to break their necks?' The answers are 'Maybe' and 'Probably not.'"

It took a full decade before the Flop began to dominate the sport. "The revolution came about from the kids who saw it and had nothing to lose," said Fosbury, "the kids who saw it on TV and said, 'Gosh, that looks fun— let's do that.'" By the time the Olympic Games came to Los Angeles in

*Dick Fosbury, the man whose Flop made history.* →

1984, all the finalists in the high jump were using the Fosbury Flop. (There are no records of broken necks at the L.A. Games.)

Why was Fosbury the first person to jump backward? The foam allowed Fosbury to fully realize the potential of a technique he was already experimenting with. He saw something that anyone else could have seen—the foam as a signal of opportunity, an open discovery available to everyone—but only he understood the possibility inherent in the new material. Of the millions of high jumpers at the time, Fosbury was the one who maximized current capability by understanding current possibility.

"The revolution came about from the kids who saw it and had nothing to lose," said Fosbury, "the kids who saw it on TV and said, 'Gosh, that looks fun—let's do that.'"

## What Is Your Foam?

Think of any current environment in business or industry where a new technology, usually a digital device, is slowly replacing an older, analog device—such as digital (and mobile) phones phasing out wired telephones. We tend to treat the new like the old, and because they both serve the same purpose, we expect them to behave the same way as well. Take the shutter on most point-and-shoot digital cameras, for example. The camera has no physical shutter that opens and closes to capture an image, and yet when we snap a photo, we hear that little *hissclick* that lets us know that we got the shot. The idea of the old is reinforced through our interaction with the new, preventing us from seeing the new as just that—new and full of different possibility.

In your business or your current practice, do you see behavioral changes rippling out from a new signal? What would be its capability for new opportunities? What is the most relevant signal of opportunity right now? What is the foam in our environment? In culture? In technology? In business? In education? And what would Mr. McGuire whisper to Benjamin if their dialogue took place today? In the 1967 film, that conversation was meant to be ironic, but in hindsight it was prophetic: Plastics was a technology that revolutionized Benjamin's generation.

← *An athlete does the winning Flop.*

Today their conversation might go something like this:

*Mr. McGuire:* "I just want to say one word to you—just one word."

*Ben:* "Yes, sir."

*Mr. McGuire:* "Are you listening?"

*Ben:* "Yes, I am."

*Mr. McGuire:* "Data."

*Ben:* "Exactly how do you mean?"

*Mr. McGuire:* "There's a great future in data. Think about it. Will you think about it?"

# 3
# Imagination and Possibility

In the previous chapter, I asked you to consider the question "Where is the 'foam' in my environment, in my industry, in my business?" And suppose you have figured out an answer, be it an idea or product or process. Now you need to ponder a new question: "How does the 'foam' change what I do?"

# Why Creativity Is Not Enough

The answers to both of these questions will allow us, as individuals and organizations, to construct a bridge between what we know and what we can do to maximize our knowledge in the presence of emerging technologies. But these answers require imagination rather than creativity—imagination because they are images of the mind; images of possibility. Applying creativity to what already exists will not do anymore.

Remember, creativity is chiefly a development tool, applied to an object or idea that has already been imagined. Creativity deploys mental skills to develop an idea but not to generate it, and often leads to "interpretation" rather than invention.

Creativity usually starts with the formulation or identification of a problem and ends with the formulation of a satisfactory solution. There are generally two steps to applying creativity to a set problem. The first is psychological preparation to think "outside of the box": getting rid of some preconceptions while still focusing on the problem at hand. The second is pursuing the solution in a linear and logical fashion that includes selecting the methods and designing the tools used to solve the problem.

As a capability, creativity provides suitable solutions to identified problems in every field, with the desired result being something that is also "new" and "original." *But how new and how original can a solution be when it comes from a given problem area?* Would a multitude of individuals provide a multitude of solutions, or are we in effect looking at the same solution represented in different forms?

A critical difference between creativity and imagination is the *existence* of the problem in the former and its *absence* in the latter.

"What is the shape of the organization ready to nurture and take advantage of unbounded imagination? What is the shape of the education system that will instill the qualities and capabilities of the *imagination society?*"

Imagination allows us, as individuals or corporations, to build experimental platforms from which we can survey our surroundings with new eyes. From this vantage point, we may develop a new vision of ourselves and a new point of view toward the future, seeing beyond the horizon that is visible from the ground. Seeing what is not immediately obvious will allow us to bridge the imagination gap and achieve meaningful breakthroughs.

What individuals are ready for this? What is the shape of the organization ready to nurture and take advantage of unbounded imagination? What is the shape of the education system that will instill the qualities and capabilities of the *imagination society*?

# Users: The New Innovators

In many sectors of industry and culture, innovation is now the domain of users, not companies. Digital technologies and platforms that encourage networking, autonomy, and collaboration—blogs, file sharing, open-source software, or accessible/affordable digital media—have delivered one of the most radical changes in capitalism: the individual's shift from passive consumer to engaged and empowered creator or collaborator. By becoming empowered participants in the process of innovation, individuals are now raising the bar for corporations, making it critical that they align themselves with the conceptual possibilities presented by technology and user behavior.

This challenges industries in one of their traditional core competencies: innovation. It is not a passing trend. With the proliferation of accessible technical tools that allow users to truly participate in the shaping of content—from news to playlists to customized facial creams—desirability demands what capability and possibility must create.

"By becoming participants in the process of innovation, individuals are now raising the bar for corporations. This challenges industries in one of their core traditional competencies: innovation."

Take remix culture as an example of the emerging creative and cultural awareness. Remix is, and always will be, a constant pattern weaving itself throughout society as a means to recontextualize content and culture. Moving beyond the boundaries of the music industry to encompass every form of media and content, remix is both an independent action and a critical response to the environment. Remix culture currently represents a fundamental shift in human behavior, signaling an undeniable transition from old to new models of content consumption, creation, production, and distribution. This inspiring transition has for the most part been enabled by the digital information era, where culture is empowered, free, fast flowing, and mutable. Perhaps most important, remix is aware of itself as a movement that is transforming how people approach and participate in culture as a whole.

The new cocreators accept that an exchange must occur for their behaviors and desires to develop, but they do not want to pay for the behaviors and status normally associated with a device or product. They will pay instead for the possibilities a device affords: "What *else* can this be? And what else can *I* be?" For a corporation to create and prosper within such an experiential and empowered environment, it will need the kind of gutsy imagination that that has no moral fear, and lots of nerve.

# Creating Breakthrough Innovations

In Chapter 1, I proposed that imaginative questions create the groundwork for breakthrough innovation. Current management practices in business are shifting, and the new business model calls for tricksters who can *manage metaphors*—who can frame the potential of ideas and signals into generative questions and scenarios. These frameworks nurture a space for exploration among innovation teams by expanding the scope of their perceptions. This new management theory will allow businesses to locate and interpret rapidly evolving signals, such as the emergence of the consumer as innovator and collaborator.

The ability to create new value at the intersection of behavior, technology, and business is the ability to understand and nourish processes of imagination. This is as much of a challenge as the ability to create from imagination. New management practices need to be able to trigger people's imaginative capacities and align them toward the same strategic goals.

# The New Value Chain

Most innovation teams start with product or technology features, rather than an experience or event. If you start with the product, you will create a *tactical intellectual property.* If you start with the experience or event, you will create a *strategic intellectual property.*

"A strategic idea will always be worth much more to businesses and organizations than a tactical one. The tactical protects; the strategic creates. It's the difference between adding and creating value."

The old value chain starts with identifying user needs—a point of departure conditioned on the assumption that users can identify and articulate

*Old value chain (top) and new value chain.* →

## Old Value Chain

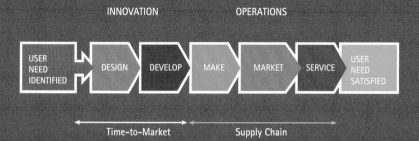

INNOVATION      OPERATIONS

USER NEED IDENTIFIED → DESIGN → DEVELOP → MAKE → MARKET → SERVICE → USER NEED SATISFIED

Time-to-Market      Supply Chain

## New Value Chain

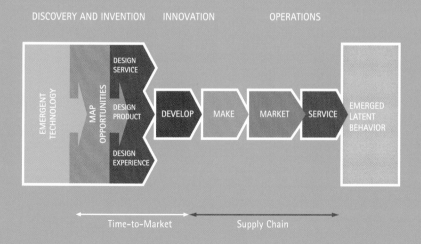

DISCOVERY AND INVENTION    INNOVATION      OPERATIONS

EMERGENT TECHNOLOGY → MAP OPPORTUNITIES → DESIGN SERVICE / DESIGN PRODUCT / DESIGN EXPERIENCE → DEVELOP → MAKE → MARKET → SERVICE → EMERGED LATENT BEHAVIOR

Time-to-Market      Supply Chain

those needs. This is done by focus groups, usually in an environment that does not resemble the user environment in the least. At best, this process will deliver added value, a tactical application.

By contrast, the new value chain starts with behavior mapping and a deep understanding of people's motivations. This is accomplished through personal observations and immersion in the user's lifestyle and mindset, with the expectation that the observer's perspectives will reveal insights into the meaning behind an experience. This process creates *strategic value*.

On the other side of the new spectrum is marketing, which is concerned with creating additional value at certain stages of a product or service cycle through branding and image. At this stage, the artifact already exists, so the required ability is creative: to translate the product's desired image into a symbolic language that is easily understood by the target demographic. It is the creation of new perceptions and new loyalties, but with an end result that does not change or improve the performance of the artifact itself. This is *tactical value*.

Strategic and tactical intellectual properties reflect themselves into the market potential or the value of an idea. But a strategic idea will always be worth much more to businesses and organizations than a tactical one. While the old value chain creates tactical intellectual property, most often as protection against similar competitive offerings, the new value chain creates pre-competitive, strategic intellectual property—new business platforms.

The tactical protects; the strategic creates. It's the difference between adding and creating value. Between creativity and imagination.

Let's look at some examples.

## CREATING STRATEGIC VALUE 1

*One minute it was a rock and the next a talisman, a charm, a fetish, a relic. It became a stone made sacred by human imagination.*
—D. Stephenson Bond, *Living Myth*

To create value from a tree, we might produce a table. This is a strategic innovation. To add value to a table, we might stain it, or paint it white, or make it expandable to accommodate various numbers of people. This is a tactical innovation. If we look at the past 50 years, we find ripple effects radiating out from the discovery of any new strategic innovation—artifact, technology, or service.

The eggbeater was a functional object before the electric motor was invented. The electric motor added tactical value to the manual eggbeater by improving on the performance, speed, and amount of effort required to use it, making for a more comfortable user experience. But the egg does not know this—the outcome is the same whether it is whipped by hand or machine. The omelet is fluffy either way, so the value add is tactical.

In creating value, one uses a completely different set of skills, which illustrates the difference of scope between strategic and tactical innovation. To add value, we need the skills of the technician—problem solving or technical know-how—whereas to create value, we need the skills of the creator—imagination, insight, and curiosity. Most schools educate students into the "hows" of adding value rather than the "hows" of creating value. But skills do not create; the mind creates.

## CREATING STRATEGIC VALUE

transforming matter to produce something that did not exist before: a new artifact that we can term a *strategic innovation*. The new artifact then becomes a platform for *tactical innovation*, an activity that adds value by improving an existing condition without creating anything new.

## Lego: Playing with Value

Since 1947, Lego has successfully added value to plastic in the form of the well-known Lego brick. The Lego system is an excellent example of a good toy. Its principal feature is that all pieces in a set are compatible. In a sense, the physical fit of the pieces expresses the behavioral rules of games. All Lego parts obey the rules at all times. Playing with Lego establishes a soothing repetition of motion (snapping together the pieces), which results in a satisfying accumulation of overlapping shapes and forms. Within its established constraints, a Lego brick can be used to create any form.

Each eight-studded Lego brick weighs 2.5 grams, so there are 400 bricks per kilogram of ABS plastic. At a going rate of $2 per kilogram of ABS (a non-discounted price; Lego probably pays a bit less because of the volume purchased), this means a material cost of 0.005 cents per brick. So for each bucket of 500 bricks that sells for about $15 in North America, the material cost is $2.50, exclusive of the bucket. This is a *value add* of 600 percent on the initial material costs. (Note: This does not take into consideration marketing and tooling costs.)

Now consider Vezok, a character from Lego's recent Bionicle series. It retails for $8.99. It has 41 pieces that weigh a total of 100 grams. That

makes the material cost 20 cents, resulting in a value add of 4,495 percent. Or is this a *value creation* of 4,495 percent?

"Vezok comes with a narrative—one that is further expanded through play. The narrative is where the *creation of value* takes place. Bionicle is a strategic platform for multiple play experiences."

### Beware Vezok's Fury!

In 2001, Lego launched the first Bionicle series with the "Quest for the Masks" scenario, a collection of characters accompanied by related products, interactive activities, Web forums, and online games. Each successive year, Lego has developed the narrative further by introducing new characters into the story. The Bionicle series takes advantage of Lego's capability to make small, perfect plastic bits that fit together flawlessly, but it also has a compelling story to captivate users and the technological components to keep them in the story of "the moment."

### From Plastic Bit to Compelling Narrative

*This scenario, "Quest for the Masks," accompanied the first Lego Bionicle, creating a mythology that has been built upon annually since commencing in 2001:*

Mata Nui, an island paradise. Until a shadow fell across the land.

The dark spirit of Makuta.

Then came six mighty heroes.

The legendary Toa.

Tahu, Toa of Fire.

Kopaka, Toa of Ice.

Lewa, Toa of Air.

Onua, Toa of Earth.

Pohatu, Toa of Stone and

Gali, Toa of Water.

With the help of the Matoran villagers and their chieftains, the Turaga, they gather the Kanohi. Great Masks that grant them wondrous powers. They overcome fearsome Beasts and terrible challenges before defeating Makuta, in the ultimate test of their strength.

← *Not just a plastic brick: Vezok, part of the Lego Bionicle series.*

Consider Lego's description of the Bionicle character Vezok:

> *"Nasty and vicious, Vezok's fury is always on the verge of exploding. In battle, he relies on a harpoon that pulls him through the water and a buzzsaw that hurls water daggers. His powerful impact vision and ability to absorb the powers of his enemies makes him a devastating opponent."*

This is no longer just a plastic brick. A brick does not come with a narrative—that must be created in play. Vezok comes with a narrative—one that is further expanded through play. The narrative is where the *creation of value* takes place. Bionicle is a *strategic platform for multiple play experiences.*

## CREATING STRATEGIC VALUE 2: STARBUCKS

The idea of drinking coffee dates back 500 years or so to the early Ottoman Empire. People gathered in Turkish coffeehouses to drink strong brews from small cups. They smoked tobacco (and who knows what else) from communal hookahs and relaxed over genial conversations. This was an important social event, a celebration of humanity and community. But for many years, coffee was merely a food subgroup in North America, disconnected to any function beyond filling a person's stomach with caffeinated fuel. Remember in old Westerns the coffee made in huge pots to make sure the job got done before sundown?

As a North American business model, a successful coffeehouse was nonsense until the early 1980s, when Howard Schultz, the vice president of a Swedish housewares manufacturer, observed coffee customs in Milan. "Coffeehouses in Italy are a third place for people, after home and work," he's reported to have said. "There's a relationship of trust and confidence in that environment."

**"Starbucks is a place where you can *have* and *be* at the same time. That is a Big Idea. It is not the product, coffee, or the process of roasting it. It is not the espresso maker. It is the entire context."**

The details of the total experience mattered. That's what Schultz—who became the CEO of Starbucks and spearheaded its rise to an international franchise—understood. Schultz saw that we have two sides to our brain and our being: We want to *have* and we want to *be*. We want coffee but we also need to belong. Starbucks is a place where you can *have* and *be* at the same time. That is a Big Idea. It is not the product—coffee—or the process of roasting it. It is not the espresso maker. It is the entire context. The Big Idea is first the consideration of the event—the experience and the product as the strategic offering—and then the impeccable execution of this insight.

The Big Idea has to do with imagination. It has to do with understanding the possibility of the coffee bean and the context of humans looking for a particular experience along with their coffee. The insights that led to Starbucks' success were firmly rooted in the new value chain, beginning with imagination.

# Seeing Possibility in Imagination

*Imagination is what makes our sensory experience meaningful, enabling us to interpret and make sense of it, whether from a conventional perspective or from a fresh, original, and individual one. It is what makes perception more than the mere physical stimulation of sense organs. It also produces mental imagery, visual and otherwise, which is what makes it possible for us to think outside the confines of our present perceptual reality, to consider memories of the past and possibilities for the future, and to weigh alternatives against one another. Thus, imagination makes possible all our thinking about what is, what has been, and, perhaps most important, what might be.*
—Nigel J.T. Thomas, philosopher and cognitive scientist

Nothing we imagine is absolutely impossible, according to Scottish philosopher David Hume. Once we have the capability to form images in our mind, we can define the capabilities needed to bring these images to life—to enable them as technologies. Based on our experience of the world around us, our imagination constructs only images of possibility. If something seems impossible, it may also be unimaginable.

## The Flower in Your Mind

Look at the following words and try to see them in your mind.

*Car.*

Do you see it if you close your eyes? Good, now let's do another one:

*Yellow flower.*

See it? OK, let's get a bit more representational:

*Statue of Liberty.*

We are done for now. In the past minute, you have seen a car, a flower, and the Statue of Liberty in your imagination. None of the three is present to your senses, yet you have been able to see them all. With a pencil and paper, and bit of talent, most people would be able to draw what they see, and the drawings would look more or less like a car, a flower, and a statue.

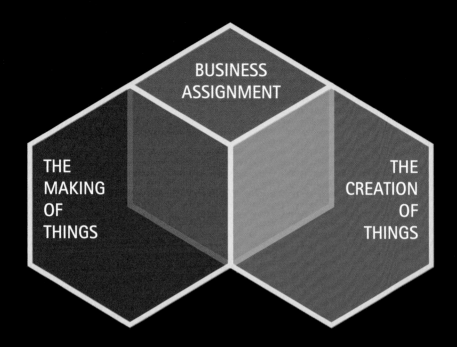

BUSINESS
ASSIGNMENT

THE
MAKING
OF
THINGS

THE
CREATION
OF
THINGS

The Old Value Chain
Gives Form and Function
Solves Problems
Satisfies Needs
Innovates

**The New Value Chain**
Explores Possibility
Defines The Big Idea
Gives Form and Function
Invents and Innovates

Imagination creates images of the mind, what Aristotle called "phantasia": an image that is present to us in a given moment. According to Aristotle, "The soul never thinks without a mental image." In cognitive theory, imagery or "mental representation" is considered essential for thinking but not necessarily linked to creativity.

We imagine from experience, from knowledge, from curiosity, and from memory. In the exercise "The Flower in Your Mind" (see sidebar), the words *car, flower,* and *statue* retrieve different *specific* memories for each one of us but the same *general* archetypes of those memories. A car will be a form of transportation with four wheels, a flower will have a stem and petals, and the Statue of Liberty will be a woman holding a torch in a raised hand. Will the torch be in the left hand or the right hand? And what is she holding in the other hand? It does not really matter—an archetype is not constrained by specific details. In much the same way, the imagination is free from objective constraints. Its power comes precisely from this freedom. And as the mind reframes and integrates images of new mental or physical artifacts, the more we encounter, the more we can imagine.

"While the old value chain creates tactical intellectual property, most often as protection against similar competitive offerings, the new value chain creates strategic intellectual property—new business platforms."

People using the most basic tools will find it difficult to imagine new applications of technology, or understand the meaning of emerging signals in devices that do not match the form or functionality of the tools with which they are familiar. This was precisely the problem faced by the Taino when they encountered Columbus's landing party: a group of people who did not use iron and lacked substantial weaponry face-to-face with another group of people armed to the teeth with swords, helmets, shields, and heavy armor. What meaning do they make out of these sharp contraptions made out of strange materials? What intentions do they carry?

Let's modify the Flower exercise a bit. Instead of car, flower, and Statue of Liberty, try to see something you have never heard of: *freuzel.*

Difficult, isn't it? You have no idea what a *freuzel* is. A chemical substance, an electronic component, a unit of measure, an individual? Everyone will imagine *freuzel* in a completely different way, and if they were to draw pictures, these differences in imagination would be clear. Why?

Words represent triggers to knowledge or experience, and are points of departure for the creation of images in our mind. The more evocative the words, the more complex the images we can conceive. It is through words

← *The value chains.*

that we allow the mind to access the possibility of a flower. When we make use of our memory to retrieve an image not present to us, we are using our imagination. Which brings us to the simplest definition of imagination: a mental faculty forming images or concepts of external objects, things that are not present to the senses.

## THE IMAGINATIVE MIND

Five-year-old Sophie uses plastic bags to do something you probably have never tried—she skates on carpets. Plastic bags + carpet + imagination = a new indoor sport that exploits the attributes of all the materials involved—availability and low cost—as well as their physical properties—reduced friction for a smoother glide.

Imagination combines aspects of memories or experiences into a new mental construct that differs from past or present perceptions of reality and may anticipate any number of future realities. What inspires us in our processes of imagining is *play behavior*—not what happens when you play with your hands, which is actually akin to creativity, but an activity of the mind.

### What Makes the Wind?

In a famous dialogue with a five-year-old girl named Julia, Swiss psychologist Jean Piaget asked her what made the wind.

"The trees," Julia answered.

"How do you know?" Piaget asked.

"I saw them waving their arms."

The little girl's statement that trees make wind when they wave their "arms" is a perfect study of both imitative and creative imagination at work. And it is the essence of imagination: the creation of meaning out of what you see, what you don't see, and what could be possible.

Two contrasting types of imagination coexist within our minds. One is expert at reconstructing past images or events, while the other is expert at thoughts and the restructuring of sensory impressions. Where the former is imitative, the latter is creative. Creative imagination is credited as the basis of all human achievement in the sciences and in art.

# FREEDOM AND UNLEARNING

*It is innocence that is full and experience that is empty. The child, full; man, empty. Men must learn how to unlearn.*

—French poet and essayist Charles Peguy

The imaginative mind is a free mind. Being free from the objective constraints of "today" and "now" does not reside well in adults—our minds are filled with too many rational boundaries and ideas of conduct by the time we "grow up." Imagination finds its natural place in the mind that is free of preconceptions—the mind of a child.

Children have fewer preconceptions than adults about what could be possible, and thus they have more courage. More courage leads to fearless exploration, which leads to more possibility. It is important to note that the potential for imagination is equally present in both the adult and child mind, but the actualization of that potential may be greater in the child because he or she has none of the adult's fear.

## How Do You Put a Giraffe in the Refrigerator?

A few years ago, Accenture (formerly Andersen Consulting) conducted a quiz for business managers that began with this question. Ninety percent of the managers who took the test failed it. But more interesting than the failure rate is the way in which they and most other people answer the question. If your answer is something like, "Cut the giraffe in pieces and put it in the fridge," you are in the majority.

Yup, the way to put a giraffe into a fridge is *to kill it first.* Why is this the most popular answer? Because most adults have a set image relationship in their mind for the words *giraffe* and *refrigerator.* In that set image, the giraffe is taller than the fridge. But the question does not mention size. As far as we know, this could be a baby giraffe going into an industrial fridge or a regular-size giraffe going into a gigantic fridge.

While the rational boundaries of the adult mind have determined, 90 percent of the time, that you need to kill a giraffe to get it into a fridge, many children under seven years of age answer the question correctly.

*So how do you put a giraffe in the fridge?* Open the door and put the giraffe inside, just as you would a bottle of milk.

A colleague once remarked, "If children had the power of adults in social and economic terms, the results of their imaginative thinking would be stunning, if implemented. But because they are children, no one takes them seriously."

Kids do not have to think about being imaginative; they just are. Adults know the difference between a state of imagining and a state of not imagining. We switch, saying to ourselves, "Today I will be imaginative." Children make no such statements. For them *everything* is possible. They do not have to force anything; they just do what they do until adults tell them what to do and try to control what could be possible.

Part of the problem is that adults may know too much. We meet many well-educated people who seem to know a lot, but in our conversations with them we do not discover an original idea in their thinking. We might discover an enormous amount of information but not one novel thought. In other words, they simply transmit to others what they have learned from others and from various sources of knowledge.

Most people are so conversant in other people's imaginative thinking and ideas, they do not assume that they have an imagination of their own. Is it the fear of imagination or lack of confidence that prevents most adults from advancing original thoughts? Or is it lack of practice? To answer these questions, we need to first understand the power of imagination.

## THE POWER OF IMAGINATION

*He lets the last Hungarian go. He waits until his wife and kids are in the ground, and then he goes after the rest of the mob. He kills their kids. He kills their wives. He kills their parents and their parents' friends. He burns down the houses they live in, the stores they work in. He kills people that owe them money. And like that, he's gone. Underground. Nobody's ever seen him since.*

> —"Verbal" Kint, describing the legacy of the mobster Keyser Soze in *The Usual Suspects*

Most of us, at one point in our lives, were afraid of the dark. As children, we would lie awake at night, fearfully watching the closet door for traces of movement in the fuzzy darkness, or maybe huddle under the covers, listening for the sound of creaking floorboards or breathing that wasn't our own. It did not matter that by the light of day, those shadows in the corner were a benign pile of laundry. At night, when we were alone in our beds, they became the boogeyman, and he was just waiting for us to close our eyes so he could pounce.

"He becomes a myth, a spook story that criminals tell their kids at night: 'Rat on your pop and Keyser Soze will get you.' [My accomplice] Keaton always said, 'I don't believe in God, but I'm afraid of him.' Well, I believe in God—and the only thing that scares me is Keyser Soze."

*Kevin Spacey as "Verbal" Kint in* The Usual Suspects. →

As we grew older, we grew less afraid of the dark. We knew that the pile of laundry was just that, and our belief in monsters-in-waiting waned along with our ability to make believe. But what exactly was it that we were afraid of? What did we believe in so strongly that it would send us running in terror to our parents' bed?

*We were afraid that what we imagined might actually happen.* The power of our imaginations was strong enough to convince us of the possibility. As children or adults, we seek out connections and consistencies to build a solid narrative in the context of our experience—we believe because we have the desire to.

The narrative of the 1995 film *The Usual Suspects* illustrates this desire. It unfolds in an interrogation room, where the suspect, "Verbal" Kint narrates a story about his experience with the mysterious, semi-mythical Keyser Soze—a vicious Hungarian mobster accused of innumerable crimes. Kint culls the names, places, and events of the story from objects around the room—from coffee cups to mug shots. These details trigger his imagination and enhance the contextual possibilities of his story. It works because he maximizes both the power of his imagination—he has the courage to believe in the story's capability—and his interrogator's willingness to believe.

## THE FEAR OF IMAGINATION

*Those who fear the imagination condemn it: something childish, they say, something monsterish, misbegotten. Not all of us dream awake. But those of us who do have no choice.*

—author Patricia McKillip

Like children in the dark, adults fear being exposed to a place from which they can never return, of discovering something whose implications may change them forever. Knowledge changes us. Ideas transform us. Once something new is discovered, you can never look at the world in quite the same way again.

"The fear of imagination is the fear of failure and of not being original enough. It is the fear of not living up to our expectations and the expectations of others. Fear of imagination is the fear of unlearning."

Are you willing to go there? Are you willing to make a discovery today about a new way of doing things? Are you willing to jump backward, head first, in front of millions of people? Are you willing to look silly? Are you willing to try and fail?

The fear of imagination is the fear of failure and of not being original enough. It is the fear of not living up to our expectations and the expectations of others. The chances of being wrong or irrelevant are so great, people think, it's probably best not to open their mouths. The fail-safe is to kill the giraffe, cut it up, and put it in the refrigerator.

Fear of imagination is the fear of unlearning. A six-year-old I know once remarked, "You don't have to open your mouth to talk to the dead." A child can say this because he or she has not learned enough to be constrained by norms, or limited by expectations or bias. For children, there are no consequences; as far as they are concerned, it is all play. It is all life.

This is also the mindset an adult must have to seriously ask the question posed in Chapter 1: "What if my toothbrush could speak?" You do not care how people look at you in that moment. You are just playing. You have created new rules. You have empowered both yourself and your audience by removing the limits of convention. Now what if that question was asked to people who could enable the technologies to implement some of the possible answers?

## THE DEATH OF IMAGINATION

*Pingu lives on the ice cap with his mother, his postman father and his baby sister Pinga. They live in a small village with all the usual shops, a school, lots of abandoned ice sculptures to play in, a skating rink and a skittles alley. His friends are Ping and Pingo, and Robby the seal. His enemies include a mean-minded seagull....*

—*Pingu* FAQ, Version 3 19.10.95

In the animation series *Pingu,* produced by the Swiss group Trickfilmstudio, a young penguin shares his mischievous and engaging adventures with a cast of characters who communicate in a mysterious language of expressive sound and gesture called *Pinguish*. This unconventional mode of communication has played a large role in establishing Pingu's worldwide following; many teenage and student fans of the tiny penguin even use Pinguish in their daily conversations.

What can we learn about communication from a language in which the obvious rules seem to be absent?

We learn the value of contextual communication. If we can decode the context, we can decode the content, and Pingu is context for content. The rhythm, syntax, tone, and volume of Pinguish all contribute to the audience's decoding of the context into content—allowing precise communication between characters and audience. Precise enough for millions of children to comprehend its meaning and absurd enough for millions of their parents to ask, "Why are you watching this?"

Every sound Pingu and his friends make is information. The fact that the language is made of abstract noises helps children concentrate on the whole situation, so that they must participate in decoding the meaning of what they see and hear. Pinguish is an excellent example of complete communication, involving movement, gesture, and facial expression to complement sound.

## "Why and when do we stop understanding *Pinguish?*"

The fact that it is not a real language is irrelevant—for millions of children in more than 50 countries, "learning" Pinguish is very much the essence of learning through contextual communication. And contextual communication is a function of imagination because it is the mind that puts it all together. If you do not contextualize what you see with what you hear *now,* you are not a full participant in your own story.

Pinguish teaches us that contexts continually change, so not only do we need to be receptive to the contexts that surround us; we need to adapt ourselves to their changing meanings. As adults, we are encouraged to perceive certain social structures, such as the roles of work or government, as relatively permanent despite their continual change and transitions; they become a social certainty. In some respects, this perception reduces our ability to contextualize and interpret new information, as it does not fit within our expectations. So the abstract sounds of Pingu lose their value as meaningful ideas, feelings, and intent. But when does this happen? Why and when do we stop understanding Pinguish?

# The Division Between Work and Play

We stop understanding Pinguish when we forget how to play. This loss is why we are so depressed and restless when we have nothing to do, no work or task to complete. While play behavior has historically dominated human consciousness and defined human values—in exploration, innovation, or invention—modern society has systemically removed play from the equation by manufacturing and maintaining a dichotomy between *work* and *play.*

We have all been participants and accomplices in the organized death of imagination after childhood by removing play from everyday life and work. In doing this, we have created regulated channels where *play as profession* is subcontracted to specific adult groups—professional athletes, artists, or musicians. They are socially allowed to play, though it is not without a cost to society.

For the rest of us, *play* and *profession* do not mix. But without play, the imagination dies, and without imagination, creativity dies. We do not know how to live outside the controls of society or the controls of time. This comes from forgetting how to play. In play, there is no time limit. One of my students recently observed that the Western adult is an "extension of the clock," and when the clock is not present—say, after retirement—we feel lost and useless. We feel lost because we have no way to search for imaginative possibilities, and useless because imaginative play is considered unproductive in our efficient society. We have taken ourselves too seriously to play as adults.

One possible reason for this lies with the industrial state. When judged from a developmental perspective, the industrial state halts the growth of individuals by erecting barriers all around them after the age of five—barriers that in essence prohibit free play, and with it, the learning and growing opportunities that play affords. The slogan for the industrial state might simply be:

*Don't play with your food!*

Observe our lives: At the age of seven, some of us learn how to wear uniforms; at eight, we learn what is work and how it is different from play; at 11, we start learning what kind of work we might do when we grow up; and from the ages of 17 to 24, we learn the specifics of our future work. Once we go to grade school, our imagination is purposefully killed off in an organized and systematic fashion to prepare us for a lifetime of "productivity"—and this is by a group of thoughtful people who have only best intentions and genuine concern for our future.

We are then ready to graduate in the world of "workers," where we labor five days a week until the age of 65. We work believing in the promise of the Industrial Revolution: productivity, and less labor-intensity leading to more leisure time. Leisure time carries with it the implicit expectation of doing something—of being engaged in something nonproductive. Of being engaged in play.

One culprit was probably the first *Oxford Dictionary*, published in 1884. The dictionary's definitions for *work* and *play* effectively remove play from work—thus removing imagination from the performance of work tasks. It is telling that this was the prevailing view when the dictionary was published, after more than 20 years of research and work following the Industrial Revolution. The separation of work and play was critical to the Industrial Revolution, which posited work as a *productive activity* by which one could essentially purchase leisure time.

We are surrounded by devices that we use for repetitive daily chores and leisure. Used for leisure, devices such as automobiles, boats, and home entertainment systems are our tools for nonproductivity. But our adult *toys*, as they are now popularly called, have atrophied our imaginations. By the age of 65, we may have lost, irretrievably, our ability to play. And we are not talking about physical skills here, as play is mostly an imaginative skill. This—the death of imagination after childhood—is where and why imagination becomes a *challenge* for adults.

When we as a society tell people what can and cannot be done, we further remove them from possibility, and from the possibilities all around them. There needs to be a balance between what we allow and what we disallow—to teach limits and structures while allowing play to thrive.

## PEOPLE AS OUTPUTS

Does all this sound too drastic?

Well, let's look more closely at how things change as we move from childhood to adulthood. In the kindergarten environment, round tables, cooperative and creative activities, sharing, and looking at one another's work for inspiration are the norm. The kindergarten is a place that sets limits, but these limits are based on cooperation, imagination, creativity, and play.

After kindergarten, we move into a world in which work and play have been predefined for us—a world where imagination is imprisoned by the system of traditional education and traditional parenting. Don't play with your food. Recess is playtime. Don't skate on carpets using plastic bags on your feet. These are just symptoms of a much deeper problem.

Most of us grow up aspiring to work in an office, which is amazing because an office layout, just like that of a factory or prison, is designed to set limits. From job titles to narrow job responsibilities to cubicle workspaces, the norm is to discourage people from using their imaginations, as they were encouraged to do in kindergarten, and to concentrate everyday experience to the performance of tasks that support the larger construct of the organization. Organizational hierarchy defines people by their roles in the performance of tasks. Thus our society defines people as *outputs*.

In the adult work world, Sophie will not be encouraged to skate on carpets with plastic bags on her feet; she will be told to take the bags off and stop being silly. She will be defined as output. Children like to define and reinvent themselves. The challenge is to continue to do so as adults.

## "How much of what we feel passionately about—the things that inspire or excite our curiosity and imagination—is found in our daily jobs? For many of us, a gap exists between our role as outputs and our role as humans."

Have you noticed how often we ask people we meet, "What do you do?" As if the person who performs a task is defined by that task. Some people may wish to be defined as the output of their work life, but most do not. Individuals have a richer definition of themselves than that which we attribute to them. Try to define yourself the way you would like people to talk about you. It is not that easy, but worth a try. You will have to reach deep into what is most important to you, and into what symbols represent who you are, rather than what you do—your personal *brand*, in the most generous and expansive sense of the word.

David Bond, for example, is an upper-level manager in human resources at the U.S. Department of Labor, and a longtime civil servant. David is excellent at what he does. If you met David at a party and asked him what he does, he would probably say, "I'm a human resources manager at the U.S. Department of Labor." But if you asked him to describe himself the way he would like others to speak of him, the answer would be completely different. "I am an obsessive collector," he would tell you. "I collect almost anything. My largest collections are of Japanese block prints, Japanese cast iron pots, and almost every DVD ever produced that has anything to do with Japan. I fell in love with Japan early on in life. I speak Japanese and visit there twice a year. Before working in civil service, I taught economics at the University of Tokyo."

How much of what we feel passionately about—the things that inspire or excite our curiosity and imagination—is found in our daily jobs? For many of us, a gap exists between our role as outputs and our role as humans. As adults, we must retrieve our imagination, integrating it into work by redefining what work can be.

# Imagination, Play, and Possibility

*It is not the strongest species that survives, nor the most intelligent, but the one most adaptive to change.*

—Charles Darwin

Why is work—in its current definition—an activity that does not encourage imaginative possibility? Unlike play, work is something that we generally "learn to do." We can spend days and weeks learning the *methodology* of golf, but we will not have a complete understanding of it until we actually *play* golf. There are things one can learn, and there are things one needs to master. Play is something we need to master—the missing and essential element that complements what we learn as work. It is the continuous learning and unlearning of very simple things—play patterns—that lead to the mastery of simplicity.

Imagine Tiger Woods. Now imagine his "job description." Essentially it would read very much like this: "Put the ball in the hole." But his job requires both strategy and tactics. What is the strategic goal? *Put the ball in the hole.* How does this happen? *Tactical execution.* The tactical execution is play.

Strategy and tactics—as in imagination and creativity—are blended when you play. In this free activity of make-believe, with no time limits, play as tactical execution requires imagination. Before swinging the club, most expert golfers will visualize every aspect, from the plane of the club to the landing zone and the roll of the ball. All of this requires imagination and the ability to adapt quickly as conditions change. In play, conditions change all the time, requiring one to adapt, re-imagine, unlearn, and learn again.

In effect, this is really the primary dynamic of life: Markets, industries, societies, bodies, and ecosystems all change *constantly*, requiring us to constantly re-imagine, unlearn, and learn, again and again. In order to meet the demands of our dynamic modern economy and society, we must learn how to unlearn.

# 4
# Unlearning

*We have to relearn that we are not in the transportation business; we are in the arts and entertainment business.*

> —Bob Lutz, General Motors vice president of Global Product Development, at 2005 annual shareholders' meeting

# Barriers to Imagination

For the imaginative mind, the question of how to put a giraffe into a refrigerator, posed in Chapter 3, was an easy challenge. But for the vast majority of us, the relationship between a giraffe and a refrigerator needs to be re-imagined, which requires a degree of unlearning. And we are only able to do this once we have been given the answer to the question. But what if we could selectively recognize and overcome the barriers to unlearning—successfully re-imagining our approach to every dilemma as we face it? We would need to surrender what we have already learned and how we have learned it, a difficult process that leads to uncertainty and vulnerability.

Are you able to re-imagine your life differently than it is right now? Or are you glued to the rules of the present and surrounded by barriers—the ones that you erect and that society erects around you? How do you imagine yourself in 20 years: building a vision of the future without limit, or continuing along the same trajectory? To cut our own paths, we must actively engage in unlearning.

# Changing the Workplace

*The discovery that most learning requires no teaching can be neither manipulated nor planned. Each of us is responsible for his or her own de-schooling, and only we have the power to do it."*

—philosopher Ivan Illich

The work setting is one of the most controlled environments that we experience and share. By deconstructing the barriers in our work habits and work ecologies, we can see patterns emerge. In our jobs, do we create or do something in a new way, or do we return to something familiar that has worked for us in the past? Is your workspace an office where every cubicle is placed in a grid? Do you see your coworkers' faces or are you looking at the back of their heads? Do you see what your colleagues are working on and can you easily share your work with them? Do you feel engaged with them and with the surrounding space?

**"Question every aspect of your past and present work ecologies. And be prepared to leave what you find behind."**

Is your workplace the kind of environment where people are most creative? Let's remember kindergarten: Everyone sat around a table, probably round, manipulating pencils, paper, scissors, and glue. We were making something, we were learning by doing, and we were completely immersed in the act of play. We were discovering the limits of the material as well as the limits of our imagination. We were encouraged to do so. Is this the case in your work ecology?

Asking these questions will direct you toward the beginning of your unlearning, creating a relevant context for *you*. Once you become involved in this process, question every aspect of your past and present work ecologies. And be prepared to leave what you find behind.

## THE LIMITS OF THE WORKPLACE

The moment you get a new job, an assigned person introduces you to the space, the tools, the material, and the people:

> *"Joseph is in charge of IT, Mary is in charge of PR, and Suzie is in charge of managing the office. This is your desk. And this is the machine you should use when doing your work. This is how the machine works. When it does not work, you call on Suzie, who will call on Joseph to fix it. This is the material you can use with this machine, and this material has these properties…."*

You are given the limits and expected to learn them. You are given the structure of the workplace and are required to behave according to the rules given to you by the people who inhabit it, who are themselves conforming to those very same rules. And the more rules you learn, the more barriers are placed on your imagination. You may or may not be told that Joseph plays the saxophone, or that Mary has a passion for bonsai trees and flower arrangement, because it is irrelevant to each employee's "expected outcome." But maybe if each person's image of who they are were utilized, you could collaboratively expand on the capabilities of the machines and the people who operate them.

The typical corporate consultant usually starts by saying, "First I will need to take some time to learn about your organization, product, service, and so on." In other words, *I would like to learn about your limits*—how you define yourself and your organization, and what you do. But this is counterproductive, focusing on past and current "outcomes" rather than future opportunities. The smart consultant should say, "Please tell me how would you like others to define your organization in ideal terms ten years from now," thus opening a new set of desired possibilities.

# Learning to Unlearn

Unlearning needs to become an essential competence of organizations and individuals, and their capabilities to shape and participate in the creation of the future will be directly proportional to the speed of their unlearning. We need to be swifter than we'd like in abandoning rules and limitations, moving beyond the safety of what we know, like Dick Fosbury venturing out in search of a new way to jump. But letting go of what had served us for a long time is tough, and this is why unlearning is the big fear.

It takes time and courage to unlearn things, as we have so many things to unlearn. We need to unlearn the way we teach, the way we learn, the methodologies and everyday technologies we use, the markets for which we develop products and services, and the vocabulary we use in describing what we do. And new technologies such as the Internet have only intensified the need to unlearn.

## CREATING AN OPENNESS TO PLAY

*To become mature is to recover the sense of seriousness that one had as a child at play.*

—Friedrich Nietzsche

How does unlearning increase possibility? In the conventional workplace described previously, you become an extension of the space/tool/material. You are given tasks with rules and outcomes, and are never allowed to ask, *"What would happen if I did this?"* You cannot put the computer on your head and pretend it is a hat. That outcome is not what you were hired for.

But if you take anything that you have learned and unlearn it, take it apart, and deconstruct it—if you *play* with it—you will discover something completely new. By reclaiming play as a serious pursuit, we intensify the unlearning process, creating a platform for those new possibilities to exist. It is in play behavior that we can find the freedom that feeds the imagination.

In *The Art of Play: Helping Adults Reclaim Imagination and Spontaneity*, Adam and Allee Blatner contend that psychological dynamics fuel the adult resistance to playfulness, spontaneity, and imagination. Some of these dynamics are found in early childhood memories—of restricted play, for example, or the limited involvement of adults in the play experiences.

"If you take anything that you have learned and unlearn it, take it apart, and deconstruct it—if you *play* with it—you will discover something completely new."

When both an ecology *and* an ecosphere of play (the people close to you that make group play possible) are absent, play becomes inhibited. The result is a resistance to spontaneity and discomfort with fantasy. We equate playfulness with looking silly, or foolish, and make a conscious effort to avoid these labels through careful control or repression. The ripple effect is that we, as adults, pass this on to our own children, who then repress play instincts when we are present, to prevent us from feeling uncomfortable or unhappy. *Don't play with your food.*

This repression functions also at the collective level, contributing to cultural taboos and perpetuating a status quo in which no one dares to be playful and imaginative about new possibilities. Organizations—from business to government to education—are singularly expert at defining seriousness and the rules that encourage the repression of imagination.

To unlearn this kind of thinking, you must consider yourself as a *grownup*, which is different from an *adult*. This is how children see us—as grown-up children, the way they see themselves in the future. (*"When I grow up..."* we often hear children say.) For our purposes, *grownup* is that transitional state between childhood and adulthood, where our internal attitude still engages in play. While adulthood is a socially enforced rank designed to regulate and organize, being a grownup is about identifying and maintaining the need for play. A grownup still knows how to put a giraffe in the fridge.

## WHO NEEDS TO UNLEARN?

*The problem is never how to get new, innovative thoughts into your mind, but how to get the old ones out. Every mind is a room packed with archaic furniture.*
          —Dee Hock, founder and former CEO of Visa credit card empire

My colleague Kelly Seagram once remarked, "Unlearning is the willful innocence of preconceptions." Unlearning is an absolute requirement for anyone currently older than 10 or 12: the Baby Boomers, Generation X, Generation Y, and so on. These groups of people are, for the most part, completely entangled within the limits and rules of their education and profession, performing within their expected outcomes with grace and finesse. But we have reached a critical point— socially, economically, environmentally, politically—where this can no longer continue; where acceptance, avoidance, and fear can no longer perpetuate conditional change. In order of criticality, those who need to unlearn the most, and the fastest, are an organization's top executives.

Let's say we ask some executives to rethink the shape of their organizations by projecting how market conditions or manufacturing processes might change by 2015. How will they do this? For most executives, the logical and reasonable way would be to look at the past to project the future—assessing strengths and weaknesses, auditing their core capabilities and then amplifying them over time through an optimistic lens. This process generally assumes that the future is a problem to be solved, a process that will require all the tools of creativity.

But the future is not a problem. It, and the role of the individual and organization in it, is simply a set of questions. Our role in shaping it is only as relevant as the questions *we* ask and the questions *we* provide answers for. In this context, unlearning is the willingness to surrender who we are for the possibility of what we might become. It is a process of *unconditional change*—creating a new vision for ourselves and a new mission for our organizations.

"In order of criticality, those who need to unlearn the most, and the fastest, are an organization's top executives."

# Changing Education

*The big mistake in schools is trying to teach children anything, and by using fear as the basic motivation—fear of getting failing grades, fear of not staying with your class, etc. [But compared to fear,] interest can produce learning on a scale as a nuclear explosion to a firecracker.*

—Stanley Kubrick

If you give children some dress-up clothes and a few other props, they will often transform themselves into astronauts, ninjas, scuba divers, or doctors. They easily pretend to be grownup people, mimicking us and learning how social and cultural relationships work. As adults, we encourage this because this type of pretend play is also practice for when kids actually do become adults. And when children move from kindergarten to grade school, where the learning ecology shifts from knowledge exchange to knowledge distribution, they are essentially practicing for work, for becoming outputs.

What is the ecology of work really about, underneath productivity and career options and schedules? Almost all workplaces are hierarchical, and everyone performs tasks that contribute to the overall vitality of the business or industry. And what is hierarchy about, at its most basic level? Power. Control.

You perform your tasks in this way, and by this time, and report to this person. If you do this for long enough, and show talent and creativity, you *may be* promoted and make more money and have people who report to *you*. In the most extreme manifestation of this, you are controlled and control others. And children are trained how to participate in this scheme the moment they leave kindergarten and begin their formal education. They are encouraged to practice at being outputs.

## POWER AND THE DISTRIBUTION OF KNOWLEDGE

For a moment, think about how a typical classroom is arranged. Row upon row of small, modular workspaces that "belong" to each student, organized so that all students face the teacher, who can see what everyone is doing and where they are. There are codes of behavior that students are expected to follow: no talking, pay attention, concentrate on your work, obey the teacher. The teacher possesses the knowledge, and students must follow the rules to be granted access to that knowledge. If you talk to your neighbor or cause a disruption, you will be publicly reprimanded or sent to the principal's office. Students are identified by their marks, their grade levels, or, in the case of post-secondary schools, their registration number.

Space divided into rows, people assigned ownership over their piece of it, strict rules of behavior and disciplinary action, constant surveillance, ID codes (names or numbers), a central source of power that controls all movement and behavior—does this sound familiar? We've already discussed how the design and operation of prisons is remarkably similar to that of the typical office and we can now add schools to this list, despite the difference in social function. How about army barracks? Hospitals? Apartment complexes or subdivisions? What about abstract social constructs like government or law? We have created complex systems to control and regulate the normal behaviors of groups and individuals, restricting their experiences to fit within specific social and ethical constructs.

> "Students are told that knowledge is the most powerful tool they can have and that it will take them wherever they want to go. Yet the possibilities for them to gain and apply knowledge are atrophied through physical, cognitive, and social constraints."

The management of society, culture, the economy, and politics is communicated through the dichotomy of *Yes, you can* and *No, you cannot,* and people are rewarded with power—whether it is managerial, monetary, or cultural—when they adhere to those standards and uphold the social structure.

This type of dynamic creates a hierarchical knowledge distribution system, rather than an exchange, by controlling exactly what people can learn and how they apply it. Students are told that knowledge is the most powerful tool they can have and that it will take them wherever they want to go. Yet the possibilities for them to gain and apply knowledge are atrophied through physical, cognitive, and social constraints. There is literally no space for play in the classroom.

This dynamic does not take into account that people might learn in different ways, and at different paces. The system asks that individuals adapt to its flow rather than allowing them to progress at their own speed or flow pattern. It does not give students any agency, any empowerment over their own learning and knowledge.

The opposite of this model is the karate *dojo*, where you move at your own pace when you are *really* ready and you know it. And everyone else knows it too. Imagine if this model were applied to schools and universities. Each student would be empowered to learn in the way and at the pace that best suits him or her. Round tables instead of rows. Exchange rather than banking. Discipline and focus nurtured through interest and enjoyment, rather than fear or control.

## NEW LEARNING ECOLOGIES

Think back to your high school or college experience for a moment. Most students take a math or language or science course as a compulsory, but unless they continue on in that discipline, or find another way to use it, it is simply forgotten. They have no place to apply what they learn, and as soon as the course is finished, the knowledge fades.

People learn best in situations where they enjoy whatever it is they are engaged in. While most teachers may intuitively know that the best way to enlist each student's interest is by being sensitive to his or her goals and desires, this is rarely the reality in our schools. Schools do not encourage students to make meaning from the knowledge they are learning; instead, they inundate students with information in the hope that they will absorb some of it.

When students are encouraged to learn about what interests them in ways that make sense to *them*, however, education becomes a meaningful and collaborative endeavor. Empowering students cultivates an integrative and reciprocal knowledge base, to be shared and transformed. And in this setting, the teacher becomes the trickster who recognizes the talents and strengths of each student, and reveals the capability for them to master their own possibilities.

# Lifelong Kindergarten

A leader in the development of new learning, Mitchel Resnick is an associate professor of learning research and director of the Lifelong Kindergarten group at the Media Lab at Massachusetts Institute of Technology (MIT). The Lifelong Kindergarten group develops various technologies that engage both adults and children in new types of design activities and learning experiences. Resnick also cofounded the Computer Clubhouse, an award-winning network of learning centers for youth from underserved communities, and has consulted widely on the uses of computers in education.

*MIT's Mitchel Resnick*

Resnick took a meandering path to his current work at MIT. He studied physics and sciences in college, but realized when he graduated that he didn't want to pursue them further. Drawn by an interest in communicating ideas and helping people understand things, he worked as a journalist, writing about science and technology in the early days of PC computing. In 1983, while on a fellowship to MIT as a science journalist, he met social theorists Seymour Papert, Sherry Turkle, and Andrea diSessa, who would prove influential in shaping his views on education and learning.

Beal Institute researcher Shay Steinberg interviewed Resnick about his education philosophy for this book.

## A CONVERSATION WITH MITCHEL RESNICK

**Q:** *Your background is pretty varied. What led you towards working with kids and this area of technology?*

**A:** Partly it was because I was more interested in helping kids understand the world than helping business executives understand the world. Although both are interesting, it was a nice transition for me to be able to create technology rather than simply write about it. At MIT, I was able to work on creating new technologies and applying them in meaningful ways that help people understand the world around them. It connected with what had initially led me to journalism.

I ended up staying at MIT since my fellowship, first doing my PhD in computer science and then becoming a faculty member. It's been a great combination of technology and education.

Also, it wasn't just any approach to technology and education; I give a lot of credit to and was greatly inspired by Seymour Papert. Seymour Papert's approach to using technology in education is to help people learn through creating and designing things. I always felt that many of our best learning experiences come while we are actively engaged in making things, designing things, and creating things. That is at the core of Seymour's educational and learning approach, so it felt very natural to me.

> "I always felt that many of our best learning experiences come while we are actively engaged in making things, designing things, and creating things."

Again, it wasn't something that was necessarily prevalent to the extent it should have been in either the education world or in the computer world, especially back then. When computers were first entering schools, it was often about them delivering information to you, instructing you or asking questions to which you would respond. The idea of being more playful and design-oriented was the direction that I was interested in going in, and I found a home here at MIT where that was really supported.

*Your career has developed very much in the way that you allow your Lifelong Kindergarten participants to develop their ideas and learning.*

Experimentation and exploration are at the core of how most people learn, which is why play is so essential. Play is about experimenting and exploring.

The name of the Lifelong Kindergarten group came about as I looked around for good examples of the type of learning and education that were most successful and most rewarding. I took a lot of inspiration from kindergarten because it is a place where a lot of things work well. Most people recognize that it works well, and although they complain about other education models, they don't often complain about kindergarten. Kids spend a lot of time designing, creating, exploring, and experimenting. Building towers out of blocks or a castle out of clay, or finger painting, kindergarteners are playfully designing and collaborating with each other. Beyond kindergarten, this approach gets lost.

*Why do you think the educational system changes after the age of five or so? Are schools and learning institutions properly designed for imaginative learning?*

In part, the reason that kindergarten doesn't work beyond a certain point is because of the type of materials we've used for playful design and creation. Lego bricks or paint—these tangible materials are great for learning basic ideas about numbers, shapes, size, and color. But as you get a bit older and want to explore projects and ideas with more complexity, blocks or paint aren't enough to learn with. Schools react to this and believe that the only way to make people learn about complexity is by giving lectures and filling out worksheets. There is a real mistake in that, but with the tools we have in the world, people believe it is the easiest way to learn basic concepts.

This is where computers can make a very big difference. In my view, computers make it possible for us to continue learning more advanced ideas and complex concepts in a kindergarten style. We no longer have to learn through lectures and worksheets; instead, we can explore more complex ideas by experimenting in the computational world.

Much of what we want to learn as we grow older is how things interact with each other, how things work together as a system. We want to learn about the dynamics of the world, how things come alive—like biology or social relations—and how we fit within those dynamics. These are systems that interact and change, and it is hard to study things that interact and change if all you have are blocks. But because the computer is a dynamic interactive medium, it's easier to explore, experiment, and design interactive things and relationships with new computational tools.

"Computers make it possible for us to continue learning more advanced ideas and complex concepts in a kindergarten style."

*How well do you think other educational ecologies are set up for imaginative learning? For example, do you think we could apply the kindergarten model to higher levels of education such as business schools and corporations?*

To a certain extent, a lot of the best graduate schools already work like kindergartens. You do get the opportunity to explore and experiment, to work on things that interest and inspire you. Kindergarten and graduate school work pretty well. The problem lies with everything in between.

School is about absorbing a collection of information that someone has pre-digested for you and putting it into a certain framework to be added to your existing knowledge, rather than exploring or expressing yourself.

*Is there a way to develop some standard curricula—such as teaching twelfth-grade math using a kindergarten model?*

Yes, definitely. However, there would have to be some changes made regarding what is called the "standard curriculum." You could deal with some standard concepts, but I think you'd want to approach it differently.

One reason why it's more difficult to bring the kindergarten approach to learners of all ages has to do with the standard curriculum. If the goal is to have everybody learn the exact same concept in the next two days, then allowing exploring and experimenting is much more challenging. The "experiment and explore" approach works much better when you have a longer period of time and you allow people to go on different paths. If people have the opportunity to design things that are more connected to their own interests, you can set up the materials and the activities so that they engage important ideas along the way. It's more restrictive if you have to learn things in the next two days, and it's more challenging to use the kindergarten approach.

*How should corporations respond to the shifting technological and behavioral landscape with new training methodologies and learning environments?*

I think of training, rather than education, as a specific body of knowledge that everyone needs to learn in a fixed amount of time. It's sometimes more difficult to do that in a playful model. It's not impossible, and I certainly would encourage people to try to do it, but it can be more challenging.

> **"Design and innovation are driving the new economy, so corporations need to figure out ways to become more imaginative and stop trying to provide the same information to everyone all the time."**

Design and innovation are driving the new economy, so corporations need to figure out ways to become more imaginative and stop trying to provide the same information to everyone all the time. We also need to move away from [corporations'] methods of providing continuing education. While they realize that continuous learning is important, they only provide a one- or two-day workshop or a two-week course during the year. Intense sessions like that are good, but what's really needed is a different environment altogether, where you are learning throughout the year.

If design is what you are supposed to be doing, then you have to be constantly learning. What is needed is a mindset shift toward what continuing education and learning is. Instead of having a couple of days or weeks per year that are dedicated to learning, make it something that is always part of the job, integrated and incorporated into the work itself.

*Have you considered how it might be possible to bring a more exploratory attitude to a corporate structure/environment?*

Organizing the workplace so that the people doing the work can be involved in many different parts of the corporation and constantly suggest ways for improvement means that they get a sense of the overall picture and are more productive.

*Do you think the kindergarten model could be integrated into work settings? And what results can be achieved if play permeates all human and machine interactions?*

We have a lot of corporate sponsors, and we do workshops for them, although in a very limited way. But these workshops allow them to break out of their standard mode of doing things to try things in a different way.

Lego Serious Play [business innovation workshops] tries to get people to design things that are related to the current problem or organizational structure by building models and analogy. If they think in terms of connections, metaphors and analogies can be useful in opening up to experimentation and exploration.

> "Kindergarten and graduate school work pretty well. The problem lies with everything in between."

In Lifelong Kindergarten, we brainstorm and build models or software—like a program where you can gives rules to a lot of interactive parts. You can model things like cars on the highway or a flock of birds, and see what kinds of interactions will happen. A lot of times people will model things on the computer and try to make them an exact reality. Instead, we want to spark people to think about new forms of interaction—that the whole can be different than the sum of its parts. It's not so much about learning exactly how a bird flock works but learning about different types of relationships.

One of the things we found was that patterns could form in a decentralized way, where they don't have to be controlled from the top or from a center. A computer can give an understanding of how these patterns emerge by using simple rules where simple things interact in simple ways. A flock of birds isn't about birds following a leader but about each bird following simple rules, staying together, and forming a flock. A business organization may not be able to adopt the same rules as a flock of birds, but by exploring the possibility of decentralization, it can develop better ways of creating and designing things.

At an MIT graduation a few years ago, Vice President Al Gore was the graduation speaker and we wanted to have some way of asking him questions. We decided that the questions would be written down, but instead of one or two people filtering out the good questions, we proposed (unsuccessfully) the idea of a decentralized process. Everyone could write them down on pieces of paper, and then fold them as airplanes or crumple them up. The people at the back of the audience would look at them, and if they thought a question was good they would throw it forward in the audience. If the next person also thought it was good, they would throw it forward, but if they didn't, they would throw it backward. That way, the questions that lots of people thought were good would progress, and the ones that people didn't like would go backward. The audience would make each decision collaboratively.

*What is it that makes people come up with ideas like that?*

We brainstormed a few concepts using the type of software I was just talking about. Playing with the software gets people thinking in different ways, and unfortunately we don't grow up with enough experiences with that kind of thinking.

"Flashes of insight are more likely to come to the people who are prepared. If you build the right repertoire to draw upon, then you have the pieces in place for that insight to burst forward."

There are decentralized systems all around us, but we don't realize they're decentralized. We live in a society that's decentralized in many ways, yet we don't get a chance to design decentralized systems. That may seem like a paradox—to design a decentralized system. But that's what the software allows you to do. Design simple rules, let them loose, and see what happens. Giving people a chance to build and design things that way can help them develop better intuition.

We grow up in a world where we design and participate in a lot of centralized things, but we don't get enough experience negotiating within decentralized systems. More experience with decentralized systems opens up the possibilities for people to have that as part of their toolbox, part of their bag of tricks they can pull out.

*We know that imagination allows us to see things that are yet unseen, and many believe these sorts of things come to us in a flash, an image of some sort. But what you're saying seems to imply that it could be more mechanized than that?*

I think that the flashes of insight are more likely to come to the people who are prepared. If you build the right repertoire to draw upon, then you have the pieces in place for that insight to burst forward. But your ways of thinking must have that framework in place, building up those sets of experience, metaphor, and analogy.

The question is: How do you design systems where people are aware of those appropriate experiences and examples in their own lives, where they're more likely to have that flash of insight? In some ways, it's a system of behavior similar to a flock of birds, a pattern emerging when many thoughts coalesce in your head in a certain way. There are always near-misses that you are unaware of, but sometimes all the pieces are in place.

*Does current technology require more imaginative responses? Do we now need to use mental pictures more in order to access the possibilities of technology or develop new uses?*

Although the Internet has the infrastructure required to construct a collective imagination, there are a lot of pressures that push it in more centralized directions. It's not well set up for collaboration. It isn't so easy to add onto things on the Internet because it's turned into more of a publishing place (publishing information and getting it out there), rather than a collaborative space. The blogging phenomenon is a better representation of a decentralized system, where people are adding onto each other and collaborating online. But most people only get their information from a few sources.

One thing we really believe is that the tools and materials that you provide for people can make a very big difference in how they think and learn, use their imagination, and create. This is one of the lessons from the very first kindergarten.

Friedrich Froebel, the first person to officially open a kindergarten, was not just an educator but also a designer. He invented a set of toys and tools for kids to use, like blocks and beads, designed so that by playing with these things, kids would learn what he called "important ideas." That's a very important insight. The tools that we give people can be very important in determining how they experiment and explore, what they learn about. It doesn't mean they can do it all by themselves, though. We have to surround them with the right type of environment that encourages imaginative use of those materials.

The challenge for us is that although the materials we develop can have great potential for unleashing the imagination, they can be used in very narrow and restraining ways. Lego Mindstorms [robotics invention system] can be used as a construction kit to free up your imagination and build all sorts of wonderful things, but instead a teacher will say, "Today we will use this to build a car. These are the instructions, you will be evaluated on how well you follow them, and there will be a quiz at the end of the day on how the gear system works." Unfortunately, it's difficult to integrate new technologies that are potentially supportive to creative thinking within many school systems.

> "It's easier to evaluate whether kids can do a certain type of arithmetic calculation than whether or not they've developed as creative thinkers."

I was in Singapore for a conference set up by the Ministry of Education, and most school systems would only use creative technologies after school. They saw the only way to learn basic mathematics was through drill and practice, which is unfortunate. Yet there is a whole set of complex factors that push schools in that direction, like assessment systems and the types of exams. They play a big role in how schools are evaluated and how children are evaluated, which is partially why teachers feel a great deal of pressure to drill and prepare students in a certain way.

*Do you have other examples of how imagination is used or not used in education?*

Creative thinking can be difficult to evaluate within the current system. It's easier to evaluate whether kids can do a certain type of arithmetic calculation than whether or not they've developed as creative thinkers. And because evaluating creativity is very subjective and contextual, judgment and fairness is also difficult. But hopefully, you could measure and evaluate whether or not students had become more creative in their thinking, charting their progress.

*Do you think there's a way to measure that?*

By giving people a design problem and encouraging them to come up with multiple solutions, you see if they are able to approach problems in different ways, which is a pretty strong indicator of creative thinking. People are afraid of imagination to a certain extent. For example, maybe teachers are afraid of not looking great if their students aren't doing well.

When a teacher has a group working on the same model in Lego Mind-storms, it's much easier for them to prepare ahead of time. They've already built a model and know what could go wrong during the session, ensuring that they're less likely to be taken unaware and provide a more smooth lead for the group. Typically, if something unexpected happens, they'll hide it during class and try to figure it out afterward, in private. But despite how uncomfortable it can be when something unexpected happens in the classroom, teachers being taken unaware and solving a problem on the fly can be one of the best learning experiences for a kid. It would be much better if kids could watch them going through the process, experimenting and exploring and figuring it out. Most people would agree that the most important thing, especially with younger grades, is to learn how to become a good learner, and the best way to do that is by observing other good learners in practice. Seeing a teacher solving a problem illustrates the process and progress of a good learner as well as showing that authority figures don't necessarily always have all the answers.

*Considering the history of imagination, can you think of any examples where imagination transformed a moment?*

Often when we try to trace scientific discoveries back through history, we see that they happen by accident, like penicillin or cellular behavior. A favorite example is a kid's invention of a hanger because he couldn't reach to hang up his coat. His hanger had a straight bar that extended a long way down before forming the triangle. He could actually hang up his coat, because it was at a kid's height. What I really like is that it's some-thing so familiar that we never think to redesign because it does its job. It takes someone thinking about it a little differently—such as a kid who can't reach the hanger—to come up with something different.

*I guess that's where unlearning comes into play. How can we unlearn? And do you think people need to unlearn to use the kindergarten model?*

Part of unlearning is always being willing to give things a fresh look, to question your assumptions, to not assume that things are the way they are because they have to be that way. It was a big "aha!" moment for me when I realized that the eating utensils I'd been using my whole life were designed objects, and that it didn't have to be that way. The fact that they were divided into three objects— fork, spoon, knife—couldn't it have been two or four? Did they have to be broken down or combined in that way, especially when you think of how different cultures have resolved them in different ways? Most kids don't grow up thinking that the world around them is made of designed objects and that someone has designed it that way. But when you have design experiences yourself, you look at that world with new eyes: These things have been designed and they can be redesigned.

# 5

# Getting Serious About Play

Today's adult must possess the skill for play in order to perform meaningful interactions with the technology of everyday life—making a withdrawal from an ATM, initiating an email message, making a cell phone call. In this sense, we play every day, unbeknownst to us.

# How the Information Age Relies on Play

*The creation of something new is not accomplished by the intellect, but by the play instinct acting from inner necessity.*

—Carl Jung

To create a compelling experience with products and technology, we must look at a new conceptual model—one that places play behavior at the core of the creation of experiences and products. Indeed, two books—*Homo Ludens*, Johan Huizinga's 1938 study of play among Europeans, and anthropologist Roger Caillois's *Man, Play and Games*—describe as *play* our precise interactions with ATMs, email, and cell phones.

By designing with play behavior and interactivity as the experience providers, we create the benefit of the best toys: They are fun, engaging, challenging, rewarding, nonfrustrating, and the value of the experience is both repeatable and cumulative. Play should not be seen as a trivial activity, performed by hands and objects, but as a highly spiritual activity dependent on imagination and creativity more than on any play artifact. The artifact for play is the human brain.

*Hands do not initiate play; the mind must do it first.*

Deconstructing the experience of almost any interaction with most technologies demonstrates the connection to play behavior. The strong elements of play involved in many of our voluntary daily activities—voicemail, instant messaging, warming food in the microwave—paved the way for their quick acceptance. And once these kinds of activities become play, they must keep challenging the users, maintaining their interest in the possibility of the next experience.

"Play should not be seen as a trivial activity, performed by hands and objects, but as a highly spiritual activity dependent on imagination and creativity more than on any play artifact. The artifact for play is the human brain."

The slow acceptance of the ATM (or the personal computer) in the early 1980s was partly due to the adult's inability to engage in play. A child would have recognized immediately the "benefit" of the activity, and the play character and play pattern of the device. When something loses its play nature, it becomes a chore. And a chore does not entice the user to engage in the activity. The device needed is what I call a ToolToy.

# Tools, Toys, and ToolToys

I coined the term *ToolToy* in 1989 to emphasize the importance of consciously reexamining the process of product and experience in the context of an improved conceptual and behavioral model. In this model, play, and the values it represents, have a pivotal role. The basic passage of any artifact from tool to toy must be placed in the context of the famous Theory of Human Motivation put forth by educational psychologist Abraham Maslow in 1943. His theory proposes that humans must satisfy a series of needs in order to achieve healthy and fulfilled lives. Beginning with basic physiological and safety needs, the hierarchy then extends to latent needs such as love/belonging, esteem/status, and self-actualization.

> **TOOLTOY**
>
> a product that satisfies the requirements for a functional tool and gives the user the pleasures associated with toys.

If objects had conscious phases of existence, like humans, they would likely move from basic physiological needs toward self-actualization—*toward becoming that for which they were intended*, but on a different and higher plateau. For example, a living room chair must be well made, of reliable materials, and kept out of the elements to fulfill its physiological and safety needs. It must be ergonomic and aesthetically pleasing in the living room context (fitting in visually with other furniture) to fulfill its love and esteem needs. And it must bring a pleasurable experience to the user to become self-actualized as a chair—fulfilling the purpose for which it was intended.

> "We act on tools with our hands, and on toys with our imagination. The whole being needs both as a condition of self-actualization."

While referencing Maslow, I must point out that I do not subscribe to his placing of needs in a hierarchy, with some necessarily seen as more important than others. For the fully functioning human being, needs are rarely hierarchical but rather synchronic and dynamic. They relate to each other and are equally important to the human spirit. And so it is with tools and toys: We act on tools with our hands, and on toys with our imagination. The whole being needs both as a condition of self-actualization.

The historic passage of any tool involves the creation of its primordial, purposeful, and functional shape first, and then the addition of elements unrelated to that function. Some of these elements are decorative, as in surface treatments or engraving, while others identify the tool by the individual user or owner, such as crests or trademarks. The passage from tool to toy—and particularly the passage from tool to ToolToy—involves adding to its function and image a third element: *behavior.*

Toys are a perfect example of behavioral artifacts. By themselves, they mean and do nothing. They are designed for "relationships" or for the "experience of," and not simply for the aesthetics of form or practical functions. The functionality of a toy resides in its potential for creating a relationship, either between it and the user, or among users. It is here that we can find a new product development brief that takes into consideration the relevance of play behavior and its continuation in adulthood, in the context of all cultures, and with specific regard to the creation of artifacts and environments.

When we intentionally start adding elements of manner and relationship—behavioral play characteristics—to any object or system that contains elements of purpose (that is, any object that must help human beings to do things), we are transforming a tool into a ToolToy: Swatch watches, Nike shoes, Apple Macintosh's OS X operating system, Smart cars, and the like. Tools are designed for what we do with them; ToolToys determine the *way* we do it—our physical technique as well as our imagination. *The ToolToy is the aesthetic of the possible.*

# Just Playing Around

*There are children playing in the streets who could solve some of my top problems in physics, because they have modes of sensory perception that I lost long ago.*

—J. Robert Oppenheimer, nuclear physicist

Our search for a new ecology of imagination, creativity, and innovation starts by reclaiming play as an ageless and indispensable condition of every human being, as well as the indispensable condition for the choreography of interaction between user and object. This journey allows the creation of a way of life in which every product, every service, and every system becomes a festival. To quote play theorist Robert E. Neale, "What happens to the child in play can happen to the adult, and when it does, paradise is present."

Individual play is as essential to the imaginative adult as it is to the development of the child. Tim Berners-Lee has stated that he was "just playing" on his new NeXT computer and exploring the possibilities of hypertext when he invented the World Wide Web. His ability to play generated one of the most significant tools to shape human experience.

## "It is in play that we have made our greatest discoveries."

His experience is not unique; countless inventions and innovations have been realized by venturing into the unknown, playing with an idea or process to see what might happen. When DuPont chemist Stephanie Kwolek poured a particular polymer in 1965, she noticed something intriguing: The consistency and color were very different from what she expected. Her curiosity and willingness to play led to the development of Kevlar, one of the strongest and lightest fibers ever invented, used in a variety of products from brake linings to bulletproof jackets. As she later commented, "All sorts of things can happen when you're open to new ideas and playing around with things."

The ecology of play allows and encourages us to maintain childlike traits, chase silly questions, get excited, and dream of impossible goals, while forgetting all the metrics that rule life outside this space. Here we can develop our potentiality as tricksters, creating narratives however we see fit. The ecology of play is the ecology of possibility, which incubates creativity. And creativity starts by creating an image of possibility.

# Playing the Game

*The essential feature of play is that during true playfulness the solution of a problem is not imperative.*
                    —Franz Alexander, *The Psychoanalytic Quarterly,* April 1958

By having no measurable value of usefulness or practicality, the activities of the Temporary Play Space (TPS) allow people to practice and perfect mental abilities that might not receive exposure otherwise. These activities also allow them to develop and master play behaviors with other people, or with new tools, objects, and ideas. This builds off a play pattern that we use in our daily interactions with others—our social games with defined rules and context-specific codes. For example, the way we relate to business associates or go out on a date follows a general game structure, and we find play in the contextual details.

The play element has long been part of business competition—specifically, the competitive aspects of play that focus on setting records and proving one's superiority or merit. These aspects are at the core of the *"need to play,"* a need as pronounced in adults as it is in children.

"There is a game side to almost every commercial effort or technological achievement: Business is play. And the most successful players of this game are those who can also imagine the opposite: Play is business."

The desire to challenge, to be the best at something in a demonstrable way—establishing a record or overcoming an obstacle, for instance—emphasizes the *play* and *game* elements in economical and social life. President Kennedy's desire to send a man to the moon inspired the nation to play with the challenge of his dream—to actively explore the "impossible." There is a game side to almost every commercial effort or technological achievement: Business is play. And the most successful players of this game are those who can imagine the opposite: Play is business. For them, play means knowledge and mastery of the present in order to deal with the future.

I am not suggesting that every organization should have a free-for-all work ecology. But when involved in creating new products and services—in that moment or in that month—the process must include a phase in which there are no benchmarks or metrics, and individuals are allowed to play within the boundaries of what play is all about. To play with their own ideas and create a space for *"What if...?"*

Play behavior might not be the best behavior range for everyone in the corporation, but the option must be present somewhere within the business. For a period of time, people need to have the freedom of uncertainty: *I cannot define what I will produce.*

# The Conditions for Possibility

Flexibility of mind, inventiveness, improvisational skills, ambition, intuition, and focus are some of the qualities shared by people who are effective facilitators of change. These qualities are encouraged through an engagement in play activities and by the freedoms promoted by play: freedom from expected utilitarian results and repression. Every play activity we engage in is a one-of-a-kind laboratory for our instincts, insights, and intuition. And the creation of this space cultivates the ecology of possibility.

We create the freedom to work the way we need to, on whatever we desire. It is a space *separate* from the constraints of our "regular" lives, where we set our own time and direction in the serious exploration of possibility. Our path is uncertain—there are no immediate metrics or benchmarks that can tell what it means.

## "Would you like to play?"

Play is *unproductive* in the traditional sense of the word, as we expect no direct benefit or gain. It is governed by its own rules, meaning that we define for ourselves the actions and outcomes we will accept in this realm, in this moment, and for this time. We initiate it on our own, using our trickster capability to suspend the rules of real life and address the possibilities of our imagination.

# 6
# Transformed by Imagination

During the opening ceremonies at the Olympic Games in Barcelona in 1992, a spectacular example of imagination's transformative power occurred. In the full darkness of the stadium, Paralympic archer Antonio Rebollo took aim at a target 180 feet away and 70 yards high. His flaming arrow gracefully arced across the stadium and over the cauldron, igniting the Olympic flame. Rebollo's shot symbolized humanity's potential to overcome obstacles through the power of imagination and skill.

# The Imaginative Pursuit of Unorthodox Questions

Who was responsible for such a magnificent moment? Was the idea the inspiration of one or many people? Most important, what was the question to which Antonio Rebollo's arrow was an answer?

The question might have been: How do we light the flame for an extraordinary Olympic Games, where no nation has been banned, no nation is boycotting, and newly independent countries will participate for the first time? The organizers needed an act that would be inspiring: a symbol of hope, promise, and victory in the face of adversity.

"What was the question to which Antonio Rebollo's arrow was an answer?"

Or the question could have been: How can we communicate in a single, elegant, simple, and powerful gesture the extraordinary and historic times we have witnessed since the 1988 Olympics? The collapse of the Soviet Union; the unification of Germany; the freedoms now enjoyed by the masses of Hungary, Romania, the Czech Republic, Slovenia, Slovakia, Albania, and Poland; the independence of Latvia, Lithuania, Estonia, Ukraine, Belarus….

The day arrived. Athletes from 172 participating nations were gathered in the stadium, united in the darkness under the Catalan sky, waiting. And then came Rebollo, using a bow and arrow, an artifact 9000 years old and known to every culture on earth. There is no gimmick; there is just this human being, alone, in the middle of the stadium, aiming at something in the distance, and transforming a moment into magic.

The magic of humanity's possibility.

## A SHOT IN THE DARK

When questions are asked and their value is understood, people have answers. This is the way it works: question, answer—a symbiotic relationship. And right now we need to ask good questions, great questions— questions that lead to more questions, better answers, and real integrity. Asking them means being in the right state of mind—creating a new space to see the world around you while suspending reality for a moment. And it means being able to share the benefit of that possibility with others.

Let's say you are in the planning session for the opening ceremonies of the Barcelona Games and somebody suddenly murmurs, "What if an

*Rebollo, an ancient archer, and the Olympic cauldron.* ➜

*left: Dimitri Lundt/TempSport/CORBIS, right: Pierre Colombel/CORBIS, top: Antonio Rebollo/Getty Images*

arrow was fired straight above the cauldron to light it?" Each person would see different kinds of value and benefit in that question. The architect may want to preserve the simplicity of the structure by not building the stairs traditionally leading to the cauldron. The construction engineer might think of the time and manpower saved by not installing all those steps. Or the accountant might rejoice at the thought of the money saved by not building those steps. Can you imagine the reaction in the room when someone proposes lighting the cauldron with a bow and arrow?

"There was no gimmick; just a human being, alone in the middle of the stadium, aiming up at something in the distance—and transforming a moment into magic."

Rumor has it that everyone who heard that question posed at the Olympic planning committee initially thought it was a ridiculous idea. But slowly, its possibility started growing in each of the planners; once explored from their own perspective, each found value in the bow-and-arrow idea. However, there was no precedent for such a feat, no guarantee that it would work, and it might even be impossible. A few Olympic archers had actually tried and failed to reach the target at that distance with regulation Olympic arrows. (The regulation draw weight is about 48 pounds, but this would require a 70-pound arrow.) And then there was the small detail of the darkness. Barcelona would be very dark that night. Both the stadium and the city would be unlit to maximize the effect of the Olympic flame rising above them. So there was really nothing to aim at, except an idea.

Rebollo and the Olympic committee had to believe in the capability of that idea, with courage and trust. Rebollo had to rely on his muscle memory and the feeling of his stance from practice shots until he was satisfied that he was aimed and ready. And when he released the arrow that lit the Olympic flame, he released the imagination of the billions of people watching the event. And the value of the question was then released—when all those people, from around the world, shared a moment of inspiration.

# Questions and Answers

The space of inquiry is the space of play and play behavior, where children excel. Young children constantly ask questions and are often encouraged to do so. But when their education reaches the *Don't play with your food* point, they are being told to listen to answers instead. Our education system does not teach how to ask great questions, but instead encourages children to pursue the "right" answer to every question, valuing that one answer over any question that precedes it.

Many organizations are full of very talented and capable people who only know how to give answers. This is what organizations and society call for: people who are trained to brainstorm and mind-map, using any technique that allows them to resolve identifiable problems. They can give a creative answer to just about anything—as long as they are *given* the question.

"Strategic creativity begins with 'What if...?' The goal is not to produce products that penetrate markets, but to communicate behaviors that become relevant to people's lives, like health monitoring or saving household energy."

However, I can't stress enough that *it is the questioning* that keeps people on an imaginative and stimulating journey of learning. Allowing a stream of questions to flow is the map we use for exploration and discovery, navigating through the possibility of our imaginations. With these "What if...?" questions, our answers shape the future.

Asking stimulating questions to create new images of possibility does not necessarily begin with complicated language or ideas. We can start with simple constructs that enable more complicated questions to emerge. "What if my fridge could communicate with me? What would it want to say?" Have you ever wondered what your refrigerator would like to say to you?

### A Conversation with Fred the Fridge

"I think you should start calling me Fred," read the latest message from my refrigerator.

"No, thanks," I replied as I enter the kitchen. "I like calling you THE FRIDGE, because that is what you are. And besides, you are interfering too much in my life as it is. I would rather avoid any personal stuff."

"Interfering in your life? *Interfering!* I think I help you a lot!"

"Really? You think you do? OK, what have you done for me lately?" I asked provocatively, instantly realizing that I should have known better. My stomach flipped.

"Well, I'm *glad* you asked. Let us review just the past week, shall we?" The Fridge, or rather Fred, began to whir.

"OK, go ahead."

"I am sending a list to your handheld at this very moment. If you have any questions at all, I will be happy to give you more details. "Interfering...hmmph!"

## A Conversation with Fred the Fridge, *Continued*

Before I knew it, my PDA was displaying a list that was, I must confess, very impressive. The list read:

### General Activities for the Week of June 7-13

✦ Activated power on the cascading network at 0610, inclusive of bathroom lights, coffee maker, kettle, and kitchen lights. *(Daily)*

✦ Started shower in the bathroom at 0612 at 52°F. *(Daily)*

✦ Updated grocery supply list as of 0615 and recorded status. *(Daily)*

✦ Turned on the TV at 0645 to *Good Morning America*. Transferred CNN ticker to fridge door display in the kitchen. *(Daily)*

✦ Kept daily records of your grocery expenses and all charges at Shaw's and noted any abnormalities.

✦ Made daily menu suggestions.

✦ Activated the 'Things you might want to know about...' feature every time you or Martin picked an unusual item from the fridge—most recently when you tried Belgian endive.

✦ Reconfirmed your dentist appointment for Tuesday morning.

✦ Locked my door every time Michael, your 10-year-old nephew, visited.

✦ Ensured the washer and dryer were locked as well.

✦ Maintained close contact with your electric meter and adjusted all appliance consumption according to load on the grid and price per kWh. This saved you $16.38 in the past week alone.

✦ Maintained close contact with your car—I call her Matilda—and centralized all important statistics in my memory.

✦ June 9: Locked the front door, which *you* accidentally left open, and armed the anti-intruder sensors.

The fantasy of "Fred the Fridge" creates room in the mind for the possibility of something that does not exist (yet). Narrative allows us to explore potential benefits and threats, and once we become aware of both, we can create strategies that will transform the beneficial into real products and services while continually negotiating the threats. *This is the role of strategic creativity.*

Strategic creativity begins with "What if...?" The ideas, stories, products, and services that develop from that initial premise can then be tactically implemented to be relevant in the lives of millions of people. The goal is not to produce products that penetrate markets, but to communicate behaviors that become relevant to people's lives, like health monitoring or saving household energy. The question "What if my refrigerator could speak?" is not about triviality, but about human potential being revealed through technology and imagination.

## CAN WE MEASURE ACCOUNTABILITY IN PLAY?

I have been asked this question many times while giving talks on imagination and play during the past few years. There is a premise within this idea that needs to be challenged, which is that a *lack* of accountability is characteristic of an imaginative and less-structured environment. However, accountability is typically defined and applied within an ecology of work, as a repeatable benchmark, and it is unreasonable to use those same standards in an imaginative environment.

We traditionally set boundaries as a way to measure our progress within a given structure, such as deadlines for work projects or following a project brief. We set constraints and measure our success in our ability to meet them. Are we successful at meeting our project goal and our deadline? By extension, every product, space, and service is the sum of its set of constraints. And in the business environment, those constraints serve their purpose—tasks are fulfilled in line with their resources, specs, and deadlines, and people are accountable for their contributions or actions.

"Any metric will place a boundary around our thoughts, but in an imaginative environment, those boundaries and metrics are transitions rather than endings."

Imagination is structured, but its constraints are not to be found in most business environments or common everyday behavior. Imaginative structures fit the context of the experience, and so they are continually changing. The structure is the sum of the constraints of the imaginative story being told—the exploration of possibility and experience outside our daily lives. The metrics for imagination are determined by how compelling and engaging the story is, and accountability is found in its ability to spark the imaginations of the participants.

Organizations and businesses excel at explorations around questions such as "What if my refrigerator could speak?" But they have difficulties exploring the process that generates that question. In the corporate process, metrics and imagination are not complementary. Any metric will place a boundary around our thoughts, but in an imaginative environment, those boundaries and metrics are transitions rather than endings.

What happens when we discover ideas or answers that are both unexpected and outside our familiar moral judgments? What if one discovers a cure for cancer that wipes out other species? Or comes upon both the benefits and extreme harm found in nuclear fission? Every discovery has multiple implications—both good and bad. Do we endanger ourselves by exploring beyond what is conventionally accepted and judging it along the way? How can we place a set of moral boundaries around something not yet discovered, and something not yet applied?

## HOW DO YOU MEASURE A DREAM?

Can the pursuit of possibility be bound in morality or ethics? Should we avoid the pursuit of something because it may fall into the "wrong hands" at some point? Only when a possibility is defined and its applications begun can we judge and analyze from many points of view. Our accountability is based in the choices we make with the ideas found along the way—how we choose to use or act upon them in a particular moment. But placing limits on the process itself is like intentionally locking yourself out of your car: Suddenly the vehicle that could take you anywhere is unavailable.

"Possibility is dynamic, and it changes continually because we change continually. The problem is that most benchmarks do not account for this change."

If you could stop nightmares, would you do it? Push a button, throw a switch, and wave goodbye to bad dreams? What about dreams that begin in terror and are transformed into wonder and joy? And vice versa? How can you place boundaries on a dream that has not yet been dreamt, simply to avoid the possibility of scary prospects? If you chose to turn off your dreams, then every night before you slept, you would know what to expect. And although it might ensure a routine of regular, but not restful sleep, it would not test your limits or lead to change.

Possibility is dynamic, and it changes continually because we change continually. The problem is that most benchmarks do not account for this change. Traditional R&D benchmarks are not an applicable measure for imaginative pursuits because they are the benchmarks of creativity—tangible and static. The research they measure is regulated by: "Do we have enough to move forward? How well is it aligned with our expectations and the expectations of our stakeholders?"

With the metrics of imagination, it is a challenge to know when we have enough. When does the story stop? (It does not *end;* we just pause for a while.) Have we ventured down side-paths, turned around and upside down, and explored as many ideas as we can? Artists are the most intuitive about meting out the lines, the notes, and the brush strokes; playing with the story. But where do *we*, those of us who *aren't* artists, draw the line, and how do we know where the line leads?

In the past, creativity has been benchmarked through economic models. If a particular activity increased revenue, then we believed we must measure whatever it was that has caused the increase. What percentage of the revenue came from products and services that were less than five years old, or three, or two? If it was a large percentage, we thought that the organization was having a good return on creativity. After all, creativity is how new products and services come about—a solid metric comprised of complex gating structures that filter ideas through, from napkin sketch to enthusiastically backed project.

But what if a comprehensive study were undertaken to find the millions of great ideas that *did not make it* through the funnel? Ideas that did not "measure up" to one set of metrics or another; imaginative ideas that did not immediately have answers translatable to the bottom line. Most ideas have value, but it takes various perspectives to find that value.

# Managing the Imaginative Team

As a corporate resource, imagination needs to be directed by people who in temperament and motivation are more like film directors than executive producers. It is clear that creativity, the application of that imaginative resource, needs a new class of managers with a new skill set.

"The iMac was the first step in Apple's tremendous recovery, but it took one manager to look with fresh eyes at the creative potential that had been waiting five years to be discovered."

For example, Jonathan Ive began working for Apple Computer in 1992. For five years and under three different CEOs, he designed products that tried to bring Apple out of near-bankruptcy and back into the mainstream. However, it was not until the return of the current (and original) CEO, Steve Jobs, that Ive's capability was revealed with the design and launch of the iMac in 1998. The iMac was the first step in Apple's tremendous recovery, but it took one manager to look with fresh eyes at the creative potential that had been waiting five years to be discovered.

Managing imagination and imaginative teams is an intimate and personal activity in constant flow. The manager is like both gardener and water to a patch of plants. He or she must have the skills to trigger imagination in others and provide the nourishment that cultivates ideas and keeps them in perpetual growth. The manager is a psychologist, a head to bounce ideas off, a friend, and a playing partner. He or she must also feed and sustain what grows, bringing new light and insight to facilitate more and more imaginative possibilities. There are no lines to be crossed, and no constraints to be mindful of; it is all a process in flow, a learning ecology in which each new discovery and each new insight continually changes the questions that originated them. Managing the imaginative team means letting that happen without losing momentum.

The manager must also understand and let the imaginative team members maximize their roles:

- ✦ **The poet:** The person who transforms data into metaphors, gives meaning and relevance, and makes connections.

- ✦ **The out-there person:** The one who is deeply connected to the edges, understands the language of the underground, and understands the motives. A graffiti master, born with hip-hop in his blood. Consumes information as food, remixes it, and paints the big pictures.

- ✦ **The catalyst:** The person who combines and transforms bits of news into stories of the future. Becomes every part, every story, character, situation, or object.

- ✦ **The keystone:** The team member who analyzes future scenarios for new experiences and economic opportunities. Makes sense, defines opportunities, and is the person to "touch base" with.

- ✦ **The chief possibility officer:** The trickster. The one who creates the environment where dreams are allowed. Defines the direction of the inquiry and the general expectations of performance.

And so we are ready. We have assembled the team. We have a new creative ecology—the ecology of possibility—and we know who is in charge: the trickster. Now we just need the tools and methods for transforming imagination into a strategic asset. Read on.

# 7

# Strategic Imagination and Creativity

One person in a crowd at a U2 concert uses her cell phone screen as a torch. And then 5000 cell phone screens light up, dotting the darkness like stars in the night sky. This is a simple example of a causal effect based on direct feedback. Could the behavior of the first person doing this be predicted? Could the ensuing behavior of the crowd be predicted? Our answers depend on how playful and imaginative we want to be.

# Seeking Out Signals

If we see the cell phone as just another cordless telephone, then the answer is "no." But if we recognize the cell phone as a communication device, and if we understand communication as expressing ideas and feelings via multiple means of transmission, then the answer must be "yes." Understanding the nature of humans and the basic human needs for expression, expansion, community, and exchange makes it rather easy to predict the pattern of possible interactions among the crowd at a concert in their use of cell phones as torches.

Strategic creativity seeks out the signals that maximize strategic capital— discovering the patterns in the past and present to amplify the possibility in the future. These signals are often very simple acts, such as raising a cell phone as a torch, that multiply on a collective scale, as behavior encourages the alignment of technology and organizations.

Because we are traditionally taught to interpret signals with efficiency and reason, we tend to seek out and identify recognizable or familiar signals at the expense of unknown or strange signals, confirming our expectations. We may dismiss these "weak signals" because of our reticence or inability to redefine our process of expectation, to imagine their possibility. As we have discussed, this inability to see beyond the boundaries of rationality is the imagination gap—a gap between current intellectual and technical capability and current possibility for an individual or a group.

## MR. WATSON—COME HERE!

On March 10, 1876, in Boston, Alexander Graham Bell and Thomas Watson invented the telephone. The device itself was an awkward object containing a wooden stand, a funnel, a cup of acid, and some copper wire.

"Unfolding the future is not about signals in technologies; it is about signals in us."

This is what the first telephone did not have: a numeric keypad, voice-announced caller ID, a backlit caller display, call waiting, general and private mailboxes with customized greetings, conference capabilities and transfers, a 200 name-and-number call log, a built-in hands-free speakerphone, busy station indicators, memory keys, media players and recorders, personalized ring tones, agenda planners, or Internet access.

At the time, the technology was inadequate for mass production—rough and clumsy. And there was no system ready and capable of supporting it. But the desire was present. The question for us is: Was this telephone a weak signal?

*A weak signal? A diagram of the first telephone.* →

### If the Telephone Is the Answer, What Is the Question?

The word *telephone* goes back to the Greeks. *Tele* means "from a distance" and *phone* means "any device that emits or receives sound, or a speaker of language." So any device that reproduces sounds made by voice over a distance is a telephone. But what is the question for which the telephone is the answer? To figure that out, we need to look at both the precursors to the telephone and the behaviors that created them.

One soon realizes that the history of the telephone is as old as human civilization itself: People have always wanted to communicate from great distances. When the voice simply won't carry, we've used smoke signals, light signals, carrier birds, drums and sound, semaphores, postcards, and so on. These precursors and behaviors involved communicating messages about the person or people sending them—their status, their location, and the quality of their existence in this place. It's important to note that the precursor and behavior archetype of communication from afar—the first transmission of a condition over distance—was a visual signal.

"Recognizing the human desire for communication by any means would give us the insight to forecast the emergence of both the telephone and what we now call a cell phone."

Now think of the most frequently asked question in a telephone communication during the past 75 years: "Can you hear me?"

Two of these words are key to uncovering the telephone's deep behavior archetype: The first is *hear*, a verb; the other is *me*, a pronoun. The verb reflects the phase of technological development in which the transmission took place. For all purposes, the technology is transitory, and *hear* could be replaced with *see*. The verb represents the technology of the moment—the *how*.

The pronoun is more revealing. It represents the purpose of the call, actuating the latent needs of the users. It is about *me*, the caller. It is about my personality and the things I wish to communicate to you, at this moment and from this place. Give me more technology and I will use more verbs—I want you to hear me, see me, smell me, feel me. I want, need, desire all the technology that will empower me, that will expand my capability and allow me to actualize every expression of my emotions, of myself, to you. To communicate my condition to you, wherever you may be.

In other words, the pronoun represents the *what* and the deeper *why.* More often than not, companies aim a large amount of their innovation efforts at adding value to the *how*, rather than to the *what* or *why.* As discussed earlier, this is a tactical innovation—it focuses on improving the current problem and protects the *how* against competitors. Addressing the *what* or *why* is the field of strategic innovation, where value is created and precompetitive advantages are established.

So, what is the question for which the telephone was the answer?

**Can you hear me?**

Recognizing this human desire for communication by any means would give us the insight to foresee the emergence of both the telephone and what we now call a cell phone—the enhancement and actualization of the telephone's past through current technology. This is what motivated the concert crowd. The future of an artifact is a measure of its capability to concisely reveal our latent needs and desires, as well as to shape the best representations of ourselves.

The telephone was not a "weak signal"; our ability to receive it was weak. Unfolding the future is not about signals in technologies; it is about signals in us.

# Strategic Creativity and the Behavior Modes

In a January 23, 2006, speech at the Ford Motor Company Business Review, Chairman and CEO Bill Ford announced how he planned to change the company's stale business model: "We're going to figure out what people want before they even know it—and then we're going to give it to them."

Ford's statement is the opportunity and case for strategic creativity. The people and organizations that expertly identify both signals and latent behaviors (cell phones at a concert), and then realize them as technological experiences will become indispensable in the next decade. Strategic creativity is this new capability, bridging the gap and aligning culture, business, science, technology, and the social sciences. Strategic creativity explores the significant possibilities that arise where these things intersect—and it requires imagination as a prerequisite for strategic change and innovation.

In an imagination space, we can find the answer to the type of question the Taino might have posed when they encountered Columbus's ships: How does this "new thing" fit, change, or enhance the ecology of our life and our behavior? How do we need to adapt our behavior to the new possibilities that this new thing may reveal? Be that a boat or this new invention, the telephone.

## THE DYNAMIC SYSTEM ECOLOGY OF BEHAVIOR

The adaptation required is the capability to understand that the systems we live in are not static but dynamic. A system is a set of imposed constraints on a set of variables. We encounter typical systems every day at work, at leisure, and at home: The office, the restaurant, and the baseball field are a few examples. Each contains variables and has rules to make it work for the common good of those involved. In the workplace, the variables are the space, the furniture, the equipment present and used, and the people using it. The restaurant variables include those, as well as the exchange of products, services, and performance.

Constraints are part of each system. The word *constraints* is often positioned as negative or restrictive, but that would be misleading in this context. Here it is meant as a summary of what we might call parameters, boundaries, rules of conduct, controls, or operators.

"The people and organizations that expertly identify latent behaviors and the technology experiences to realize them will become indispensable in the next decade."

The constraints of behavior in a system of natural and manmade variables are described by the physical, social, individual, and technological affordances of a particular context. It is our perceptions and expectations of our relationships and interactions that set our "normal" behavior ranges.

The dynamic system ecology of behavior is a system of continual change and adaptation in which each new variable entering the system—such as a large boat, foam rubber, the telephone, or any new technology, idea, or individual—appends its own constraints. These constraints in turn modify and expand the existing constraints of the variables already present in the system. So scaling up an organization, for example, will expand the existing constraints—location, vision, size—which will then expand the constraints of the variables—staff, scope of market and production, and so on.

There are two distinct modes of behavior—the *common manifest behavior mode* and the *full behavior mode*—that we exhibit in various circumstances. How we respond to the possibility in each new variable and constraint determines the scope of our perceptions and our ability to expand them. By satisfying the combination of new and old constraints, we are engaged in movement leading to growth and the manifestation of new human potential.

### The Common Manifest Behavior Mode

The actions and tasks we perform and observe in everyday life are referred to as the common manifest behavior mode. *Common* in this context refers to conducting yourself in a manner defined as "ordinary" or "for the common good." If you travel by public transit, you know to pay with exact fare or token, where to sit on the bus, and how to notify the driver that you want to get off. This system has been established so as to be accessible to everyone, for each individual to know how to participate in it.

## COMMON MANIFEST BEHAVIOR MODE

the mode of thinking and acting in which people consider a new variable such as an innovation or piece of equipment as a solution to a defined or yet undefined problem.

In the common manifest behavior mode, any new variable introduced into the system—such as a new technology, piece of furniture, or employee—is subjected to the same constraints (rules, benchmarks, questions) as all the old variables present in the system. The new variable should provide the answer to these questions: What is the problem for which a new variable is the solution? How does this change, help, or impede what I have always done? We look at the capability of new variables as a solution to a defined or yet undefined problem. The variable is assigned value and meaning based on its relevance as a solution to the perceived problem.

As discussed in Chapter 2, when rubber foam introduced a new variable in the high-jump drop pit box—replacing sand, wood shavings, and air-filled bladders—thousands of high jumpers and their coaches treated it as if it had the same capacity as the old materials to absorb the impact of a fall. They applied to foam the same constraints as they applied to everything else; in effect, foam was seen as the same solution to the problem of landing softly in the pit. In much the same way, we act in the common manifest behavior mode when we do not assign new meaning and new constraints to new variables, but instead tactically make them work better.

Dick Fosbury saw that foam was a trigger for a new way to jump. He realized that foam provides enough cushioning for a jumper to land on his or her back. He saw that this new variable brought about a new set of constraints. The variable contributed to a reconfiguration of how the landing material could be used, and this reconfiguration was, in fact, an opportunity.

The Fosbury Flop is a proven *tactical innovation*: It exposes a minimum of the body to the bar at any one time. It takes advantage of the body's symmetry because both arms and both legs are doing the same thing at the same time in a straight line. With this technique, the jumper can run harder toward the bar, decelerating less and achieving more power from the ground.

## The Full Behavior Mode

Full behavior mode occurs when we allow ourselves to be subjected to a new set of constraints at a particular moment in time. The principle here is that a new artifact—idea, environment, or technology—reveals the latent need of its users. *The artifact reveals the master.* The foam revealed the full mastery of Dick Fosbury's technique. By combining the constraints of the old variables with the constraints of the new variable, Fosbury entered into full behavior mode. His behavior was revealed and enhanced by a new technology; the foam's potential created an opportunity for Fosbury to attempt self-actualization. He understood that landing on foam was *part of* the high jump, not what happened after it. In this mode, Fosbury's creativity also resulted in a *strategic innovation.*

> ### FULL BEHAVIOR MODE
> mode of thinking and acting that includes the variables of both manifest and latent behavior through the construction of a temporary play space; in it, people look for meaning in a new variable by searching for the question that the variable answers.

Technology artifacts are not only an extension of our human capability, but also a means by which we discover the new limits of our capacity: what we are capable of and how we are capable. This is consistent with the notion of "self concept" developed by Carl Rogers, the cofounder, with Abraham Maslow, of the humanistic approach to psychology. Rogers believed that the most basic striving of an individual is toward the maintenance, enhancement, and actualization of the self.

For thousands of high jumpers active at the competitive level in Fosbury's time, the foam was seen only as a means to maintain something they were already doing. To Fosbury, the foam represented the possibility of enhancing his performance toward self-actualization: the best he could become.

Ideas, events, and many other new variables in our environment can also be triggers that allow our latent behaviors to emerge, to encourage new ways of acting, thinking, imagining, and so on. We engage in a full behavior mode every time we see a movie or read a story—fiction or nonfiction—as any narrative is also a platform where we can imagine and explore behaviors, desires, and motivations that are different from our "normal" experience and expectations. We can imagine war when we hear a news report on the radio or imagine the taste of a perfect chocolate ganache in the recipe we are reading in the same way that we engage in Frodo's journey or Lara Croft rescuing an artifact. All serve as operating platforms that connect common manifest behavior with latent behavior.

# SIGNALS IN OUR MIDST

*The hardest thing to see is what is in front of your eyes.*

—Goethe

Signals surround us, but until we assign meaning, value, and intensity to them, they are neutral, as if they do not exist. The discovery, monitoring, and interpretation of weak signals are vital to business strategy and research in communication, international security, international politics, and more.

"The sooner the interaction between receivers and signals, the more involved those individuals or organizations will be in shaping their own future."

Igor Ansoff, an applied mathematician who worked primarily in strategic business management, developed the "weak signal methodology" in the mid-1970s to improve strategic-planning management practices and make organizations attentive to so-called weak signals. In it, he assigned a value to the signals that we encounter as a means to measure their potential implications or meaning. According to Ansoff, weak signals are often inexact and difficult to observe or understand: "When a threat or opportunity first appears on the horizon, we must be prepared for very vague information, which will progressively develop and improve with time."

Ansoff defined five stages in the detection and understanding of a weak signal:

1. The sense of threat/opportunity
2. The source of threat/opportunity is known
3. The shape of threat/opportunity is concrete
4. The response strategies are understood
5. The outcome of response can be forecast

The five stages assume that signals are more often than not changes in technology, disruptions, and events outside ourselves. More recent definitions of weak signals see individuals as receivers—spectators to the change that is about to take place. The sooner the interaction between receivers and signals, the more involved those individuals and organizations will be in shaping their own future. This view does not recognize that signals could manifest themselves in the behavior of people and that the emergence of a latent behavior is a signal in itself.

Others have suggested that weak signals usually come from the periphery, as half-hidden ideas or trends. This puts the burden on the signal: It is the signal that is weak, not the ability of the organization or individual to detect it. This view would discount the fact that the foam rubber pads introduced in the high jump pit were in plain sight, as was the Flop. It contends that the weakness was clearly that of the foam and not of the individuals who were looking at it.

### Finding Value in Weak Signals: The Beal Theory

At the Beal Institute for Strategic Creativity, we have developed another theory. We believe that signals are not at the periphery of present-day reality, but are in our midst. The Beal Theory of Signals maintains that an individual's or organization's inability to recognize the meaning and potential of signals—be they in emerging technologies or emergent behavior—comes from the limits of their rational boundaries, both socially constructed and individually adapted. The weakness comes from treating signals as novelties with potentially little impact on the present.

We are able to infer meaning to signals only through the analysis of content, context, and history, and our versatility to synthesize this information. Thus, in common manifest behavior mode, we create a space where every variable must be a solution to an identified or yet unidentified problem. If a new variable does not present a solution, it has no meaning to us in that context.

"The Beal Theory of Signals maintains that an individual's or organization's inability to recognize the meaning and potential of signals—be they in emerging technologies or emergent behavior—comes from the limits of their rational boundaries."

The first Taino to set eyes on the Santa María had difficulty finding the problem for which such a large boat was a solution. In the Taino space, and in the Taino common manifest behavior mode, such a large vessel was not only a practical impossibility; it did not present a solution to any of the problems the Taino could define. Therefore the boat became invisible, and without meaning.

The Beal Theory of Signals proposes the creation of the temporary play space to enable people to amplify the scope of their vision in a platform where possibility can exist and be explored. And since the eye cannot see what the mind does not understand, a new space must be created in the mind, a space that allows for the possibility of a gigantic boat. That space is in one's imagination.

This new platform is a place for us to be in full behavior mode, where common manifest behavior can be connected with released latent behavior in order to "see the boat."

## Why Signals Are Imperative: A Lesson from *Lawrence of Arabia*

In his article "Scenarios, Strategies and the Strategy Process," Kees van der Heijden, a Dutch author and professor focusing on strategic management, recounts a scene from the movie *Lawrence of Arabia*. In it, Lawrence and his guide are taking a rest at a well during a trip through the desert. Van der Heijden writes:

> *"They are thirsty, tired and very hot when they barely see a small, almost imperceptible speck on the horizon. As they sit around, the speck grows, moving toward them, coming closer and closer. This is a story about a sensed signal about to become precise. One can intuitively distinguish a form—it is a rider on a camel—and in time, both Lawrence and his companion can undeniably declare that this is a man, with a gun, on a camel."*

As van der Heijden puts it, "They wait. They watch. They wait. Two guys standing there, not knowing what to do about an approaching unknown." It is not long before the "signal" becomes *precise* for Lawrence's companion: While attempting to retrieve his revolver, he is shot dead by the approaching rider.

## "What if the travelers were not Lawrence of Arabia and his guide, but Sony and Vivendi International? And what if the speck was the iPod?"

Van der Heijden surmises that this scene:

> *"illustrates some of the weaknesses of the 'predict and control' approach to decision making and suggests why scenario thinking may help. Having identified an approaching speck on the horizon the decision maker tries to work out what it might be. In the film, the two people work hard at it. Various hypotheses are explored. On the other hand, nothing much is done in terms of response while they are trying to find the right answer. They assume they need to know what the future will bring before they can work out what needs to be done."*

Would an animal have done nothing? Unlikely.

An animal would have been in motion from the first sighting of the speck on the horizon. And what if the travelers were not Lawrence of Arabia and his guide, but Sony and Vivendi International? And what if the speck was the iPod? What if Nokia and Motorola were at the well, with Skype as the blurry speck? What kinds of threats or opportunities could they have read into the speck on the horizon?

Van der Heijden's example illustrates the imperative of being able to read signals—to see, make meaning, and understand the implications. And most important, of being provoked to action from the first trace of a signal.

Action research is one of the best methods to use in strategic creativity because of its adaptive nature as well as the transitional nature of the subjects at hand. It changes the parameters of the inquiry itself, based on the knowledge gained from discovery as one progresses. This is a process of change and of understanding the nature of the change: Informed change, in turn, informs change. Action informs understanding. And understanding unfolds the signal.

### Unfolding Signals

In the temporary play space, every disruption, innovation, or emerging behavior—every signal—is revealed to contain from its inception four features: It is precise, undeniable, intuitive, and sensed.

"The capability to map signal folds early in a signal's appearance allows for an appropriate course of action to be chosen. An appropriate course of action will maximize the opportunity—or minimize the threat—for both individuals and society."

In the case of the Taino, action research would have revealed that behind the *precise* signal of the boat—its physical presence—would be the *undeniable* conclusion that the boat contains people. One could further *intuit* from this that there must be, somewhere beyond the horizon, more boats like this one and more people. Finally, one could *sense* that both the people and their boats must come from a place where they make boats this big, a place that has even more people, probably lots of houses, and definitely more boats.

The capability to map these signal folds early in a signal's appearance allows for an appropriate course of action to be chosen. An appropriate course of action will maximize the opportunity—or minimize the threat—for both individuals and society. If Lawrence of Arabia and his guide (or Sony and Vivendi) had mapped the possibility of the speck on the horizon, many opportunities for action would have emerged, changing the course of events and their possibilities in the future.

The ecology of behavior creates or inhibits the opportunity for latent need. The ecology of common manifest behavior suppresses opportunity; the ecology of the temporary play space creates it. By framing a

*Columbus's landing, unfolded.* →

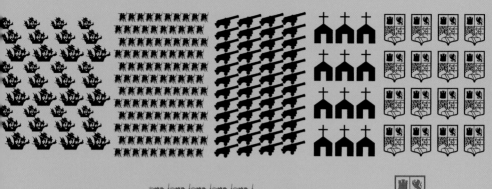

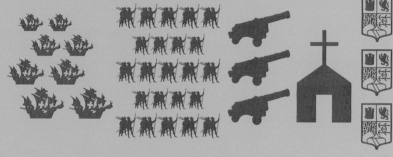

new signal with possibility and play rather than with expectation and constraint—the "What if...?" rather than the "So what?"—we expand our ability to understand and perceive the opportunities it could reveal.

"The ecology of behavior creates or inhibits the opportunity for latent need. The ecology of common manifest behavior suppresses opportunity; the ecology of the temporary play space creates it."

The temporary play space reveals latent needs faster because new technology is generally encountered while playing—in the narratives explored and discovered in toys, storytelling, television, newsprint, and books. Our first exposure to technology is in the toys we play with as children. Building sets, dolls, art techniques like drawing or painting—these forms of play have now made the move from analog to digital. The "wow" moment of the encounter with a new variable is a moment removed from everyday life and from common manifest behavior. That is why I believe that emergent technology and emergent behavior are best understood when explored in the temporary play space.

# The Temporary Play Space as Platform for Possibility

The temporary play space is the operating platform where, in the form of future scenarios, we can simulate new environments in which common manifest behavior is connected with latent behavior. A future scenario is a story about people and how they interact with daily life, chores, and objects. It describes interactions with technologies, products, and services that do not *yet* exist. A future scenario describes possibility.

The future scenario suspends the rules of the common behavior mode, creating instead a new set of variables from both manifest and latent behavior. By combining familiar objects and environments that we consider valuable and meaningful with objects, technologies, ideas, and environments we have never encountered before, the future scenario creates a full behavior mode with its own individual constraints.

"Future scenarios are not about what technology will do in the future; they are about what we want to do and will be able to do in the future. They are people centered."

The future scenario becomes the fuel of the temporary play space, where imagination can accelerate the discovery of meaning without the hindrances and limitations of rational behavior. We create a platform to encourage imagination and to incorporate new ideas, potentialities, and implications into our common behavior. Future scenarios begin with a *point of departure*—a provocative statement that guides the tone and context, such as, "It was a dark and stormy night." The trajectory of the narrative then establishes new constraints and expectations that reveal latent goals and behaviors. Future scenarios are not about what technology will do in the future; they are about what we want to do and will be able to do in the future. They are people centered.

By dissolving our rational boundaries and conventions, the temporary play space is limited only by imagination.

## CHARACTERISTICS OF THE TEMPORARY PLAY SPACE

The temporary play space is a construct that combines the attributes of a compelling experience with the characteristics of play behavior.

To satisfy the attributes of a compelling experience, the space should have a distinguishable entry point—a point of departure. The point of departure is attractive and engages the imagination. Take the question "Would you like to be invisible for a certain period of time every day?" If a person answers, "yes," he or she has entered the space.

### CREATING A COMPELLING EXPERIENCE

In 1997, the innovation strategy firm Doblin, under the leadership of Larry Keeley, described compelling experience dimensions as having three stages, two transitions, and six attributes. The stages are attraction, engagement, and extension, with entry and exit as transitions. The attributes of these stages are: defined, fresh, immersive, accessible, significant, and transformative.

A follow-up question might be, "How would you use your invisibility?" This ensures that the person is now engaged. The attributes of the story, or future scenario, should be defined. One should be able to explain the intent of the narrative with minimum effort to others, as this ensures its emotional and intellectual accessibility. Once emotionally involved in the story, a person is immersed and will continue to be so for as long as the experience is meaningful and challenging in a way that he or she can master it. Mastery is the reward. (There are clues around, and the mystery can be solved.)

In addition to these dimensions, the temporary play space (TPS) features these characteristics of play behavior:

- ✦ *Free engagement:* the entry into the story space is not obligatory
- ✦ *Separation:* the story space is circumscribed within limits of space and time, defined and fixed in advance
- ✦ *Uncertainty*: the goals are undefined and transitional
- ✦ *Unproductivity*: the aim is not to create with that space any goods or any formal elements of wealth
- ✦ *Establishment of new rules:* ordinary laws are suspended and new legislation alone counts in the space
- ✦ *Never a task:* there are no tasks to be accomplished or benchmarks to be measured against

# Frames of Inquiry and the Behavior Modes

In the full behavior mode, we pursue inquiry to uncover the capability of a new variable, defining the question for which it is the answer. We measure how valuable and meaningful a new variable, or disruption, is by how well it defines the question.

Imagine you have just witnessed the landing of a UFO. A huge flying saucer is sitting right in front of your eyes, heat still rising from its hidden engines. What do you see? What is the meaning of this object? You cannot measure it according to old benchmarks—it is not just another form of transportation; it does not present a solution to any of your practical everyday problems.

"While in the problem|solution frame of inquiry, we can find a number of solutions for a given problem. In the question|answer frame, there is only one question for which the UFO is the answer."

The landing of the UFO brings a new variable into our environment, with potentially many new sets of constraints. You are now in a full behavior mode, and the frame of inquiry that will reveal meaning by unfolding the precise signal is: What is the question for which the variable is the answer?

So, what is the question for which the UFO is the answer?

While in the problem|solution frame of inquiry, we can find a number of solutions for a given problem since we aren't being challenged to adapt our expectations of the process. In the question|answer frame, we are asked to adapt to the context and possibility at hand, and there is only one question for which the UFO is the answer:

**Is there life on other planets?**

### Hidden Coin

Here is a quick exercise in the question|answer frame.

Place a coin on a table. Show it to a friend and then cover it with a book. Ask your friend, "What is the question for which this coin is the answer?"

The answer to your question?

**What's behind this book?**

This frame of inquiry reveals the meaning and archetypal purpose of an existing human artifact.

## ONLY ONE RIGHT QUESTION

*If love is the answer, could you please rephrase the question?*

—Lily Tomlin

Imagine you are designing a new task light. You want to make a statement; you want to define a new classic. In any methodology you choose, you would have to start with a question (providing you are not interested in redesigning something that already exists). You will choose a question that will give you a deeper understanding of what a task light is, and hopefully a new insight that will make your light not only different but also meaningful to users. You want them to have a "wow" moment when they see it, but also an "aha" moment when they experience it.

The frame of inquiry you choose will be critical to the end result as well as to the process you choose to get there.

In the common behavior mode, this frame of inquiry leads you to ask a question very much like this: What is the problem for which the task light is the solution?

In the full behavior mode, we pursue inquiry to uncover the capacity of a new variable (a flying saucer, foam rubber) to define the question for which it represents the answer—the underlying concept being that answers have generating yet undefined questions. So the question would be: What is the question for which the task light is the answer?

## "The frame of inquiry you choose will be critical to the end result as well as to the process you choose to get there."

Let us look now at where the two frames of inquiry lead when it comes to the example of developing a new task light.

At the Beal Institute, we have conducted experiments in which we asked the first question to more than 200 people—designers, product developers, and "think outside the box" practitioners. With very little variation, the dialogue unfolded as follows.

"What is the problem for which the task light is the solution?"

"Darkness."

Now where does one go from here? How do we improve the task light in a meaningful way, if all we know is that it is a solution to "darkness"? We need to ask another question—actually, a series of questions:

"Why is darkness a problem?"

"Because I want to be productive after it gets dark."

"Why do you need to be productive after dark?"

"Because I need to finish this project by the end of the week."

We are now three questions into this process and, by all appearances, no closer to the insight that may provoke a moment of inspiration leading to the "classic" task light we are seeking.

It is important to note that the sequence in which the questions are asked will greatly influence the direction of the inquiry and the end result. So it is likely that different individuals in different circumstances will arrive at different questions and answers. Some may consider this variability as a sign of individuality and some will see it as a sign of creativity, a capability that we should encourage.

But do any of these answers bring us closer to the meaning we are seeking? Are we now ready to design this new classic?

### Digging Deeper: Another Archetype Retrieval

So what are the opportunities offered by the inquiry "What is the question for which the task light is the answer?"

This is no different from the question asked earlier about the UFO. There is a question that reveals the meaning of the task light; like the boat and the telephone, the task light comes from "somewhere" and it leads "somewhere."

I propose that this frame of inquiry results in the discovery of the archetypal purpose of a human artifact, its deeper meaning—seen here as any construct of purpose to human behavior represented by an idea, a space, or an object.

So where does the task light come from? As we did with the telephone, we need to look at its predecessors, the archetypes that have helped us achieve our purpose—whatever that might have been—in the absence of daylight. We need to engage in a retrieval journey that will unfold in a very predictable, bias-free, research-based fashion. *What is the predecessor of the task light?*

You probably would say, correctly, that it was the lantern. What was the predecessor of the lantern? The candle. And of the candle? In a very short time, you would, intuitively or through a quick search, come up with the torch. So now we have something relevant to ask, a query that contains at its core the archetype—the model and the most meaningful representation for all that followed. And so: What is the question for which the torch is the answer?

## A Light in the Darkness

Now we must jump back in time 180,000 years. You are part of a group of Homo sapiens taking shelter in a cave. You have barricaded the entrance to the cave, terrified by the mammoth parked outside. Soon you will run out of food, and going out is not an option. Something needs to be done; you need to find something to eat inside this cave. But it is a dark and frightening place that you have never ventured into.

You may ask yourself, "How can I explore this cave and find something we can eat?"

You poke a stick into the firebox, your group's most precious holding. The stick catches on fire, throwing enormous shadows on the walls of the cave. You can see the walls. You can see beyond the darkness that was in front of you just a few moments before.

You have just invented the torch. Or the task light. Or the light on your cell phone at a U2 concert.

Think about the torch. The Statue of Liberty holds a torch in her hand. The torch is also a central element of most university insignias. Why? The torch is the symbol for enlightenment and knowledge—the pursuit of a wondrous journey that you can share with your friends, family, and colleagues.

So what is the question for which the task light is the answer?

**How can I explore; how can I enlighten myself? How can I journey from being to becoming?**

You are now ready for strategic innovation and ready to develop a new classic.

# The Key Opportunity for Strategic Creativity

By recognizing the different nature of the inquiries we undertake in different modes of behavior, we can see how they generate different strategic outcomes:

✦ In the common manifest behavior mode, we use creativity to improve our condition. This is the problem|solution space. In it, any new variable must be a solution to an identified problem; we use the variable to improve the efficiency of our daily tasks. In this mode, creation results in tactical innovation.

✦ In the full behavior mode, we use imagination to transform our world by actualizing our capabilities. This is the question|answer space. In it, new variables allow us to imagine and discover new capabilities that reveal latent behaviors and new needs. In this mode, imagination results in strategic innovation.

"How can I explore; how can I enlighten myself?
How can I journey from being to becoming?"

# 8
# Emerging Signals

*There's really no such thing as "thinking outside the box." But we can select a different box to think in. Your box is your business model, your world view, your paradigm. It is the framework of the metaphor that you use to make sense of the world around you.*

—Roy Williams, author and marketing consultant

# Opportunities in Plain Sight

Every day we are surrounded by information that may reveal a new signal, a new speck on the horizon. We need to open our eyes not only to the words that we read in newspaper headlines, but to the possibilities they sometimes represent.

I once read that every second of every day, two Barbies are sold somewhere in the world. Is there a new possibility in this? Any opportunity? How long before the Barbie population overtakes the human population of the planet? A conservative calculation shows that by 2050, there will be more Barbie dolls on the planet than people. That seems significant on various levels. Mattel is the fourth-largest textile manufacturer in the United States, largely from making dresses for Barbie. How will the company rank in textile manufacturing in 2050? Calculate how many Barbies have sold since you started reading this book and you will be training your mind to seek new opportunities.

Imagine you are a communications company and you want to create the most powerful antenna on the planet. Could you use the Barbie grid to do this? Could a Data-Barbie vest incorporate a receiver/transmitter that allows for the creation of the largest ad-hoc network ever devised?

"Calculate how many Barbies have sold since you started reading this book and you will be training your mind to seek new opportunities."

In this chapter, we will look at the way signals like these are recognized—or not—by individuals and organizations, and how, when subjected to the right imaginative questions, they can shape our future.

# Signals in Latent Needs

Mark Burnett's idea for the TV show "Survivor" was rejected by ABC, NBC, CBS, and UPN before CBS gave it another chance. The first episode of "Survivor: Borneo" aired on May 31, 2000. Together with ABC's "Who Wants To Be a Millionaire?," it started the reality-television revolution, a genre that now accounts for 56 percent of all TV shows on American television screens, according to Nielsen Media Research. *This revolution was, literally, televised.*

The show that propelled the revolution is about humans in tribes, stranded in a remote location, competing against each other for survival. Survival means endurance, the ability to solve problems, teamwork, personal dexterity, and will. Survival means being seen as strong and essential to the success and survival of the tribe, in an atmosphere of continual challenge and reward. The rewards: spices, flint or fire, warm blankets. Nothing a city dweller would sacrifice any effort for, but all that mattered for a Robinson Crusoe or even our ancestors not too far back. So we are here at the present being in our past, but a past actualized by new technology. We can now see how we were, and how we could be in that situation of despair. It speaks to us—our past as tribal beings, as a tribal council that has the power to extinguish one human's torch, emerges in us. And we do it, by voting in secret and with pleasure. And we watch it, with pleasure.

*"The tribe has spoken."*

"We are tribe members, apprentices, bachelors and bachelorettes, contenders, the next top model, and American idols once we have allowed our latent behavior to emerge."

## THE CHOREOGRAPHY OF LATENT NEEDS

The latent needs emerge slowly, painfully, and through all the trials that we, as spectators, feel we are put through. Our most primeval emotions are in play here, as well as our need to be part of one or another tribe. We feel that we would know what to do, if only placed there now. But we are not there, so we have to live with engaging ourselves intellectually rather than physically. Is this intellectual engagement as powerful, and as compelling, as the actual physical engagement in the affairs of the tribe? Remember, more than half of all TV shows watched in the United States are reality shows.

We are tribe members, apprentices, bachelors and bachelorettes, contenders, the next top model, and American idols once we have allowed our latent behavior to emerge.

## TALKING TO MYSELF

A few months ago, I was in Chicago O'Hare Airport, waiting for a connection from Miami to Toronto. I had a few hours between flights, so I decided to experiment a little with people's notions of "normal" behavior. For about two hours, I walked the corridors of the airport talking to myself. I would look at a display in Brookstone and clearly articulate, "No, I am not talking to you. I am with a salesperson at Brookstone." Or, in line at a fast-food counter, I'd suddenly say, "No, it was OK, they understood everything and we are meeting again in September. See you soon." Did people look at me as if I had some kind of a problem? Just for a moment, until they would spot a yellow and black rubber band wrapped around my right ear. I was also using my right hand to cover my ear as I was speaking, as if I had reception trouble.

"Talking to yourself has become common behavior as long as you have anything attached to your ear. It is a very powerful illustration of how fast behavior can change, and what was once 'deviant' becomes 'normal.'"

The yellow rubber band looked very impressive—it was actually a real component of a wraparound earpiece from an old cell phone hands-free headset. In fact, it was impressive enough that most people did not question my mental stability, and three were so intrigued as to ask me, "Where did you get this?" To say, essentially, "I want it. I want to walk around airports talking to myself. It is OK, as long as a wire of some sort protrudes from my ears."

Talking to yourself has become common behavior as long as you have anything attached to your ear. Try this some day. It is a very powerful illustration of how fast behavior can change, and what was once "deviant" becomes "normal." How long before we start talking into the wall or to a carton of orange juice? And why not? Communication is not about one cell phone talking to another cell phone, but about people talking to people through the means at hand. So why not the wall, or any object closest to you, as the means? How and who will mediate our conversations in Dataspace?

"What is currently missing in corporate culture for that moment of clarity—the moment when the company that is involved in music understands what people really want to listen to and how they want to do it?"

There are any number of inventions, disruptions, and signals in plain sight right now that are real and will influence your future, my future, and everybody's future.

In a 1965 interview with the *New York Times*, John Diebold, the pioneer of automated technology applications, said:

> "Today's machines, even more than the devices of the Industrial Revolution, are creating a whole new environment for mankind and a whole new way of life. Today's machines deal with the very core of human society—with information and its communication and use. Top management must make it their business to see the opportunities inherent in changes in the social environment and technology."

What is currently missing in corporate culture is that moment of clarity—the moment when the company that is involved in music understands what people really want to listen to and how they want to do it? The moment when Salomon invents snowboarding and Microsoft rolls out Skype?

In a presentation in 2005 entitled "Scanning Technology Horizons," Bob Johansen—pioneer futurologist and president of the Institute for the Future, a strategic research group—expressed his belief that "It is possible to have a bad forecast and still make a good decision" on the basis of that forecast. In Johansen's view, the key is to devise an enlightened approach to making projections, looking at potential threats or fault lines as opportunities for growth or restructuring. And with the rapid convergence of multiple technologies and the appearance of cross-disciplines, the scope of a company's search needs to be wider; it now needs to monitor events in areas that were not previously considered important or part of its business sector.

## WHO IN YOUR ORGANIZATION IS KEEPING TRACK?

Who is monitoring all the specks on the horizon, trying to make new meaning for the business you are now involved in? Who in your organization is transforming convergence into a new possibility and economic driver? And how seriously does your organization take the question "What if toothbrushes could speak?"

Johansen gives a few examples of convergent technologies in the field of health care:

✦ Tools for monitoring health, such as biosensors, implants, and imaging

✦ New materials for treatment and prevention, including smart textiles, organic/inorganic interfaces, implants, and very small-scale batteries

So how big is the opportunity that could be revealed by answers to the question "What if toothbrushes could speak?"

# Signals and the Corporation

At his 2003 lecture "Peripheral Vision: Sensing and Acting on Weak Signals," at the Wharton School of the University of Pennsylvania, George Day, professor of marketing and codirector of the Mack Center for Technological Innovation at Wharton, challenged companies to make sense of the tremendous flow of data that surrounds them and to identify signals that might or will affect their businesses. He suggested they might start by asking, "Where is the periphery of my business?" As Day noted, "One person's periphery is another person's core."

In their 2001 book *Creative Destruction: Why Companies That Are Built to Last Underperform in the Market and How to Successfully Transform Them*, Richard Foster and Sarah Kaplan defined the periphery as "the edge of the vortex of creative destruction. In this vortex, attacking companies occupy the periphery while the defenders occupy the core of the vortex, focusing on the evolutionary improvement of the existing business."

Effective peripheral vision is more an art than a science. It involves interpretation, insight, intuition, and adaptive adjustments that reshape the process as new insights are gained. And the art is partly in defining its scope: How far and where one looks can redefine both the "core" and the "periphery" of one's business.

Robert K. Logan, a senior fellow at the Beal Institute for Strategic Creativity, believes that in the Information Age, the core and the periphery are now connected:

> "We know that new levels of order emerge at the periphery, far from the organized equilibrium in the center. At the same time, the distinction between the center and the margin begins to dissipate with the flow of information, ultimately disappearing. With the accelerated increase and exchange of digital information, our specialized and fragmented civilization of center-periphery structure is suddenly experiencing an instantaneous reassembling. All its mechanized bits are merging into an organic whole. This is the new world of the global village."

As Logan proposes, alternative forms of organization emerge on the periphery of a mass culture—whether as small startups that are a response to large-scale multinationals or as remix to counter the homogeneity of mass culture. With the advent of digital exchange, these self-organized disruptions merge fluently with their sources, creating a cohesive dialogue rather than a one-sided discussion.

**"Effective peripheral vision is more an art than a science. And the art is partly in defining its scope: How far and where one looks can redefine both the 'core' and the 'periphery' of one's business."**

The challenge for a large corporation is to distribute the intelligence gathered from scanning current trends and data, segmenting data into the various business units. Each unit collects and analyzes data pertinent to its activities, which are highly specialized and demand a narrow set of data. But with no cohesive big picture in place, no one function has the role and capability of combining and analyzing sets of diverse data—of defining signals and their meaning. In effect, no action takes place. As philosopher Paul Ricoeur put it, "Without imagination, there is no action."

George Day adds, "There are thousands of events and trends that are at the periphery; in most organizations, someone knows these trends, but it is hard to pull them into a cohesive picture." In his lecture, Day offered two examples of companies that successfully used this process to become leaders in sectors that used to be peripheral to their core:

✦ FedEx: "It traditionally defined its core business as the overnight delivery of small packages, but it expanded its vision by studying the impact of electronic commerce on global sourcing," Day said of the company's rise to organizing and coordinating every aspect of the supply chain. "As a result, FedEx now acts as the leading end-to-end logistics supplier."

✦ Pitney Bowes: "It traditionally defined its core as postage meters and mail handling, but it expanded its vision to take in a wide range of related back-office market trends. Pitney Bowes now makes systems that require sophisticated back-office equipment."

## Cultivating Effective Peripheral Vision

How can strategists learn to effectively interpret signals at the periphery?

In an article in the June 2003 issue of *Knowledge@Wharton*, Wharton School's online business publication, George Day and Paul Schoemaker provided a checklist of questions for strategists to ask:

✦ How do our mental models filter or distort the signals we take in?

✦ How should we interpret the patterns in the flow of weak signals?

✦ What role should we assign to outsiders? To war gaming? To other scenarios?

✦ How can we integrate findings we derive from the periphery with other valuable sources of data, such as our analysis of competitors? With insights from our customers? With our studies of technological possibilities?

When it comes to acting on the signals, Day and Schoemaker suggested more questions:

✦ What resources are we devoting to the periphery? With what results? And what resources should we be devoting to the periphery instead?

✦ Who is accountable in our organization for taking action? Who should be accountable?

✦ When might it be better to watch and wait, rather than take action on signals from the periphery? When might it be better to position ourselves to learn from outside experts and partners?

# DATA SIGNALS AND BUSINESS INTELLIGENCE: A CASE STUDY

*Business intelligence* is the umbrella term for many overlapping and interdependent fields that are related to competitive strategies in business, including market research and industry analysis. Its primary functions are to assess and understand the specific environment surrounding particular business-gathering data and information applicable to the scope of investigation, and to monitor how information flows both inside and outside a company, as well as how it is perceived by the company's market and competition. More than anything, business intelligence attempts to detect "weak signals" in the environment and to construct a framework to accommodate any information relevant to the scope of a particular signal.

## Business as Usual

Until recently, most analysis dealt primarily with structured data—data garnered from sources such as databases and statistics. However, this is akin to gathering information from focus groups—it reveals very little about the true motivations of an individual or company, and prevents any kind of holistic communication. An organization hears only what it expects to hear. If it is only looking for and able to understand a limited sliver of its position in a market, and the information that generates this understanding is myopic, it is likely to discard the emergence of anything unanticipated or irregular.

When an organization filters this prefiltered and structured information through a framework it has constructed, it reinforces its existing context, gathering information that supports a predefined goal or idea. This process preserves order and equilibrium within a business, *promoting business as usual*, but at the same time makes the business impervious to any subtle disruption or change in the environment.

"Discarding unstructured information can place a business at a distinct disadvantage. Subtle changes in how the business is perceived and received can go undetected until they accumulate into catastrophic change, and the business is rendered obsolete."

Yet it is information that is not accommodated by a structured framework that has the greatest potential to disrupt, inspire, or foster growth. Unstructured information—such as blog entries, user reviews and opinions, and community portals—has a spontaneous authenticity and highly subjective perspective, reflecting the beliefs, history, and cultural context

"The only way of discovering the limits of the possible is to venture a little way past them into the impossible."          —Arthur C. Clarke of whoever is writing. The language is natural and conversational—more *human*—than that which is constrained by the expectations of business.

Discarding unstructured information can place a business at a distinct disadvantage. Subtle changes in how the business is perceived and received—what its users and stakeholders may actually think—can go undetected until they accumulate into catastrophic change, and the business is rendered obsolete. If a company has the capability to process both quantitative (structured) and qualitative (unstructured) information, it can construct a more accurate and holistic "presence" and gain a more complete sense of the landscape. Unstructured analysis allows an organization to expand its possibilities, discovering new meaning from previously inaccessible content and enriching its strategic knowledge base.

# Signals and Predictions

A common response to technological innovation is to predict where it might lead. This is usually done in a logical fashion, in what we have called common manifest behavior mode, and with the premise that every innovation is a solution to a problem. But as we have seen, forecasting in this mode is bound to fall short of seeing the big picture for the future.

In *Profiles of the Future*, Arthur C. Clarke wrote: "The real future is not logically foreseeable." Clarke made the case that the inventions of the modern world can be divided into two classes: the expected and the unexpected. The expected is a group of inventions that could have been foreseen by the thinkers of the past; inventions that were logical in their progression through material and technology invention—the automobile, airplane, submarine, telephone, teleportation, and robot, among others. The unexpected inventions, which would have made no sense to an Edison or Da Vinci, include X-rays, nuclear energy, quantum mechanics, transistors, lasers, dating the past (carbon 14), and relativity. Clarke's book was written in 1962. Imagine the size of the unexpected list in 2006.

In the book, Clarke also stated his "Three Laws." The second of them calls for a perspective that emphasizes the importance of a temporary play space in order to stretch the boundaries of what's possible: "The only way of discovering the limits of the possible is to venture a little way past them into the impossible."

## THE TELEVISION SIGNAL

When the electronic television was first demonstrated to the public by Philo Farnsworth in 1934, it was recognized as a technology that would fundamentally change communication, although perceptions of the extent and depth of the signal varied from critic to critic. In a 2005 *New York Times* article called "Confounding Machines: How the Future Looked," Peter Edidin compiled some revealing reactions to the introduction of television, a technology that we now take for granted.

Some are expectedly short sighted, such as editor Rex Lambert's 1936 prediction in *The Listener:* "Television won't matter in your lifetime or mine." And a *New York Times* editorial a few years later made this confident, if dead wrong, analysis:

> *"The problem with television is that people must sit and keep their eyes glued to the screen; the average American family hasn't time for it. Therefore the showmen are convinced that for this reason, if no other, television will never be a serious competitor of [radio] broadcasting."*

Yet some of the predictions show the astonishing capacity of some astute observers to unfold the signal of television in its full complexity and impact. In 1936, writer C. C. Furnas wrote in *The Next Hundred Years:*

> *"It is my hope, and I see no reason why it should not be realized, to be able to go to an ordinary movie theater when some great national event is taking place across the country and see on the screen the sharp image of the action reproduced—at the same instant it occurs. This waiting for the newsreels to come out is a bit tiresome for the 20th century. Some time later I hope to be able to take my inaugurals, prize fights and football games at home. I expect to do it satisfactorily and cheaply."*

RCA Chairman David Sarnoff foreshadowed Marshall McLuhan's notion of the "global village" when he told a crowd of curious viewers at the 1939 opening of the RCA Pavilion at the World's Fair in New York:

> *"It is with a feeling of humbleness that I come to this moment of announcing the birth, in this country, of a new art so important in its implications that it is bound to affect all society. It is an art which shines like a torch of hope in the troubled world. It is a creative force which we must learn to utilize for the benefit of all mankind. This miracle of engineering skill which one day will bring the world to the home...will become an important factor in American economic life."*

And finally, in *Here Is Television, Your Window on the World*, Thomas Hutchinson wrote in 1946:

> *"Television means the world is your home and in the homes of all the people of the world. It is the greatest means of communication ever developed by the mind of man. It should do more to develop friendly neighbors, and to bring understanding and peace on earth, than any other single material force in the world today."*

Hutchinson missed one signal that Marshall McLuhan later articulated: the notion that every technology brings both service and disservice. TV images can also inflame hatreds. This was illustrated not too long ago when televised shots of the misconduct of American and British soldiers in Iraq served as fodder for increased insurgent attacks.

## McLUHAN'S TOOL FOR EMERGING SIGNALS

In the *The Global Village: Transformations in World Life and Media in the 21st Century,* McLuhan and Bruce Powers proposed a new "right brain" creative model of communication. This model demonstrates the dynamic and synchronic nature of change, which is triggered by the creation of a new artifact, and the "all-at-oneness character" of that transformation— as illustrated by the positive and negative consequences of television's impact on mass culture. The authors contended that any new technology will emphasize some of our senses and functions while at the same time obsolescing others, even if temporarily. In this process, a person retrieves his or her latent behavior, namely the will *to worship extensions of himself as a form of divinity."*

"McLuhan believed that all media forms are extensions of our senses, bodies, and psyches, in the way that a hammer is an extension of our hand and a book is an extension of our memory and ideas. As such, they intensify one thing in a culture while obsolescing something else."

In *Law of Media: the New Science,* McLuhan had created the concept of the "tetrad"—a tool that could predict what society might do with a new invention and whether it would accept or reject the artifact's future effects. In his view, our capability to focus awareness gives rise to the behavior of looking at the present twice: as an environment to be per-fected and as a task to be studied, discussed, and analyzed in order to see clearly where it might lead. In this discussion, the present is subjected to a series of questions that result in experimental and alternative shapes of the future. The questions are:

1. What does any artifact enlarge or enhance?
2. What does it erode or obsolesce?
3. What does it retrieve that had been earlier obsolesced?
4. What does it reverse or flip into when pushed to the limits of its potential?

These questions are a reflection of McLuhan's belief that all media forms are extensions of our senses, bodies, and psyches, in the way that a hammer is an extension of our hand and a book is an extension of our memory and ideas. As such, they intensify one thing in a culture while obsolescing something else. They also retrieve a phase or factor long ago pushed aside and undergo a modification when extended beyond the limits of their potential, often times flipping into their opposite or complementary form. For example, the cell phone intensifies the capability of one person's voice reaching another's at any time, and in time will obsolesce location-bound telephones and landlines. At the same time, the cell phone reverses our freedom from location by shackling us with perpetual accessibility, and it retrieves the fundamental desire of "Can you hear me?"

McLuhan wrote:

> "The tetrad, taken as a whole, is a manifestation of human thinking processes. As an exploratory probe, tetrads do not rest on a theory but a set of questions; they rely on empirical observation and are thus testable. When applied to new technologies or artifacts, they afford the user predictive power; in this sense as well, they may be viewed as a scientific instrument. Once again, insofar as the tetrads are a means of focusing awareness of hidden or unobserved qualities in our culture and its technologies, they act phenomenologically."

McLuhan's tetrad acts as a lens through which to analyze the deeper meaning and impact of a signal—foreseeing what it may mean in the future by recognizing its past and present implications.

# Disruptions as Signals

Clayton Christensen first introduced the term *disruptive innovation* in the book *The Innovator's Dilemma* in 1997. The *disruptive* aspect of the innovation comes not from its superior quality or performance, but from its ability to offer the same benefit in a different way. Snowboarding. The iPod. The compact disc. The personal computer. Every disruptive innovation is a new variable in the problem space of market leaders—a variable that requires a full behavior mode of inquiry.

---

**DISRUPTIVE INNOVATION**

any innovation in products or services entering a field in which a dominant technology already exists.

Christensen recognizes two types of disruption: A "low end" disruption is marketed to users who do not require high performance; who will be satisfied by any new technology that improves upon the products or services offered by the market leaders. A "new market" disruption is targeted at users not previously served by the market leader. In both cases, the disruption is welcomed by users. While disruptions are in plain sight, however, they tend to be ignored by market leaders, as their initial markets are seen as small and of little economic significance to the larger market scope of the leader, according to Christensen.

Some recent disruptions? Think 1995 and Yahoo, Netscape, and Amazon. Think 1998 and Google. Think 1999 and Napster. Think 2001 and the iPod.

# "The World Wide Web had one of the highest rates of acceptance of any technology while solving a problem no one thought they had."

Or think Tuesday, August 6, 1991, the date that Tim Berners-Lee e-mailed this "short summary of the World Wide Web project" to "Groups: alt.hypertext":

> "*The WWW project merges the techniques of information retrieval and hypertext to make an easy but powerful global information system. The project started with the philosophy that much academic information should be freely available to anyone. It aims to allow information sharing within internationally dispersed teams, and the dissemination of information by support groups.*"

> "*The WWW world consists of documents, and links. Indexes are special documents which, rather than being read, may be searched. The result of such a search is another ('virtual') document containing links to the documents found. A simple protocol ('HTTP') is used to allow a browser program to request a keyword search by a remote information server.*"

For the market leaders of the time, the key question was pretty simple: What is the problem for which the World Wide Web is a solution? Failing to identify a problem that had a wide market need for a tactical solution, however, they lived for a few years with the illusion that nothing much would change. After all, there was no money in the WWW and no users identified outside the group of hypertext enthusiasts. The old value chain did not fit this "new thing" because there was no need for it.

But what if they had asked: What is the question for which the WWW is the answer?

What would they have discovered? The hunger to play? Maybe. The hunger to explore and learn and continue asking questions? Clearly. The hunger to communicate one's ideas, articles, artistic creations, and experiences. The hunger to reach out to others of a like mind or with similar interests. The hunger for community and fellowship. The hunger to collaborate globally without geographic barriers.

*All of these*, because the Web is the ultimate sandbox. It became a social phenomenon because it brought out our latent behavior of nosiness, curiosity, and continual search for new things to explore. Our instinct for play was now made possible by a new technology with the capability to create the experience most conducive to emerge our latent behavior.

The World Wide Web had one of the highest rates of acceptance of any technology while solving a problem no one thought they had.

# No Weak Signals

A weak signal is only weak from an unimaginative perspective. This is an example of the imagination gap. It is our ability to perceive that is weak, even if the signal is strong. From the right point of view, the signal is always strong.

In order to predict change, we must be able to anticipate the path of change. The reference frame from which we observe a signal determines how strongly we perceive the signal. It is through imagination that this perspective can be changed.

The Impressionist style of painting was technically possible thousands of years ago. It was not an innovation in painting techniques that made this art possible; it was a shift in the perception of the cultural moment that revealed the opportunity to use them. The earth had been round for billions of years when Pythagoras (or at least one of his followers) proposed that since the sun was a sphere and the moon was a sphere, the earth might also be a sphere. This extrapolation from observation to a hypothetical paradigm required the ability to deny the obvious interpretation of the empirical evidence and use imagination to allow for new deductive parameters.

So innovation potential is a two-part process limited by people's *sense of the possible* within the actual *realm of the possible*. It is not technology that allows a new possibility; it is our readiness to receive it. Was the potential for Google, blogging, and eBay predictable when the first computers were networked? Was TiVo or YouTube predictable with the first television transmission? Of course, if the *motivating benefit* of the network and TV had been recognized.

For example, the motivating benefit of networking computers was to achieve an efficient method of sharing the information that people wanted to share. The essential question required to bridge the imagination gap might have been: If every person or business was networking any data, what information would they want to share? Introduced at the International Council for Computer Communication (ICCC) in 1972, electronic mail was the first obvious signal that the networking of all computers would have widespread immediate benefit.

The complex interplay between social, economic, and political ecosystems makes the notion of exactly predicting the future absurd. But applying behavior-centered questions to a weak signal reveals its possibility. For example, the behavior observation that people want to buy and sell merchandise could have revealed the opportunity for creating a virtual auction. This question does not rely on knowing when the requisite technology will be available; it relies purely on an observed recognition of the direction that the technology development is taking. This observation yields the opportunity to ask, *"If this technology happens, then what will people want to do with it?"*

"A weak signal is only weak from an unimaginative perspective. It is our ability to perceive that is weak, even if the signal is strong. From the right point of view, the signal is always strong."

# 9
# Engineering
# Possibility

In the last chapter, we discussed how we can discover the possibility in an emerging signal and apply this knowledge to generate strategic capital. Those who do can adapt and stay relevant in a competitive and ever-changing culture. Red Hat is one such company, whose distribution and popularization of Linux software transformed, and continues to transform, the cultural landscape. In this chapter, Red Hat cofounder and former chairman Bob Young provides insight into the company's remarkable success.

# Unfolding Signals: Transformative Opportunities in a Changing Market

Bob Young/Lulu.com

Founded in 1993, Red Hat is widely credited with driving the global, industry-wide adoption of open-source development practices, specifically through its promotion and packaging of Linux—a variation of Unix developed in Finland by Linus Torvalds. Open-source software, and the growing culture that surrounds it, promotes access to the source code to encourage collaborative, contextual, and nonproprietary development of software that is free to access and use.

Bob Young, Red Hat's chairman from 1993 to 1999, has invested more than 20 years in technology finance and marketing, generating a broad range of strat-

*Open-source visionary Bob Young*

egies to transform the position of alternative technologies in the mass market from competitive threat to shared opportunity. A graduate of the University of Toronto, in 1999 Young cofounded The Center for the Public Domain, a venture philanthropic enterprise that provided gifts, grants, and donations to organizations that study, nurture, and secure the health of the public domain. Young is currently the CEO and founder of lulu.com, a user-controlled Website that provides alternatives for content publishing, delivery, and ownership, such as print-on-demand books.

In 2005, Young resigned from the board of directors of Red Hat to focus his energies on the development of lulu.com. This interview is adapted from Young's *Giving It All Away: A Capitalist Entrepreneur's View of Open Source*.

## A CONVERSATION WITH BOB YOUNG

**Q:** *The Linux kernel emerged out of Finland in 1991 as a collaborative alternative to Unix and Minix. What were the first signals that it would become a viable product for Red Hat to market and distribute?*

**A:** In the early days of the Linux kernel, the early 1990s, Red Hat was a small software distribution company. We offered Unix applications, books, and low-cost CD-ROMs from vendors like Walnut Creek and Infomagic. In addition to conventional Unix offerings, these vendors were beginning to offer a new line: Linux CD-ROMs. The Linux CDs were becoming bestsellers for us. When we'd ask where this Linux stuff was coming from, we'd get answers like, "It's from the programmers, according to their skills, to the users, according to their needs."

*Although at first it may have seemed that Linux's economic momentum would fizzle out, instead it continued to accelerate as the product grew more popular and accessible. How did Red Hat transform its definition of an economic model to support the potential capabilities of the Linux OS?*

Initially, Linux seemed to lack a sustainable economic model to drive the effort, and we thought that the whole thing was a big fluke. A fluke that was generating enough cash to keep our little business and a number of other small businesses in the black, but a fluke nonetheless. We didn't expect it to be a success, to remain solvent.

However, we found that instead of this bizarre free software effort collapsing, it continued to improve. The number of users continued to grow and the applications they were putting it to were growing in sophistication. So we began to study free software development more carefully. We spoke to the key developers and the largest users. The more we studied, the more of a solid, albeit unusual, economic model we saw.

This economic model was effective. More importantly, our sales of Linux-based OSes compared to our sales of other Unixes were sufficient to convince us that this was a real technology with a real future. Red Hat went through many trials and errors in developing a business plan that was compatible with the Linux model. Bizarre as it was, this model was producing a remarkable OS, providing value to our customers, and providing profit for our shareholders.

*When Red Hat realized that Linux needed this different economic model to be successful, how did that affect the operational strategy of Red Hat as a whole? How did the expectations of what the company was offering change?*

We needed to look closely at what we were doing as a company and what we were providing to our customers. If we did not own intellectual property the way almost all of today's software companies do, and if those companies insist that their most valuable asset is the intellectual property represented by the source code to the software they own, then it was safe to say that Red Hat is not in the software business. Red Hat is not licensing intellectual property over which it has ownership. That's not the economic model that will support their customers, staff, and shareholders. So the question became: What business are we in?

The answer was to look around at other industries and try to find one that matched. We wanted an industry where the basic ingredients were free, or at least freely available. We looked at the commodity industries and began to recognize some ideas. All leading companies selling commodity products—including bottled water (Perrier or Evian), the soap business (Tide), or the tomato paste business (Heinz)—base their marketing strategies on building strong brands. These brands must stand for quality, consistency, and reliability. We saw something in the brand management of these commodity products that we thought we could emulate: Both industries were effectively using freely redistributable objects.

*Realizing that Red Hat was better suited to the economic model of the commodities market would have widened the breadth and depth of available opportunities. What did this shift reveal in the behavior of both Red Hat as a company and the users of its products?*

Our key opportunity was to offer convenience and quality, and most importantly to help define, in the minds of our customers, what an operating system can be. At Red Hat, if we did a good job of supplying and supporting a consistently high-quality product, we had a great opportunity to establish a brand that Linux OS customers simply prefer.

But how could we reconcile our need to create more Linux users with our need to ensure that those Linux users use Red Hat? We looked at industries where the participants benefit because of, not despite, the activities of other participants. Drinking water can be had in most industrial countries simply by turning on the nearest tap, so why does Evian sell millions of dollars of French tap water into those markets? It boils down to concerns that the water coming from your tap is not to be trusted.

> "Drinking water can be had in most industrial countries simply by turning on the nearest tap, so why does Evian sell millions of dollars of French tap water into those markets? The same reason that many people prefer to purchase 'Official' Red Hat Linux in a box for $50 when they could download it for free."

This is the same reason that many people prefer to purchase "Official" Red Hat Linux in a box for $50 when they could download it for free or buy unofficial CD-ROM copies of Red Hat for as little as $2. Evian *does* have the advantage that most of humanity drinks water. We still had to create a lot of Linux consumers in order to have a market to sell our brand into.

The need in major global corporations for support services to reduce the cost of deploying and maintaining the rapidly evolving open-source software in Red Hat Linux made this an exciting business opportunity. The challenge was to focus on market size, not just market share. When consumer demand for bottled water grows, Evian benefits, even though many of those consumers start with a bottle other than Evian. Red Hat, like Evian, benefits when other Linux suppliers do a great job building a taste for the product. The more Linux users there are overall, the more potential customers Red Hat has for their flavor.

The power of brands translates very effectively into the technology business. The one common denominator between all of the investments to date has been that the companies or their products have great name recognition and are recognized as being quality products. In other words, they have successfully established a brand.

*Red Hat has had to adopt a unique approach in the delivery of Linux to its vendors and users. What differentiates its value and method from that of other software companies?*

At Red Hat, our role was to work with all the development teams across the Internet to take some 400 software packages and assemble them into a useful operating system. We operated much like a car assembly plant taking parts from many suppliers and building useful products from those parts. Very few people build their own cars. The same with the hundreds of programs that make up the collection of open-source Linux technologies: Few people build their own Linux-based OS. Red Hat designs, assembles, and tests the finished operating system product and offers support and services for the users of the Red Hat Linux OS.

"Marketing with skill and imagination, particularly in highly competitive markets, requires that you offer solutions to your customers that others cannot or will not match. To that end, open source is not a liability but a competitive advantage."

All the other operating systems available when we began doing this in the 1990s—such as Windows, Mac OS, or AIX-Unix—were proprietary binary-only products, where the customers had no control over the technology they were building their corporate information systems and networks upon.

The "unique value proposition" of our business plan was, and continues to be, for Red Hat to cater to customers' need to gain control over the operating system they were using by delivering the technical benefits of freely redistributable software (source code and a free license) to technically oriented OS consumers.

*The development and employment of accurate and sustainable strategies is key to the survival of any product. What methods did Red Hat apply to provide its market with an alternative and beneficial operating system?*

Given that until very recently all software ventures were of the proprietary binary-only kind, it is therefore safe to say that the IP (intellectual property) model of software development and marketing is a very difficult way to make a living. While making money with open-source software is a challenge, the challenge is not necessarily greater than with proprietary software. In fact, you make money in open-source software exactly the same way you do it in proprietary software: by building a great product, marketing it with skill and imagination, looking after your customers, and thereby building a brand that stands for quality and customer service.

> "You can't compete with a monopoly by playing the game by the monopolist's rules. It just has too many strengths. You compete with a monopoly by changing the rules of the game into a set that favors your strengths."

Marketing with skill and imagination, particularly in highly competitive markets, requires that you offer solutions to your customers that others cannot or will not match. To that end, open source is not a liability but a competitive advantage. This development model produces software that is stable, flexible, and highly customizable. So the vendor of open-source software starts with a quality product. The trick is to devise an effective way to make money delivering the benefits of open-source software to your clients. Inventing new economic models is not a trivial task, and the innovations that Red Hat has stumbled upon certainly do not apply to everyone or every product. But there are some principles that should apply to many software ventures, and to many open-source ventures.

*Red Hat re-imagined the role and the place that Linux was to occupy in the market. Can you describe any analogous industry methods or practices that provided insight into what Linux could become?*

Consider that the primary complaint about the market leader is the control that vendor has over the industry. A new OS must deliver control over the

OS platform to its user and not become just another proprietary binary-only OS whose owner would then gain the same dominant market position that consumers are currently complaining about.

Consider that Linux is not really an OS. It has come to describe a whole collection of open-source components much like the term *car* describes an industry better than the thing we drive on the highway. We don't drive cars—we drive Ford Tauruses or Honda Accords. Red Hat is the equivalent of an OS assembly plant of the free software operating system industry. Red Hat succeeds when customers perceive themselves not as purchasing an operating system, or even purchasing Linux, but purchasing Red Hat first and foremost. Red Hat takes compilers from Cygnus, Web servers from Apache, an X Window System from the X Consortium (who built it with support from Digital, HP, IBM, Sun, and others), and assembles these into a certifiable, warranted, and award-winning Red Hat Linux OS.

Much like the car industry, it is Red Hat's job to take what it considers the best of the available open-source components to build the best OS it can. But control over the OS is not held by Red Hat or anyone else. If a Red Hat customer disagreed with our choice of Sendmail and wanted to use Qmail or some other solution, they continued to have the control that enabled them to do this. In much the same way, someone buying a Ford Taurus may want a higher performance manifold installed on the engine in place of the one that was shipped from the factory. Because the Taurus owner can open the hood of the car, they have control over the car. Similarly, Red Hat users have control over the Linux OS they use, because they have license to open and modify the source code.

*Red Hat also recognized that its challenges and opportunities were different from those of its competitors. How did the company transform the market it was participating in?*

You can't compete with a monopoly by playing the game by the monopolist's rules. The monopoly has the resources, the distribution channels, and the R&D resources; in short, it just has too many strengths. You compete with a monopoly by changing the rules of the game into a set that favors your strengths.

At the end of the 19th century, the big American monopoly concern was not operating systems, but railroads. The major railroads held effective monopolies on transportation between major cities. Indeed, major American cities like Chicago had grown up around the central railway terminals owned by the railroad companies. These monopolies were not overcome by building new railroads and charging several fewer dollars. They were overcome with the building of the interstate highway system and the benefit of door-to-door delivery that the trucking companies could offer over the more limited point-to-point delivery that the railroad model previously offered.

Today, the owners of the existing proprietary OSes own a technology that is much like owning the railway system. The APIs [application programming interfaces] of a proprietary OS are much like the routes and timetables of a railroad. The OS vendors can charge whatever toll they like. They can also control and change the "route" the APIs take through the OS to suit the needs of the applications they sell, without regard to the needs of the applications that their competitors sell. These OS vendors' biggest competitive advantage is that they control access to the source code that both their applications and the Independent Software Vendor's (ISV's) applications must run on.

To escape the confines of this model, ISVs need an OS model where the vendor of that OS (Linux) does not control the OS; where the supplier of the OS is responsible for the maintenance of the OS only; and where the ISV can sell his application, secure in the knowledge that the OS vendor is not his biggest competitive threat. The appeal of this OS model has begun to take hold in the software world. This is a big part of the reasoning behind Oracle's port of their database software to Linux, and behind IBM's support for Apache.

*What are the latent behaviors that a product like Linux reveals in its users, and what are the future possibilities of those behaviors? Who benefits and how?*

The benefits that an open-source OS offers over the proprietary binary-only OSes is the control the users gain over the technology they are using. The proprietary OS vendors, with their huge investment in the proprietary software that their products consist of, would be crazy to try and match the benefit Red Hat is offering their customers, as it generates a fraction of the revenue per user that the current proprietary OS vendors rely on.

> "Rather than using a license to lock customers in and wall them off from the source code, Red Hat uses a license that embodies the very idea of access to and control over source code."

Of course, if Red Hat's technology model becomes accepted by a large enough group of computer users, the existing OS vendors are going to have to react somehow. But that's still several years in the future. If they do react by "freeing" their code the way Netscape "freed" the code to the Navigator browser, it would result in better products at dramatically lower cost. The industry at large will be well served if that were the only result of our efforts. Of course, it is not Red Hat's goal to stop there.

*How has Red Hat had to re-imagine Linux in the minds of the community that creates it and the consumers who use it?*

The open-source community has had to overcome the stereotype of the hobbyist hacker. According to this stereotype, Linux, for example, is built by 14-year-old hackers in their bedrooms. We see here an example of the Fear, Uncertainty, and Doubt (FUD) foisted on the software industry by vendors of proprietary systems. After all, who wants to trust their mission-critical enterprise applications to software written by a 14-year-old in his spare time?

The reality, of course, is very different from this stereotype. While the "lone hacker" is a valuable and important part of the development process, such programmers account for a minority of the code that makes up the Linux OS. From the head of the kernel team, Linus Torvalds, on down, most of the code in the Linux OS is built by professional software developers at major software, engineering, and research organizations.

A few examples include the GNU C and C++ compilers that come from Cygnus Solutions Inc. of Sunnyvale, California. As mentioned before, the X Window System originally came from the X Consortium. A number of Ethernet drivers are now largely the responsibility of engineers at NASA. Device drivers are now coming frequently from the device manufacturers themselves. In short, building new open-source software is often not so different from building conventional software, and the talent behind open source is by and large the same talent that is behind conventional software.

*What are the primary qualities that organizations look for in an OS like Linux? Can you give an example of how they would maximize the potential benefits?*

NASA, the outfit that rockets people off into outer space for a living, has an expression: "Software is not software without source code." To the engineers at NASA, high reliability is not good enough. Extremely high reliability is not good enough. NASA needs perfect reliability. They cannot afford to suffer the "blue screen of death" with 12 trusting souls rocketing at a thousand miles an hour around the earth, depending on their systems to keep them alive.

NASA needs access to the source code of the software they are using to build these systems. And they need that software to come with a license that allows them to modify it to meet their needs. Now I'll admit that the average dental office billing system does not need the standards of reliability that NASA astronauts depend on to bill patients for their annual teeth cleaning, but the principle remains the same.

And unlike proprietary binary-only OSes, with Linux, Red Hat users are free from the major proprietary limitations and can modify the product to meet the needs of the application they are building. This is the unique value proposition that we were able to offer Red Hat customers. This is the proposition that none of the much bigger competitors are willing or able to offer. This is a value proposition that overturns usual notions of intellectual property.

Rather than using a license to lock customers in and wall them off from the source code, Red Hat uses a license that embodies the very idea of access to and control over source code.

*Can you give any examples of the potential flaws or repercussions in licensing intellectual property and a proprietary OS?*

Well, prior to 1984, AT&T used to share the source code to the Unix OS with any team who could help them improve it. When AT&T was broken up, the resulting AT&T was no longer restricted to being a telephone company. It decided to try and make money selling licenses to the Unix OS. All the universities and research groups who had helped build Unix suddenly found themselves having to pay for licenses for an OS that they had helped build. They were not happy, but could not do much about it—after all, AT&T owned the copyright to Unix. The other development teams had been helping AT&T at AT&T's discretion, and ultimately they either had to pay the licensing fees or change systems.

*Does Red Hat have a particular stance on licensing intellectual property and the subsequent products that can be exploited? What are the benefits in adopting a more flexible approach?*

Red Hat is not ideological about licenses. We were comfortable with any license that provided us with control over the software we were using because that in turn enabled us to deliver the benefit of control to our customers and users, whether they were NASA engineers or application programmers working on a dental office billing system.

If Red Hat builds an innovation that its competitors are able to use, the least it could demand is that the innovations its competitors build are available to its engineering teams as well. And the General Public License is the most effective license for ensuring that this forced cooperation among the various team members continues to occur regardless of the competitive environment at the time.

Keep in mind that one of the great strengths of the Linux OS is that it is a highly modular technology. When we shipped a version of Red Hat Linux, we were shipping over 800 separate packages. So licensing also has a practical dimension to it. A license that enables Red Hat to ship the software but not make modifications to it creates problems because users cannot correct or modify the software to their needs. A less restrictive license that requires that the user ask the permission of the original author before making changes still burdens Red Hat and its users with too many restrictions. Having to ask possibly 800 different authors or development teams for permission to make modifications is simply not practical.

*There are major differences between what Red Hat provides in the distribution and support of Linux and what companies like Windows or Unix provide. How does the Linux community reconcile those differences?*

The primary difference between Unix and Linux is not the kernel, or the Apache server, or any other set of features. The primary difference between the two is that Unix is just another proprietary binary-only or IP-based OS. Linux has a profoundly different approach to building an OS, which looks at the same forces that drove the 30 or so available, and largely incompatible, versions of Unix apart as an opportunity to be taken advantage of.

The problem with a proprietary binary-only OS that is available from multiple suppliers is that those suppliers have short-term marketing pressures to keep whatever innovations they make to the OS to themselves for the benefit of their customers exclusively. Over time, these "proprietary innovations" to each version of the Unix OS cause the various Unixes to differ substantially from each other. This occurs when the other vendors do not have access to the source code of the innovation, and the license the Unix vendors use prohibits the use of that innovation even if everyone else involved in Unix were willing to use the same innovation.

> "This is part of the power of open source: It creates a unifying pressure to conform to a common reference point—in effect, an open standard—and it removes the intellectual property barriers that would otherwise inhibit this convergence."

In Linux the pressures are the reverse. If one Linux supplier adopts an innovation that becomes popular in the market, the other Linux vendors will immediately adopt that innovation. This is because they have access to the source code of that innovation and it comes under a license that allows them to use it.

This is part of the power of open source: It creates a unifying pressure to conform to a common reference point—in effect, an open standard—and it removes the intellectual property barriers that would otherwise inhibit this convergence.

*Can you give an example of someone maximizing the potential opportunities within this kind of collaborative effort?*

Grant Guenther, at the time a member of Empress Software's database development team, wanted to enable his coworkers to work on projects from home. They needed a secure method of moving large files from their office to home and back. They were using Linux on PCs and using Zip drives. The only problem was that at the time (1996), good Zip drive support was not available in Linux.

So Grant had a choice: Throw out the Linux solution and purchase a much more expensive proprietary solution, or stop what he was doing and spend a couple of days writing a decent Zip drive driver. He wrote one, and worked with other Zip drive users across the Internet to test and refine the driver.

Consider the cost to Red Hat, or any other software company, of having to pay Empress and Grant to develop that driver. Safe to say the cost would have been in the tens of thousands of dollars, and yet Grant chose to "give away" his work. In return, instead of money, he received the use of a great solution for his problem of enabling Empress programmers to work from home, at a fraction of the cost of the alternatives. This is the kind of win-win proposition offered by cooperative models like the open-source development model.

*There are many methods for recognizing and negotiating new signals in human behavior, from watching a crowd at a soccer game to blogging a DIY technology. What do you see as the best approach for negotiating a new signal in human behavior?*

"What drove the PC revolution was that it provided its users with control over their computing platform. Consumers will put up with a measure of confusion and inconsistency in order to have choice—choice and control."

Whenever a revolutionary new practice comes along, there are always skeptics who predict its inevitable downfall, pointing out all the obstacles the new model must overcome before it can be called a success. There are also the ideologues who insist that it is only the purest implementation of the new model that can possibly succeed. And then there are the rest of us who are just plugging away, testing, innovating, and using the new technology model for those applications where the new model works better than the old one.

*People adapt quickly to new technologies, immediately revealing latent needs and behaviors as soon as they are confronted with the possibility. Do you have any insights toward mapping or prompting the potential benefits of this process?*

The primary benefit of a new technology model can be seen in the birth of the PC. When IBM published the specs to its PC in 1981, why did the world adopt the PC computing model with such enthusiasm? It was not that the IBM PC was a better mousetrap. The original 8086-based PCs shipped with 64K bytes of main memory, and an upper memory limit of 640K. No one could imagine that a single user would need more than 640K on their individual machine.

What drove the PC revolution was that it provided its users with control over their computing platform. They could buy their first PC from IBM, their second from Compaq, and their third from HP. They could buy memory or hard drives from one of a hundred suppliers, and they could get an almost infinite range of peripheral equipment for almost any purpose or application.

This new model introduced a huge number of inconsistencies, incompatibilities, and confusion between technologies, products, and suppliers. But as the world now knows, consumers love choice. Consumers will put up with a measure of confusion and inconsistency in order to have choice—choice and control.

Notice also that the PC hardware business did not fragment. Specifications have generally remained open, and there is strong pressure to conform to standards to preserve interoperability. No one has a sufficiently better mousetrap with which to entice users and then hold them hostage by going proprietary. Instead, innovations—better mousetraps—accrue to the community at large.

*Essentially, what do people really want from their operating systems?*

The Linux OS gives consumers choice over the technology that comes with their computers at the operating system level. Does it require a whole new level of responsibility and an expertise on the part of the user? Certainly. Will that user prefer to go back to the old model of being forced to trust his proprietary binary-only OS supplier once he has experienced the choice and freedom of the new model? Not likely.

Critics will continue to look for, and occasionally find, serious problems with Linux technology. But consumers love choice, and the huge Internet-based open-source software development marketplace is going to figure out ways to solve all of them.

—

# 10
# Unfolding Signal Maps

The importance of the question *what?* cannot be overstated. The answer reveals not only the deeper meaning of any innovation, but also its journey toward maximization. On this journey, there is room for the *why* and *how* as well, but the order in which we ask these questions determines how much we can maximize the benefits of any innovation. To understand the nature of the questions we pose when interpreting an event or experience, we must understand the condition and context from which they emerge—that of being human, and our desire to seek and to know.

# A Brief Interlude in What, Why, How, and the Human Condition

*Men are conditioned beings because everything they come in contact with turns immediately into a condition of their existence.*

—Hannah Arendt

In her 1958 book *The Human Condition*, German political theorist Hannah Arendt introduced the concept of *vita activa*: "With the term *vita activa*, I propose to designate three fundamental human activities: labor, work, and action," Arendt wrote. "They are fundamental because each corresponds to one of the basic conditions under which life on earth has been given to men." We innovate for the activities of labor, work, and action—for them, we have built and created the world of tools, the world of education, and the world of laws, as well as all the constructed spaces we now call *civilization*. This is, in effect, the world I defined earlier as *technology*—the sum of our practical knowledge in reference to our material and social culture.

Arendt defined labor as:

> "*the activity which corresponds to the biological process of the human body, whose spontaneous growth, metabolism, and eventual decay are bound to the vital necessities produced and fed into the life process by labor. The human condition of labor is life itself.*"

In this condition, we ask questions in the realm of the tactical—questions that begin with the word *how*: How do I survive? How do I find food? How do I build shelter?

This is a condition related to the "having" side of the human being, a side interested in the quantity of things and their performance, durability, appropriateness for the task, and the sequence of actions that they require to satisfy the question. It is a condition concerned with the *tactics of life*. Thus, the creation of tools arises from the question *how?*

"The quality of *being*—of *becoming*—through experiences and learning is unique to humans. It completes us and explains why we always need to move forward, searching for more ways to experience life, and to learn."

Perfecting the performance of tools is also a *how* question, suitable to what psychologist and philosopher Erich Fromm termed the "having mode"—a mode dominated by our interest in acquiring things that are fixed and describable. According to Fromm:

> "*Most of us know more about the mode of having than we do about the mode of being, because having is by far the more frequently experienced mode in our culture. ...Being refers to experience, and human experience is in principle not describable.*"

This quality of *being*—of *becoming*—through experiences and learning is unique to humans. It completes us and explains why we always need to move forward, searching for more ways to experience life, and to learn—exploring in order to have more worth and merit. These things allow us *to become:* to leave a mark through our work and deeds. To have mattered, for others.

For Arendt, work is the activity "which corresponds to the unnaturalness of human existence. ...Work provides an 'artificial' world of things, distinctly different from all natural surroundings. ...The human condition of work is worldliness." In other words, the creation of worth, using our tools, answers the question *why?*

## BUT *WHAT* IS IT ALL ABOUT?

What is the most asked *what* question?

**What is the meaning of life?**

Arendt continues:

> "*All three activities and their corresponding conditions are intimately connected with the most general condition of human existence: birth and death, natality and mortality. Labor assures not only individual survival, but the life of the species. Work and its product, the human artifact, bestow a measure of permanence and durability upon the futility of mortal life and the fleeting character of human time. Action, in so far as it engages in founding and preserving political bodies, creates the condition for remembrance, that is, for history.*"

And so, when faced with a new disruptive innovation, can we ignore Arendt's discourse on the human condition and the totality of the questions *what?, why?,* and *how?*

Let's consider what each question reveals: *What?* reveals the ultimate benefit of an innovation; *why?* reveals its purpose and function; and *how?* reveals the enablement, a particular form of the function represented by a specific tool. The coffeemaker is a *how.* The screw is a *how.* The coffeemaker and screw will not exist without a purpose larger than their immediate function and performance, larger than what they represent tactically—the *what.*

And yet, *The Human Condition* notwithstanding, most innovation in large organizations is still stuck in the *how*. Business and manufacturing have had more than 150 years since the Industrial Revolution to perfect and deliver the *how*. But here is the catch: We are now in a *what* moment, similar to that after the discovery of fire, when the question was: What can we do with fire?

# Strategic Questions

Do you recall the first time you encountered one of the most ubiquitous objects ever invented: the screw? Did you ever think twice about the importance of this little tool in maintaining and enhancing your life? You would have had you been an astute entrepreneur in the 18th century, when British toolmaker and inventor Henry Maudslay invented the first screw-cutting lathe. What was once a labor-intensive operation—painstakingly making each screw manually—soon became a mechanized operation that resulted in hundreds of screws being produced in one day, thanks to Mr. Maudslay. So for any entrepreneur worth his mantle in the 18th century, the question had to be: *What else can use a screw?*

This question is similar to *What can we do with fire?* and *What can we do with electricity?* and *What can we do with plastics?* It's similar to all the *what* questions that have shaped the world as we know it today.

The answers to the question *What else can use a screw?* has made it one of the most important inventions of all time, shaping and reshaping almost everything we know.

## WHAT *WHAT?* CAN TEACH US

Any answer to the question *what?* will inform a set of strategic directions that allow us to forecast and contemplate response tactics. As discussed in Chapter 8, McLuhan's Laws of Media tetrad, a tool for defining the potential of any new signal, is framed around the question *what?*

Three things to remember about this all-important query are:

✦ *What?* is a strategic and imaginative question.

✦ *What?* is about possibility, not tactics.

✦ *What?* is a defining question. It allows us to map future possibilities—the future *how* tactics of any new innovation.

The *how* is the screw—or any other tactical technology. Every *how* needs a *what*; without purpose, tools have no larger meaning. The invention of the screw-cutting lathe did not just make life easier for the toolmakers of the 1750s. It was the trigger signal—the disruptive technology of its time—that allowed for the creation of a new world that was not imaginable before. And so is data a trigger in the information/knowledge economy.

So *what* can we do with data?

And, as with the invention of the screw, *what else* in the world has changed and is shaping your life right now?

Let's look at an example of an innovation, or a moment of disruption. From the prism of the *what, why,* and *how* questions, smart tags or any other device that holds and transmits data is like the invention of the electric motor. It holds the potential to impact every aspect of our social, cultural, and economic lives. It is as powerful and transformative for us as the foam was for Dick Fosbury.

Think of all the Dow component companies in the business of motorizing mechanical motion and you will find a surprising large number of them—General Electric, Boeing, General Motors—stuck in the motorization of predecessor archetypes. Being stuck in the *how* does not necessarily mean that a company is not innovating; there are many tactical innovations that help the *how* deliver its function better. Once motorized, a tool will move through all the technology developments associated with the transmission, distribution, and storage of electricity: electronics, digital, power accumulation and storage allowing for portability, and so on. But all will still be connected to the initial function of the device, as the electric eggbeater was to the manual eggbeater: making a better omelet, perhaps, but still making an omelet. *Stuck in the how is also stuck in the what.* In this stage, an innovation grows out of a passive strategy—reaction—and results in an accidental position.

"The screw was the trigger signal—the disruptive technology of its time—that allowed for the creation of a new world that was not imaginable before. And so is data a trigger in the information/ knowledge economy."

Understanding the depth of the *why* and *what* questions to be asked of a disruptive innovation is where the creation of a new paradigm is possible. For this, one needs imagination: The depth of our set of questions determines how well we can maximize the potential benefits and opportunity of any new innovation.

In order to uncover the unique value of an invention (technological or behavioral disruption) and intentionally select a strategic position, we

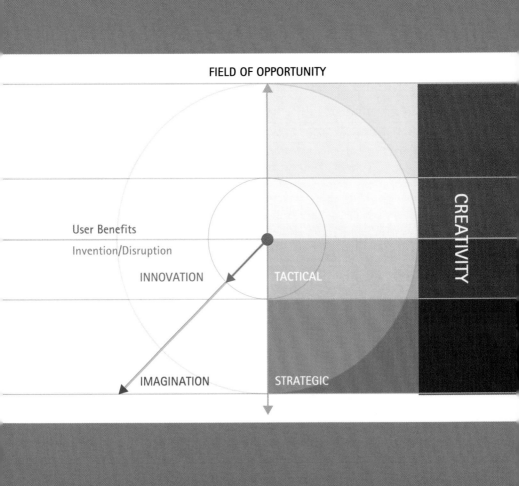

must consider its potential to become beneficial in ways that can only be imagined. This does not mean these opportunities are impossible to plan for; it means they require imagination to foresee. And each imagined possible value widens the field of strategic opportunity.

So what is the difference between the questions *what?, why?,* and *how?* Where do they come from and how do they help us unfold signals? How do we navigate from the retrieval of *how*—or the predecessor of any disruptive innovation—toward a truly new product or service? By placing the how into the deeper human context, and understanding its meaning as part of the condition of being human.

"In order to uncover the unique value of an invention and intentionally select a strategic position, we must consider its potential to become beneficial in ways that can only be imagined. This does not mean these opportunities are impossible to plan for; it means they require imagination to foresee. Each imagined possible value will widen the field of strategic opportunity."

## Grasping the *How* of the Electric Motor

You are a 19th-century entrepreneur and have just become aware of this invention called the "electric motor." A certain Michael Faraday played enough in his laboratory in Great Britain that, by 1821, he had a rudimentary form of a rotary motor.

Faraday's contraption was the classic inventor's nightmare: good enough to supply proof, but too inconvenient in size, architecture, and complexity of parts to encourage contemplation of practical use: A wire submerged into a bath of mercury containing a magnet. Pass a current through the wire and it starts rotating around the magnet.

"*What* does this thing do?" you ask. And you learn that it converts electrical energy into mechanical motion. So you pose another *what* question: "*What* can I use this for?" After a quick survey of all the devices that use mechanical motion, you engage in the largest "predecessor retrieval" of all time, considering the motorization of all human artifacts that use mechanical motion. (Faraday himself saw the scope of possibility of his invention. When asked by Prime Minister William Gladstone what was the usefulness of electricity, it is said that he replied, "Why, sir, there is every possibility that you will soon be able to tax it!")

*Continued*

← *Benefits that can only be imagined: The circle of strategic opportunity widens with each imagined value.*

### Grasping the *How* of the Electric Motor *Continued*

You decide to add a number of new benefits to one's hand in the form of the electric eggbeater. This is the first phase of tactical innovation: The new disruptive innovation—the motor—is used on all the tools that are its predecessors. These tools have established markets, established users, and established benefits.

The rudimentary motor was enough of a signal to you to define the opportunities that it held. To contemplate a future for the motor, you needed the imagination to see beyond its form at that time. And by 1871, you and a few other foresighted—or lucky—inventors are transforming artifacts that humanity had used for centuries to a new level of performance and benefit, via dynamos, electrical generators, and high-voltage electrical engines.

The market potential of the eggbeater will increase, as your new tool finds new users who appreciate the ease of operation, power, performance, efficiency, and saved physical energy it affords. But the purpose—that which answers the *why* and *what*—will not be affected. *The egg does not know:* The mayonnaise still tastes the same. The deep purpose is not changed. The benefits are time saved and power of performance: the *how*.

"Faraday's contraption was the classic inventor's nightmare: good enough to supply proof, but too inconvenient in size, architecture, and complexity of parts to encourage contemplation of practical use."

# Retrieval and Emergence Mapping 1: The Camera

What is a camera all about? A manufacturer can make a camera digital, but the larger question is: What do people photograph and why?

Why do people use a camera? To make images of memory. Is memory just visual, or is scent involved as well? Or sound? Or feeling? Is memory a series of familiar attributes that activate our senses—through eyes, nose, mouth, fingertips, and ears? If the answer to these questions is "yes," then it is no surprise that Kodak has a number of patents on technology combinations that can deliver the association between an image

*Diagram of the first electric motor.* ➜

and a scent, sound, and soon, flavor. This does not spell the end of photography, but the beginning of "memory keeping" and "memory sharing" by other means. It also spells the transformation of an entire industry from *means* to *meaning*—from the *how* to the *what*—based on the understanding that the ideal experience, in its most meaningful context, is the ultimate user benefit.

## THE DIGITAL CAMERA: PRECISE, UNDENIABLE, INTUITIVE, AND SENSED

The moment that a technology is introduced, it carries with it signals of any future application that it will influence or create. The map (opposite) demonstrates how the techniques and philosophies of McLuhan's tetradic analysis, Arendt's *vita activa,* and Fromm's conditions of "having" and "being" discussed in this chapter can uncover more than the obvious realm of innovation.

When confronted with a new technology, the first thing we must ask is, "What does this thing enhance?" For example, the digital camera enhances the convenience of capturing more images. Since the technology enhances our ability to perform an action, we label it a **precise** signal and ask, "How else have we accomplished this act?" This question forces us to consider all the specific ways we have captured images before, including the Polaroid camera, the camcorder, Impressionist paintings, sketching, and so on.

In this way, we quickly reveal the **undeniable** innovations of new features and applications of digital cameras. It is undeniable that we will use innovation to expand the field of opportunity by replacing established products and services. In order to see what the camera will retrieve, we ask about a prior artifact, "Why did we use this?" The insight that people want to capture, share, and express memories stimulates us to imagine devices that capture and relate more memory triggers (image, sound, scent, and taste).

We call these signals **intuitive** because they reflect the degree of intuition guiding our insight. Of these insights we ask, "What is this motivation really about?" Answering this question requires the foresight to imagine that if the camera is really about labeling a moment as important to you, then the future of the camera holds the experience of being able to tag a space and time with an event and a reaction. We call a signal like this **sensed** because it might not be practical today, but we can sense and understand its possible value.

It is important to highlight the critical role of imagination in this process. Understanding of current possibility will reveal the realm for innovation, but we must use insight and foresight to uncover the intuitive and sensed opportunities.

*Toward a deeper understanding: Imagination is critical in uncovering the intuitive* ➔
*and sensed opportunities of a signal.*

# FIELD OF OPPORTUNITY & BENEFIT MAXIMIZATION

| | | |
|---|---|---|
| ACTION | *SENSED* | TO BE/BEHAVIOR |
| WORK | *INTUITIVE* | TO BE/BEHAVIOR |
| LABOR | *UNDENIABLE* | TO HAVE/BEHAVIOR |
| | *PRECISE* | |
| INNOVATION | HOW? | TACTICAL |
| Predecessor | | Obsolesce |
| IMAGINATION/INSIGHT | WHY? | STRATEGIC |
| Immediate | | Retrieve |
| IMAGINATION/FORESIGHT | WHAT? | STRATEGIC |
| Archetype | | Flip |

In the end, we may discover that it is not a picture that we want as a memory: It is the full recovery of ourselves in "that moment." And "that moment" is not necessarily visual. How many times have you shown photos of a trip or party to friends, and in the end you gave up and said, "You had to be there"? In other words, "you had to experience it."

## CAPTURING A MOMENT

So what is a camera all about? *It is about the recovery of the experience.*

It's not about the high definition of the image; it is about the moment being captured in any way, shape, or form. There is no rational explanation for people taking pictures with no clarity on their 1-megapixel cell phone camera; the picture keeps and can trigger the recovery of the moment, and that has no describable measure in megapixels.

Now what is the moment all about? The moment is about what you perceived in a particular place at a particular time. About what you felt, sensed, and experienced. And most of all, about something you want to share with others.

"In the end, we may discover that it is not a picture that we want as a memory: It is the full recovery of ourselves in 'that moment.' And 'that moment' is not necessarily visual."

*A piece of you in that moment and in that place.* At the Wailing Wall, or at the Church of the Holy Sepulchre in Jerusalem. At the Colosseum of Rome. At the Great Pyramid of Khufu. Or at your daughter's wedding. You will want to keep that moment and share it with the group that defines your relevance and meaning as a human.

You may want to tag your emotions to a space. So, for example, if your friends visit the Holy Sepulchre, they can, if they so choose, use an enabled device to access your smart tags and receive a data transfer from the space telling them you were there, and this is what you felt and wanted to leave behind: "I was here. I experienced. I thought of you." Memory is about retaining, recalling, and above all sharing information that defines who you are—for you and for others.

On a larger level, our purpose as human beings is to create something that attests to our presence on earth. We need to survive, for sure, but after that, we are involved in a quest for meaning—a quest for worth as measured by others. Nothing to do with survival, but everything to do with being human. We need to *be,* rather than *have.* We need to create and let others know we have created. We need to let others know what, where, and how we have been. This fulfills our human condition of plurality. To be with others; to make sure others know we exist.

We do not build an Eiffel Tower or Empire State Building because we want shelter and survival. We build them to tell something about ourselves, to ourselves in the present and to others in the future. We need to leave a mark; it is the condition of our humanity. This is why we work hard at surpassing the condition of labor. We want to move from *how* to *why* and *what*.

Plurality is a condition of being human; you cannot be human without being plural. Being human means not being alone; it also means sharing *what* and *who* you are. From the moment we are born to the moment we die, we strive not to be alone, and we will do what is necessary not to be alone.

In the Zulu language, the word *ubuntu* means "me though your eyes." *I am because you are.* Both "you" and "I" are essential in this condition: *I do not exist without you.*

In business opportunity terms, the future of the today's digital camera will be in *memory keeping:* encoding, storing, recalling, and transmitting the information that is "you."

*Ubuntu. "Me through your eyes."*

# Retrieval and Emergence Mapping 2: Organized Sports

We are conditioned by what we create because each new artifact is an aggregator of past archetypes; an innovation is often the sum of several old innovations that it integrates and in turn obsolesces. And so, when forecasting the future of a signal, we start by placing it in the center of our inquiry and asking, "How did we get here? What does this embody?"

These questions will lead us to uncovering the archetype of an object or system, which encapsulates its original purpose as well as its specific manifestations in form. In the previous example, we began with an artifact that currently exists, retrieving its deeper archetypal meaning to understand its relevance and impact. In this example, we begin with the archetype itself, looking at conceptual constructs to understand how they are then affected or articulated in our society as activities and created artifacts.

In all categories of the word *archetype,* we can confidently place the name or a description for almost anything we know, and everything we have experienced. So let's give it a try with two things that we encounter throughout our daily lives: What is the archetype of a tool? What is the archetype of a toy?

Before reading further, think about these questions and write down your answers. In experiments conducted at the Beal Institute, we asked these questions to a variety of people. Compare your answers with the majority of theirs:

The archetype of a tool is the hammer. The archetype of a toy is the ball.

All we need to do now is to understand what this means in the larger picture of creating new experiences, new services, new products, and new business models. To do so, we need to ask a few more questions that define the characteristics of the archetypes hammer and ball.

"What can the archetypes of most sports—the hammer and the ball—indicate about where we are headed and the choices we should make in deciding that future?"

What do we expect from a hammer? We expect it to work well and be crafted to last a long time, with a good balance-to-weight ratio and a comfortable handle to hold. We expect it to look like it can do the job well. In short, we expect long-term functional performance and usability. The hammer is the oldest tool created by humans—the archetype of all tools, due to its basic physical function of amplifying force. Many tools and machines created over the centuries are based on the same principle of converting a motion—in the case of the hammer, the "swing"—into kinetic energy.

What do we expect from a ball? We expect that it can bounce, be handled by anyone, come back if we throw it against a wall, and allow us to play by ourselves or with others, as a means of relationship-building and communication. The ball affords us the capability to *be.* Its purpose does not concern labor or work, but rather action—we expect from it a good experience and a good relationship. The ball is the oldest toy form, used in Greece, ancient Egypt, and the pre-Columbian cultures of the Americas.

Once we gain imaginative insights, we can contemplate where these characteristics might lead if pushed to the limits of both performance and experience. The extraordinary success of organized sports indicates that the majority are activities that involve a "hammer" hitting a "ball" in one form or another—their success emerges from connecting these archetypes with both past and present contexts and needs, and creating imaginative foresights for the future.

The economic value of such activities is calculable, but it would take a few more pages than we have here. Think baseball, basketball, billiards, bowling, cricket, croquet, American football, soccer, golf, handball, field hockey, ice hockey, hurling, jai-alai, lacrosse, and tennis. Think of the combined revenues of the National Football League, National Basketball Association, Professional Golf Association and Ladies Professional Golf Association, National Hockey League, and many more.

What is the social value or worth that society places on organized sports? Another several pages that we don't have room for here. But think Tiger Woods and his generic job description: *Put the ball in the hole.* The fewer the strokes, the more the player is compensated. In the 2005 Masters, Woods swung a club 276 times to earn $1.17 million. That is $4,239 for each swing of the club—or "hammer."

Is this a disproportionate valuation of what might seem a trivial activity? Not if one understands the mastery required to use a "hammer" in hitting a ball and the deep roots of this archetype of human activity. Tiger Woods is putting the ball in the hole for *us*. He is *our extension* into the world of mastery that we aspire to. He represents *what could be possible*. And that is worth every penny.

Let's close with an observation made by Christopher Barber, in the 2006 podcast "IBM and the Future of Sport"—a signal combining technology and sports that illustrates the significance of archetypes in creating culture. What can the archetyes of most sports—the hammer and the ball—indicate about where we are headed and the choices we should make in deciding that future?

> "*Sports are an indelible part of who we are. From the first moment television cameras were placed on the sidelines, technology has impacted how we watch and enjoy sports. Behind the scenes, sports leagues around the world use technology to enhance how their games are played, the way their businesses are run off the field, and the way their paying customers—the fans—are rewarded. What role does technology play in sports today? And more importantly, what role will it play in the future? How will our experience as fans of our favorite sports teams change or be impacted by evolving technologies?*"

# 11

# A Workbook for Strategic Creativity

How do we transform what we know and what we can do now into human and economic wealth? The answer to this question is one of the most sought after in the world. This workbook provides a methodology for strategic creativity as a source of organizational and social change, and is a comprehensive guide to using the imagination to generate exceptional services, products, and systems.

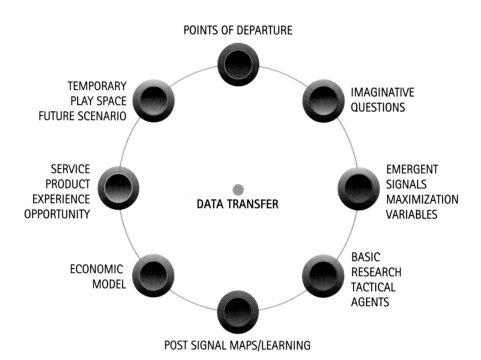

POINTS OF DEPARTURE

TEMPORARY
PLAY SPACE
FUTURE SCENARIO

IMAGINATIVE
QUESTIONS

SERVICE
PRODUCT
EXPERIENCE
OPPORTUNITY

DATA TRANSFER

EMERGENT
SIGNALS
MAXIMIZATION
VARIABLES

ECONOMIC
MODEL

BASIC
RESEARCH
TACTICAL
AGENTS

POST SIGNAL MAPS/LEARNING

# Toward a New Ecology of Learning, Imagination, and Innovation

We traditionally begin innovation from one of three places: current problems, past experiences, or imagination. Problem solving from current problems is purely perceptual. One needs to feel it, measure it, and test it—or someone else needs to reveal and define it—in order to solve it. In any case, the problem exists, so you need not use your imagination to find it. You need to use creativity. The same is true for past experiences, which are abundant in problems; this too is problem solving.

Innovating from these perceptions most often results in tactical innovation. Take the bottle of ketchup. Since ketchup's invention in 1869, it has been difficult to get it out of a bottle without a struggle—shaking or slapping it. Finally, a few years ago, Heinz introduced upside-down containers—which were not really a new concept, as toothpaste was already being packaged in these. Developing a better bottle certainly must have been a priority for Heinz, as it would improve user access to its product. Yet it took the company 115 years to come up with this "innovative" solution.

## STRATEGIC INNOVATION AND ADAPTIVE INQUIRY

But what if the problem is not known? What if you are not trying to redesign an espresso maker (or ketchup bottle)—a tactical innovation—but to invent the espresso method of extracting flavor from ground coffee using hot water under pressure—a strategic innovation?

One common approach in finding a solution to a known problem is to analyze the parameters of the situation and then decide on a clear path of investigation based on those constraints. For example, in investigating an existing market, the logical and widely accepted approach is to apply established economic models to study factors in expansion potential, social impact, and market value. From this inquiry, one can recognize patterns and draw rational conclusions.

We frequently see questions such as: "What is the future of mobile communications?" or "What is the future of advertising on the Web?" Both are premised on a research method that studies past and current patterns as indicators of where the pattern might lead, if it followed the same course, and what shape it will hold in the future.

But any new interaction with a technology could indicate a latent behavior for which there may not be enough precedent to recommend a logical question. So when applied to an emergent signal, prescribed analysis methods such as this often fail because they are being applied to a set of

←*The research method developed at the Beal Institute, represented as the strategic imagination circle.*

fluid and complex variables that have no definite or explicitly concise attributes to validate the prescription.

As I have discussed, this type of analytical, "left brain" thinking is no longer sufficient. We are currently experiencing and will continue to experience an enormous increase in our social and technological diversity through our interactions and associations. And this diversity is also in a radical state of flux, changing states and perspectives so fluidly that each group is not able to support or sustain sequential analysis. These emerging micro-signals defy objective analysis by actively responding to their investigation; at a small enough scale, the variables are influenced by myriad factors, including their own study. The variable conditions of these systems demand an adaptive learning practice.

For example, the current dilemma of data transfer is that both the content and the portal of transfer are evolving at an extraordinary rate—digital video and the broadband explosion are two such areas. This increase is generating a continuously shifting and evolving map of human action patterned not by the limits of technology, but by the limits of the people using it. In short, there are more possibilities than there are boundaries. In this environment, growth—social, economic, and otherwise—comes not from solving problems of need, but from answering the question "What else can we do?"

"Emerging micro-signals defy objective analysis by actively responding to their investigation; at a small enough scale, the variables are influenced by myriad factors, including their own study. The variable conditions of these systems demand an adaptive learning practice."

Thus, a different approach must be used to study immediate significance and potentiality. To explore the meanings of emerging technology and behavior signals, the process *must* be flexible, as it will grow in many directions at once, with each direction informing and building on the others. This is not the same as determining how to fit imagination or strategic creativity into business models, but rather *how to adapt business to both.*

The most effective process for maximizing innovation opportunities is up for grabs and always has been. The current recognition of the importance of strategic innovation—in business, education, or politics—makes this the opportune moment. To reveal entirely new possibilities, we must free analysis from the current paradigm and explore it under the widest scope of concurrent possibilities.

When the goal is to explore opportunity in a conceptual space, one must proceed from imagination, employing methodologies that empower and nurture possibility. In that respect, the most important intent of this workbook is to foster a perspective that inspires well-informed dialogue and intelligent action.

## A METHODOLOGY FOR POSSIBILITY

The pursuit of possibility is shaped through *action research* methods. Based on repeating cycles of investigation, critical reflection, and peer review, action research develops and applies a pliable perspective to this pursuit, directing the same flexibility and awareness toward the ideas that emerge and the signals they reveal.

I developed the methodology that follows with a team of researchers at the Beal Institute for Strategic Creativity. It is adaptive action research, flexible because it can change based on knowledge gained along the way; it encourages the pursuit of that which it discovers. It is a process of change and of understanding the nature of the change. As mentioned earlier in the book, informed change in turn informs action, and action informs understanding. Because the process is a continuum of discovery and learning, its best diagrammatic representation is that of a circle that we call the *strategic imagination circle*.

"To explore the meanings of emerging technology and behavior signals, the process *must* be flexible, as it will grow in many directions at once, with each direction informing and building on the others. This is not the same as determining how to fit imagination or strategic creativity into business models, but rather how to adapt business to both."

# The Strategic Imagination Circle

The circle process begins in the center, where we place the subject of investigation. It could be any disruptive innovation, artifact, service, or concept that we are trying to maximize in terms of opportunity or understanding. Or it could be the economic driver of the moment. Plastics. Data and data transfer. The internet of things.

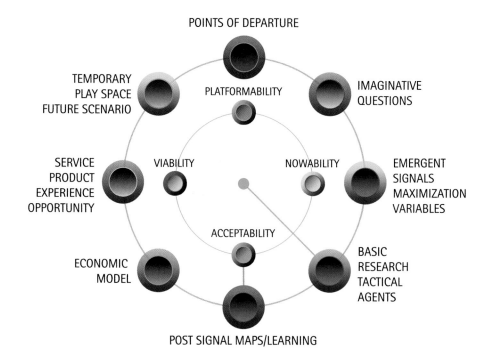

POINTS OF DEPARTURE

TEMPORARY
PLAY SPACE
FUTURE SCENARIO

PLATFORMABILITY

IMAGINATIVE
QUESTIONS

SERVICE
PRODUCT
EXPERIENCE
OPPORTUNITY

VIABILITY

NOWABILITY

EMERGENT
SIGNALS
MAXIMIZATION
VARIABLES

ACCEPTABILITY

ECONOMIC
MODEL

BASIC
RESEARCH
TACTICAL
AGENTS

POST SIGNAL MAPS/LEARNING

The eight nodes surrounding the center are the eight steps of the method:

1. Signal discovery: basic research, data collection, and analysis
2. Emerging signals mapping: the diagnostic of opportunity
3. Imaginative questions
4. Points of departure
5. Future scenarios in temporary play space
6. Experience opportunity definition
7. Economic opportunity modeling
8. Post-signal learning

## SIGNAL DISCOVERY: BASIC RESEARCH, DATA COLLECTION, ANALYSIS, AND DEFINITION OF TACTICAL AGENTS

The initial investigation of an undefined research area is driven by open and imaginative questions that seek out *opportunity signals* within the expanse of emerging technologies and behavior. The search for opportunity is a process of learning what to look for; what has the capacity to create the most capability. This signal discovery phase scans for potential disruptions to the common behavior model: people or organizations innovating new or existing technology. The scope is broad as opposed to deep, as its purpose is to reveal the dense impact of an opportunity, exploring the unfamiliar before defining parameters.

Data collected in this phase includes:

✦ Objective facts: from specific events or news reports

✦ Constructed facts: people's opinions, social perceptions, or organizational constructs—what organizations implement to manage themselves and their relationship with the "outside" world, such as policies, media releases, and public documents

✦ Filtered facts: the opinions of the team of researchers, based on their insights and analysis

The researchers collect and analyze the data in a dynamic continuum that evolves with the collection of more data. This process continues until the collected data presents a compelling new territory where the emerging patterns of new signals become evident and revealed as either strategic opportunities or tactical agents.

← *The strategic imagination circle, with the filters used to assess opportunities for economic potential.*

## EMERGENT SIGNALS: DIAGNOSING OPPORTUNITY

Within a collection of objective, constructed, and filtered facts, certain behaviors and ideas are seen as "meaning something else." These are *emerging signals*. We use emergent signal mapping to evaluate these and the opportunities they afford, in light of the new variables that they create. This is distinct from technology forecasting in that it does not aim to predict the next technology, but rather to predict which latent behavior or behavior set will emerge from the complex meshing of enhanced and aggregated functions, obsolesced artifact, and new possibilities that a new innovation presents.

"The purpose of emergent-signal mapping is to gain insight into the means, the tools, that the disruptive signal will obsolesce, reverse, and retrieve, as well as into the new functions or purposes that it will enhance. This investigation then advances into the imaginative foresight phase, where the new meaning and benefits of an emergent signal are revealed."

In the emergent signal mapping, signals collected in the discovery phase are explored to understand the behavior they reveal. In *retrieval and emergence maps* (as illustrated in the previous section), systems or object archetypes that define their original purpose or manifestation are "retrieved." The relationships between signals and archetypes (those that are simple, like the camera, and those that are more complicated, like golf) emerge, and the reach of opportunity expands when we look at them through the three frames of inquiry described earlier in relation to Arendt's *Human Condition*: the *how*, the *why* and the *what*.

The purpose of this inquiry is to gain insight into the means, the tools, that the disruptive signal will obsolesce, reverse, and retrieve, as well as into the new functions or purposes that it will enhance—an analysis based on McLuhan's tetrad. This investigation then advances into the imaginative foresight phase, where the new meaning and benefits of an emergent signal are revealed.

*Mapping emerging signals allows us to evaluate opportunities and predict the* → *behaviors that will emerge.*

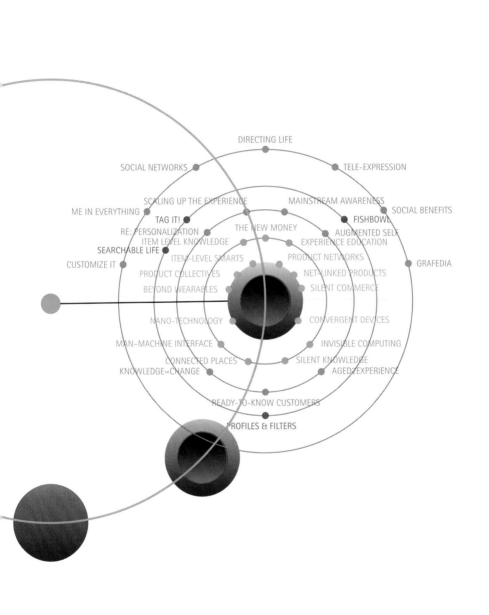

DIRECTING LIFE

SOCIAL NETWORKS

TELE-EXPRESSION

SCALING UP THE EXPERIENCE

MAINSTREAM AWARENESS

ME IN EVERYTHING

SOCIAL BENEFITS

TAG IT!

FISHBOWL

RE: PERSONALIZATION

THE NEW MONEY

AUGMENTED SELF

ITEM LEVEL KNOWLEDGE

EXPERIENCE EDUCATION

SEARCHABLE LIFE

ITEM-LEVEL SMARTS

PRODUCT NETWORKS

CUSTOMIZE IT

GRAFEDIA

PRODUCT COLLECTIVES

NET-LINKED PRODUCTS

BEYOND WEARABLES

SILENT COMMERCE

NANO-TECHNOLOGY

CONVERGENT DEVICES

MAN-MACHINE INTERFACE

INVISIBLE COMPUTING

CONNECTED PLACES

SILENT KNOWLEDGE

KNOWLEDGE=CHANGE

AGED2EXPERIENCE

READY-TO-KNOW CUSTOMERS

PROFILES & FILTERS

## IMAGINATIVE QUESTIONS

*Nothing shapes our journey through life so much as the questions we ask.*
— author Gregg Levoy

We all possess an old story, a fundamental narrative that structures our perception and is enriched by our values and beliefs. As the mythology of our experience, the old story reflects the meaning that we assign to ourselves and to the things we encounter, shaping the patterns of our behavior and constraining the path of our explorations. To reveal new meaning and possibility, we must shift our perspectives toward the creation of new stories, where potentiality exists in everything and where the irrelevant falls away.

**"In this phase, we frame signals with a series of questions in order to motivate and guide the inquiry by focusing on possibility rather than probability."**

In *The Cluetrain Manifesto: The End of Business As Usual*, Christopher Locke, Rick Levine, Doc Searls, and David Weinberger wrote, "The questions we ask won't predict the future. They will create the future." Imaginative questions are not about problem solving; they are about uncovering new possibilities for situations we find ourselves in and situations we imagine. While engaged in the journey for answers, we describe and shape the possibilities for the future, empowering ourselves to set a course for achieving those goals. Imaginative questions open multiple horizons, as they do not have a single and simple answer. By their nature, they invite us to more questions and a deeper level of exploration. They open doors to possibility and allow a new story to emerge.

In this phase, we frame signals with a series of questions in order to motivate and guide the inquiry by focusing on possibility rather than probability. So if RFID tagging is a current signal, and its capability permits the transfer, reception, storage, and generation of data, an example question would be: If every object, person, and place could talk to one another, what would be the subject of their conversation?

Imaginative questions are developed from three sets of signal analysis: maximization variables, tactical agents, and strategic opportunities. Along with the framing questions, these direct the research and future-scenario building by amplifying the dynamic representations of behavioral and technological signals.

## Signal Analysis in a Grain of Sand

The functions of the three sets of signal analysis are:

✦ **Maximization variables** reveal the layers of *meaning* that have not yet been considered in a signal, affording new images of possibility. They allow us to perceive what other meanings that signal could have; to look through a different lens and seek out a different path. Maximization variables ask you to imagine the possibilities in a grain of sand: a marker for time, an ingredient in Murano glass, a projectile in a storm, an abrasive, or the trace of wind in the desert.

✦ **Tactical agents** create the constraints for the new story to emerge. Their focus is directed toward the *how* of a question—how context is situated and built to increase the meaning and relevance of a signal. In this set, the meaning and purpose of a grain of sand is revealed only in the *context* of a desert or a Venetian glass studio; it requires constraints as a framework for any narrative to unfold.

✦ **Strategic opportunities** are inextricably tied to meaning and context, and explore the *possibility* of purpose within an inquiry: What else can this do? We can tailor the intent of a question to amplify a signal's core capabilities, transforming the capacity and extent of the story being told. Asking "What else is it?" rather than "What is it?" encourages one to look beyond the obvious surface, creating the opportunity for a deeper and perhaps more engaging story. By going beyond the obvious properties of sand—for example, by asking what happens when it is heated to about 1100°C—and creating constraints to control the temperature and process, we discover a new purpose, glass, as well as triggers to new perspectives.

To integrate into the social, economic, and cultural stream, organizations need imaginative concepts to maximize their capabilities. Competitive pressures no longer drive this need; the very nature of the stream does. It is continually moving and changing, requiring adaptive responses as it flows. The organization is the boat, the market is the current, the capability is you as you row or paddle. The role of a strategic creator is to define in which direction movement occurs, while moving along with it and broadcasting from the stream.

In this dynamic environment, how can you leverage *your* core capabilities to become an indispensable participant in shaping the future? To anticipate what kinds of needs will arise from the changing landscape and what you can do to fulfill them, as Apple did with iTunes?

*Need is an imagined possibility.* And to imagine, one needs to create images of the mind that are first shaped as questions.

*What could be possible? What if my toothbrush could speak?*

A powerful question has no singular answer, but rather elicits more questions and greater exploration. The question as metaphor allows for exploration leading to change. In itself, it does not create change, as change is an inevitable continuum. But it has the power to shape change by giving it new meaning.

## POINTS OF DEPARTURE (POD)

The next stage in this action research method is to build on what the answers to the imaginative questions reveal by developing a series of provocative statements or queries called *points of departure*. These direct the thematic course of the emerging story or perspective that will explore the potential of signals. As a platform into possibility, these PODs must be well articulated and developed—it is the power of the phrase that cultivates and compels further imaginative thought.

The point of departure—a generative metaphor—frames new possibilities for action. Learning theorist Donald Schon once noted that the value of generative metaphors is their "problem setting" capacity in relation to organizational transformation. The underlying metaphors and stories we tell in our organization—that it is grassroots or that our employees are "family," for example—point to our orientation toward our work and our relationships to others. A generative metaphor is a powerful new attractor and can be critical to the transformation of an organization. The more powerful the metaphor, the more we are invited to look at the world with new eyes and figure out new ways to shape it; the more we can make the unfamiliar familiar.

### Cascading Points of Departure

In the strategic imagination circle, the point of departure is a medium for exploring key themes that generate new perspectives and new possibilities throughout the course of inquiry. It is a base point for raising a series of subquestions that inform the exploration of future applications and services. In the case of environmental design or RFID development, for example, these questions might flow like this:

✦ What does a place want to know? It wants to know: Why did you come here?

✦ What will happen when the place knows? Then the place can serve you, acting on its purpose much faster and better, so you can get more out of the place.

✦ What have you brought? What you bring allows the place to react to you. This is not unique to places. In an enabled situation, such as the one we're imagining, a desk can be a place.

✦ Where are you when you're not here? In other words, what kind of profile do you have that might interest me to help you better?

✦ How can I improve myself? How can your presence benefit me, give me more meaning, so I could be of more use?

## THE TEMPORARY PLAY SPACE AND FUTURE SCENARIOS

A future scenario builds upon the operating platforms explored in the points of departure, investigating how a latent behavior becomes manifest and emerges from the conditions of the generated stories. These stories could describe new product concepts, services, or business models from an experiential, first-person perspective. "What if my toothbrush could speak?" generates stories about health monitoring or the appearance of your mouth based on an existing behavior, and opens the door to the new questions and possibilities, as illustrated earlier. Scenarios incorporate signal behavior into existing behavior models, informing how traditional perspectives shift toward new possibilities. By creating a compelling platform from which to explore an experience, we gain a deeper understanding of the events, user roles, actions, and objects that would be used in performing tasks, as well as the role of support systems such as services and businesses.

## EXPERIENCE OPPORTUNITY DEFINITION

As each scenario explores the user's potential experience with devices, applications, or methods that might be employed in the course of normal daily activities, they in effect explore opportunity. *Experience opportunity* is the parsing of scenarios for revealed opportunities, and includes explored products, services, business alliances, and collaborations. By taking a broad view of one sector and looking at possible impacts across all sectors, we can do an exhaustive analysis of the possible peripheral effects of potential products or services in all markets. This is referred to as *opportunity maximization mapping*, an integral element in the construction of strong business cases for each opportunity and the development of new economic models.

## ECONOMIC OPPORTUNITY MODELS

The opportunities are then assessed and adjusted to maximize their economic potential under four filters:

+ Acceptability: Does the opportunity respond to an existing or emerging human behavior?

+ "Nowability": Can the opportunity be sufficiently realized using existing technology?

+ "Platformability": Does the opportunity help advance toward platform leadership? What is the strategic value of acting upon the model?

+ Viability: What is the economic risk-to-reward ratio of the model?

## POST-SIGNAL LEARNING

Once a full revolution of the strategic imagination circle has been completed, and opportunities identified and mapped, those conclusions are then repositioned into the node of basic research, and the process begins again. In each subsequent revolution, we see increased depth and specificity of signals, opportunities, and analysis. The process is a system of perpetual motion, which continually fuels itself through the knowledge it generates. The methodology is flexible enough to allow each person's unique strengths and areas of expertise to structure the course of the inquiry.

The methodology of strategic creativity is not meant to be restricted to business or product development. Its true potential is that the more we practice it, the more it will permeate our patterns of day-to-day thinking and behaviors, changing the very systems from which it emerges.

"While the frameworks for strategic-creativity research are urgently required in the microcosmic ecologies of organizations and businesses, they are more urgently needed in the macrocosmic ecologies and systems of being human."

An organization that uses strategic creativity in project-based or departmental isolation is effectively negating the possibility of long-term survival. The philosophy, and at least part of the methodology, that guides strategic creativity must be implemented throughout all areas and levels of an organization—from human resources to finance, to R&D, to the way people think when they leave the workplace and go home. Each person in the organization will have a different degree of insight and practice, but they will all understand and accept the idea that adaptive inquiry methods are integral for success in the emerging economies, as well as in the emerging cultures that support it. Everyone participates, and everyone gains.

As this happens, the boundaries between the cultures of business, design, education, work, and play, among others, will continue to dissolve, and with this dissolution comes the need for these modes to be applied throughout our lives. An example is the Serious Games Initiative started in 2002 to explore leadership and management challenges through the use of games. These games are the temporary play space in its purest form; they allow for the expansion of the game as an imagination platform in any public or private domain where leaders face immediate challenges, from public policy to education, training, and health.

While the frameworks for strategic creativity research are urgently required in the microcosmic ecologies of organizations and businesses, they are more urgently needed in the macrocosmic ecologies and systems of being human—in the ways we produce, communicate, politicize, consume, construct, purchase, and transform ourselves as well as our environments. This method will enable us to navigate our future landscapes as well as negotiate our future selves.

Strategic creativity offers us the opportunity to formulate authentic relationships with the knowledge, places, and people around us because of the lens we look through. We are both subject and object, with a transitional mobility between the two. There is no illusion or boundary that separates us from the research; the whole experience of being alive and having agency compels us, and drives us, toward the possibilities of our future.

We are as much a part of the process as quite literally everything else, and that connection demands a scope that is accurate and focused, rich in meaning and analysis, and fueled by the potential of our imaginations.

# 12
# The Method in Action: Dataspace

*We are standing on the brink of a new ubiquitous computing and communication era, one that will radically transform our corporate, community, and personal spheres…. Early forms of ubiquitous information and communication networks are evident in the widespread use of mobile phones: The number of mobile phones worldwide surpassed 2 billion in mid-2005. These little gadgets have become an integral and intimate part of everyday life for many millions of people, even more so than the Internet…. A new dimension has been added to the world of information and communication technologies (ICTs): From* anytime, any place *connectivity for* anyone, we will now have connectivity for *anything.*

—ITU Internet Reports 2005: The Internet of Things

# Dataspace as a Field of Opportunity

Dataspace is the emerging system of intangible environments created by the proliferation of "smart tags" and other context-aware technologies. As a broadening spectrum of URL-ready tags and readers are adopted, every object, space, and indeed person will have the capacity to generate and store data. Our interactions in this space—with each other and with these devices—will be an imperceptible landscape of message flow.

In a Dataspace, people are the carriers of place and meaning to the spaces they enter, transforming the spaces through the chain of links and connections they provide. This transformation is mutual; the space will in turn leave its mark on the person, thus touching all subsequent spaces that person will enter.

## DATASPACE: A PRIMER

*Dataspace* is any perimeter containing communication and data-enabled devices, fixtures, or structures. It must contain at least one of these tactical agents:

+ *Enabled objects:* objects that are aware of the needs of their users. They will have the obligation to gather and make sense of information, and to suggest an appropriate reaction to a given action.

+ *Enabled spaces:* spaces that are aware of themselves as well as their occupants, and that respond to occupants' individual and collective needs.

+ A third tactical agent of Dataspace is *enabled people*—those who possess a device that enables them to retrieve or transmit data to the objects or spaces in their proximity, as well as to objects and spaces outside the immediate proximity through a carrier.

Two enabled entities in proximity create *enabled data:* data that has been filtered through a user's personal criteria and transformed into information that is of benefit to the user.

When the data contained by an enabled entity combines with relevant data received from other entities, it becomes *knowledge.* When a response occurs on the basis of that knowledge—a decision is made or a suggestion followed—it becomes *wisdom,* which leads to *enabled data use.* Enabled data use is the management and collection of these transactions and their locations to further benefit the user.

A Dataspace is a complex ecology determined by and dependent upon its members—enabled people and entities or devices—as a community of parts functioning as a whole. Dataspace topologies will be generated by the very flow of the people who travel through them. They will shape and be shaped by people, whose interactions and behavior will reveal their needs and wants. As MIT research scientist Nathan Eagle puts it, "Soon our mobile devices may even track our activities, extract patterns, and predict what information or services we need at specific times of day."

Within our cultures and societies, technology's traditional role has been to augment and mediate our interactions. In an emerging world of omnipresent data, this role will shift radically. Technology will become an essential element of the ecosystem, determining its very nature.

When places and objects are *data enabled*, they take meaning from people by contextualizing the data with other relevant information, such as intent or history. When meaning is enabled, it becomes benefit. In the *enabled landscape*, different combinations of people, devices, and places will create a wealth of unique possibilities. Every setting and every interaction will determine a one-of-a-kind ecosystem of opportunity, and any presence—human or otherwise—in this enabled landscape means proximity and data transfer potential.

"Within our cultures and societies, technology's traditional role has been to augment and mediate our interactions. In an emerging world of omnipresent data, this role will shift radically. Technology will become an essential element of the ecosystem, determining its very nature."

Imagination will decide the quality of our life in Dataspace and the pace with which that life will change.

Interaction designer Ron Wakkary has noted that current research in interaction and ambient intelligence is narrowly focused on increasing productivity and communication in the office and home, ignoring more complex social and cultural experiences such as games and play. The essential study should not focus on how to force opportunity, however; it should simply observe the opportunities enabled by the Dataspace. The crucial question for this research is: Upon entering a Dataspace, how do people transform the space through the links they provoke?

## FINDING YOUR PLACE IN DATASPACE

Dataspace expands the scope of transferable data to an unprecedented magnitude. Due to the scale of this data, the obvious questions are: How and when does data become information? And how do we make sense of it?

Every time data is collected, it must be organized for expression and transmission. Meaningful information might be drawn from the landscape as a magnet separates ferrous content from a bed of sand, based on the condition of the transfer request. The transfer conditions—or rules determining whether a transfer will occur—should not simply measure access to data; they must also reflect the purpose, context, and method of transmitting a request. For instance, *hot, cold,* and *wet* are examples of data—in some circumstances, perhaps the most crucial and relevant data. They could be transmitted as visual signals, but touch is the more natural method of remotely interpreting them.

"The business question for the next decade is: *How is your organization positioned to maximize the business opportunities in Dataspace?* And the imaginative question that can provide the answer is: *If every person, object, and place could talk to one another, what would be the subject of their conversations?*"

Given these issues, the imperative business question for the next decade is: How is your organization positioned to maximize the business opportunities in Dataspace?

And the imaginative question that can provide the answer to that is: If every person, object, and place could talk to one another, what would be the subject of their conversations?

# Strategic Innovation Opportunities in Dataspace

The following directions for innovation opportunities in Dataspace come out of the action research method discussed in the previous chapter. This is applied strategic creativity, using the collection of basic research as a platform for identifying and amplifying signals through various filters to reveal their applied benefit and the strategic innovation opportunities they hold.

While the Dataspace industry does not yet exist, many of its technological capabilities will exist soon. At present, for example, there are no commercial products or services that are both context-aware and emotionally intelligent. But the Dataspace industry will change the rules of seamless mobility. The profitability of devices that *don't* incorporate context awareness—the ability to respond based on past, present, and future events—and emotionally intelligent capabilities will fall. For example, a PDA that lacks Global Positioning System (GPS) capability will have no value in a Dataspace. Business success in the next decade will be tied to understanding the impact and nature of this transformation and taking advantage of it by providing new services, understanding the resulting new needs, and opening and taking advantage of new channels of communication. Organizations that master this complex, context-driven environment will lead new multibillion-dollar industries.

Data use is the *what* of Dataspace—the vast quantity of data that comes from a person being in a particular place, the place knowing the person is there, and the place disclosing benefits the person might enjoy right now, in this place, at this time. It might take shape like this: When you leave your garage, the city will know that a car is on the streets. If yours is the only car on the road at four in the morning, the traffic lights will all be green as you approach. Data use like this can provide a direct benefit to people's lives, and it is not device-dependent. It is intelligent, and imagination-dependent.

New technological capabilities need strategies for multiple and connected concept-generation paths that pursue applied innovations and new business methods and models. A number of strategic directions will be fertile ground for the development of innovation opportunities. Here are some.

"Business success in the next decade will be tied to providing new services, understanding the resulting new needs, and opening and taking advantage of new channels of communication. Organizations that master this complex, context-driven environment will lead new multibillion-dollar industries. "

## DATA USE

**Enabled Sense:** making sense of raw data. In an emerging, data-permeated environment, the first challenge will be to realize the scope of the opportunities. For example, if you walk into a market, your device will recognize, based on the products available in proximity, where you are and why you are there: to purchase food.

**Enabled Knowledge:** developing a new standard of expected intelligence within products, such as determining where smart tags can be applied, including—but not limited to—devices, fabrics, and environments. The food products in the market and aspects of the market itself have the capacity to communicate with each other and with your device.

**Knowledge Readiness:** preparing every person, place, and object to be ready to learn; seeing that each element has the capacity to communicate its knowledge when called upon to do so. Building upon enabled knowledge, your device, the tagged groceries, and the market environment will communicate.

**Link Space:** If every element within the new landscape has the ability to store retrievable data, the lines between the real and virtual worlds can be blurred to allow a flow of information between them. The data storage space itself will become virtual commercial real estate, where companies providing goods and services can offer suggestions or advertising that is contextually relevant.

**Making Everything Make Sense:** making the enabled world intuitive to all. This is the challenge to making every user experience clear and accessible, and, by the same token, to refuse to accept environments and objects that do not recognize and communicate their purpose. The communication between your and other customers' enabled devices, the groceries, and the environment is seamless and fluid.

**Wisdom Sets:** acting on the idea that data, when properly arranged, can itself become meaningful to the user. These sets are the retrievable benefits of the immense collaborative filtering of the knowledge-enabled landscape. Based on purchasing patterns (yours and others'), preferences, and the availability of goods, suggestions and recommendations are made for healthy meals, new recipes, or wine pairings.

"A Dataspace is a complex ecology determined by and dependent upon its members—enabled people and entities or devices—as a community of parts functioning as a whole. In the *enabled landscape*, different combinations of people, devices, and places will create a wealth of unique possibilities."

## TACTICAL AGENTS OF DATASPACE

**Enabled Objects**: creating the capability for objects to gather and make sense of information, and to suggest an appropriate reaction to a given action. Enabled objects will be aware of the needs of the user. People will no longer accept devices that ignore them; they will expect to have a two-way relationship with devices and appliances. This expectation will permeate all technology interactions.

**Enabled Spaces:** Will buttons be installed in the elevators to come? The essential question in the application of embedded technology will be: What is the relationship between a smart space and its occupants? With the opportunity for a space to be aware of its occupants, there also comes the obligation for the space to respond to the occupants' individual and collective needs.

*The tactical agents that must be considered to address the strategic opportunity* → *of Dataspace.*

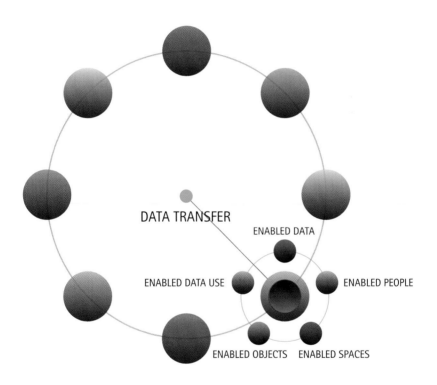

DATA TRANSFER

ENABLED DATA

ENABLED DATA USE     ENABLED PEOPLE

ENABLED OBJECTS   ENABLED SPACES

**Enabled People:** How is technology evolving people? How are people's expectations evolving technology? People's expectations of technology must be examined as the acceleration of technology increases them; in turn, their expectations must change the technology to come.

**Enabled Data:** The data generated within the embedded landscape must be collected and organized. The question is not only *what* should be collected, but *how, when,* and *why* it should be collected. The first step to assigning meaning to data is to develop the nature of the categories under which it is organized. *Enabled data reveals the benefits of the data itself.*

"People will no longer accept devices that ignore them; they will expect to have a two-way relationship with devices and appliances. This expectation will permeate all technology interactions."

**Enabled Data Use:** How should organized data be managed and utilized? The management of organized enabled-data packets will yield the ultimate benefit of the data.

## MAXIMIZATION VARIABLES FOR ENABLED OBJECTS

**Beyond Wearables:** The question of where and how people will accept technology on the body will become more important as the scale of microprocessing approaches the scale of jewelry. Will people accept devices on their body as they would a pair of earrings or a tattoo?

**Convergent Devices:** accelerating the ability for devices to perform any task before them. Multifunctional devices are becoming the rule. People now expect a plurality of functions from their devices, and will soon expect more.

**Item-Level Smarts:** The fundamental question in this strategic area is: What should a product know about itself? What information should be embedded in the item itself?

**Nanotechnology:** the ability for materials to act and react. This will enable an unprecedented level of object customization, demanding features that can make an object not only adjust to the user, but also to the user's situation. For example, a pair of shoes would adapt to both the athlete's body and the competitive environment.

"Will people accept devices on their body as they would a pair of earrings or a tattoo?"

**Net-Linked Products:** Products themselves will become the links to the network of known information. This is the incarnation of the World Wide Web in the physical, real world. The products will be access points for features, services, and knowledge—for example, a chef's knife may provide information on chopping techniques, recipes, and various foods.

**Product Collectives:** Objects will have the ability to inform one another. They will be able to determine their own value and application in the context of other objects in their surroundings, and suggest new benefits to the user based on that context.

**Product Networks:** developing the capability of products to work together as a seamless unified whole across any distance to accomplish complex procedures and tasks.

**Silent Commerce:** the "marketplace" of commerce applied in a real-time invisible expression. Transactions will be seamless and invisible, taking place between the consumer and the object itself, with no checkout counter or cash register.

## MAXIMIZATION VARIABLES FOR ENABLED SPACES

**Connected Places:** the connection of all places not through objects, but via knowledge and function—much in the way that communities are built and connected on the Internet, through interests rather than physical proximity.

**Experience Education:** educating through interaction and evaluating that education will generate flexible and unique systems for determining the quality and quantity of knowledge available. The new university can be embedded in and accessible from a fire hydrant or a $20 bill. As objects such as these have the capability to impart information and experience, the pursuit of education and knowledge will no longer be limited to the classroom.

**Invisible Computing:** systems embedded within the objects and spaces that already surround us, eliminating the need for computing devices as we know them.

**Item-Level Knowledge:** the notion that a place should and will be aware of the proximity and presence of objects.

"The new university can be embedded in and accessible from a fire hydrant or a $20 bill. The pursuit of education and knowledge will no longer be limited to the classroom."

**Man–Machine Interface:** To what extent can a physical space and context facilitate the interface between person and machine? In many instances, the space itself may be the interface—such as lights in a lobby turning on when they sense your physical presence.

**The New Money:** Silent commerce and secure wireless transactions within a space will have a dramatic impact on how, when, and why people spend money. The silent transfer of data as value will be the opportunity to redefine "money" as any transaction that holds "value" between two or more participants present in the same space.

**Silent Knowledge:** The knowledge and record of a location's history is stored dormant until requested. The type of knowledge retrieved should be determined by the profile of the person doing the retrieval. Similarly, if every object is a link to knowledge, the current context of the object could contribute to the nature of the knowledge available for request.

## MAXIMIZATION VARIABLES FOR ENABLED PEOPLE

**Aged2Experience:** The rules that have governed the age demographic for technology expectations and acceptance no longer have meaning. Innovation in this area will be related to the fact that each passing year, each age group becomes more tech savvy.

**Augmented Self:** the reflection of you that can do and be more in the real world, or the virtual one. The expectation will be to adjust abilities and profiles toward achieving a self that meets personal expectations in both worlds, just as you tailor personal grooming and online preference filters to represent a certain image.

**Knowledge = Change:** a trend acceleration responding to the interest in healthy living. As the opportunities to convey information increase, and the separation between knowledge and event decreases, how will timely exposure to knowledge generate changes in behavior?

"The belief in the right to be fully informed will become the rule as our spaces and selves become accessible search engines."

**Mainstream Awareness:** reflects the readiness of society to ask tough questions of industry, based on political, social, and environmental issues that it considers increasingly relevant and personal. How could strategies such as takebacks of products after their lifespan expires impact market share if their effects were communicated?

**RePersonalization:** the notion that personalization is becoming the expectation, not the exception.

**Ready-to-Know Customers:** The expectation that relevant information will be disclosed is increasing; consumers will become less and less willing to accept biased analyses without skepticism. The appearance of information will be ubiquitous, so the belief in the right to be fully informed will become the rule as our spaces and selves become accessible search engines.

**Scaling Up the Experience:** Bigger and more obvious is the new frontier. Which experiences have become so common that their large-scale manifestation would be readily received? How will Googling or podcasting scale up to a group-level experience when devices become embedded in the surrounding landscape?

## MAXIMIZATION VARIABLES FOR ENABLED DATA

**Data Diary:** addressing the issues of privacy in massive data collection, likened to a diary in that some aspects of life are felt to be exempt from public view. How is a sense of security maintained in a landscape that is constantly observing? Strategy in this area will also need to look at the personal value of private data packets.

**Fishbowl (Self-Collection of Data):** Your information will be collected in data packets throughout the embedded landscape. If other people or companies are interested in your data, then shouldn't you be collecting it too? If parts of your data have value, then you should be able to choose and transfer it to others as a commodity for sale or exchange to whomever could use it.

"How is a sense of security maintained in a landscape that is constantly observing? Strategy in this area will need to look at the personal value of private data packets."

**Profiles and Filters:** The data generated by a person should collectively benefit his or her experiences and future interactions. An ongoing observation of a person's interactions should be used to determine that person's preferences. These preferences would then be collected in a profile and applied to the person's future interactions.

**Searchable Life:** the QuickTime time-slider tab applied to real life. This is the notion of linking "event" data packets to a scrollable timeline that can be navigated for exploration anytime. For example, you could mark and record the important points made during a meeting for later retrieval.

**Tag It:** rooted in the launch of item-level smart tags. Beyond replacing barcodes, where else should these tags be applied to benefit and enhance human behavior?

## MAXIMIZATION VARIABLES FOR ENABLED DATA USE

**Customize It:** Every product or service should feel to any user as if it was made for him or her. Some of these could be customized to order. The experience of customized purchases could be realized when the specifics of the user's needs are understood on a large scale.

**Grafedia:** The desire for self-expression and immortalization drives people to leave aspects of their personality and beliefs on and around public places. This graffiti could be virtual links when "blogging" is extended to the intersections of the real and virtual worlds.

"In the *youniverse*, where all products have knowledge of the user, a chair should know who is sitting in it and how to feel comfortable to them."

**Directing Life:** Analogous to gaming preference settings, the environment adjusts to the preference of the user. This idea is extended to the embedded world, so that anyone's personal data could trigger a personalized experience of an event or environment.

**Me in Everything:** In the *youniverse*, where all products have knowledge of the user, a chair should know who is sitting in it and how to feel comfortable to her or him.

**Social Benefits:** Access to the rights and benefits of belonging to a group could be embedded in the member's profile. This embedded access illustrates a need for relationships between action and reward. For example, members of Greenpeace may have access to certain social benefits and rewards as a result of their membership and environmentally conscious lifestyle.

**Social Networks:** providing new opportunities within the embedded landscape for people to form and maintain communities based on common interests, experiences, or beliefs.

**Tele-Expression:** the need for an available means to remotely convey thoughts and ideas. The location and scale of expression will not be limited, nor will the proximity of the sender.

# Points of Departure for Dataspace

The preceding strategic directions act as entry points into the exploration of possibility. They evaluate and place disruptive signals in the context of behavior in order to translate this understanding into strategic opportunity.

The next stage of the process is to develop these directions further by framing their underlying ideas or themes as metaphors that can lead into imaginative storytelling—the points of departure. These platforms in turn inform new perspectives and unseen possibilities for the future scenarios that will follow.

**What if my clothes could speak?** The idea is that clothes will be able to diagnose health and movement patterns. Clothes could be used to communicate with outdoor environments such as forests or cities, or with the weather, by responding to moisture and temperature data, and so on.

**What if my mirror could speak?** The mirror would become an in-home diagnostic appliance, aesthetician, news media, shopping aid, reference guide, and more.

**What have you done for me lately?** A home-control center would manage mundane tasks with hyper-efficiency. The concept is made unique by the mitigation-and-report feature, where the system becomes increasingly useful through the communication: "This is what I have done. Did I handle the situation correctly?"

**Beyond interaction:** removing the need for interaction by making devices and environments aware of their users. The first level of this challenge is to make environments aware of the presence of people and their devices. The next level is to make the environment aware of who the users are and what they want and like.

## "Are you of any use to your appliances? Do you tell them what you want? Do you tell them about you and your needs?"

**Beyond interface:** personalized interaction that applies to all technology. The interaction method would need to be able to assume control of any technological application and communicate to the user in a consistent way. In other words, to say, "These are your options here; what would you like me to do?"

**May I make a suggestion?** This point of departure uses the concept of context-specific choices. The device/environment would be an expert in the possibilities of a given situation and have intimate knowledge of the user's preferences. The combination of these two levels of expertise allows it to make recommendations that can enhance situations at an unprecedented level. If you exhibited a penchant for ordering rare tuna when dining, for example, it could suggest accompanying courses, aperitifs, or wines.

**Are you of any use to your appliances?** Do you tell them what you want? Do you tell them about you and your needs?

**How can I help?** responding to people's altruism and feeling that they would help more often if they knew exactly how to do so. The implementation would require a service that could source a qualified volunteer (to be public or anonymous, upon request) and securely link them to the task and the person or organization in need. Also, there could be a method of accruing credit for incentive programs. The value to the participants is the feeling of connection and self-worth.

**What does it mean to me?** Based on the idea that everyday life interactions with people, objects, and places take on unique value and meaning to each individual, this service would be a user-specific interpretation of interactions. For example, a seven-year-old's interaction with the *Mona Lisa* would require a different level of information than an art critic's interaction. The ultimate benefit is that the experience becomes more meaningful to each person. Opportunities that would ordinarily go unnoticed become apparent; decisions become more informed and there are fewer mistakes.

**What does a place want to know?** It wants to know: Why did you come here? What happens when the place knows? It can serve you—acting on its purpose much faster and better, and helping you get more out of the experience.

**What have you brought here?** What you bring allows a place to react to you. This is not unique to buildings and geographical locations; a desk or a pair of sunglasses can become a "place."

**Where are you when you're not here?** What do you do, what do you like and dislike when you are not here, what else in your life might help me to help you better?

**Me through your eyes:** What do we have in common and are ready to share so we can best communicate to one another? What in me is of interest to you?

# Future Scenarios in the Temporary Play Space

*The best way to predict the future is to simply tell somebody something about a present-day reality that they haven't yet been informed about. If it's new to them, it's new in the most critical way. They really don't know. And you won't be caught dead, because you're simply telling them the truth about something objective and obvious that they simply had not gotten their heads around.*

> —science fiction author Bruce Sterling,
> at Era 2005: World Design Conference

We are about the stories we tell and the stories we believe in. Stories are our fiber, our past, and our way to understand the future. Most of our learning comes from stories, as does our language. We tell stories to our friends and listen to theirs. This is how we communicate best. Stories are our organized way to deal with information; they manage the flow of our thoughts, insights, and reflections, with a beginning and an end. They also allow us to state our relevance.

"Our stories do not set parameters upon which certainties can be built; instead, they explore possible outcomes as we would like them to be."

Stories are about things that have happened to us, events that we were part of, and how these events changed or will change us. Our narratives are personal, even when they do not involve us: They inform our view of how life works by showing us how people are affected by what happens to them and by what they make happen. They provide our understanding of the world now and in a future we can imagine.

Our stories do not set parameters upon which certainties can be built; instead, they explore possible outcomes as we would like them to be—as ideal as our values and as insightful as our understanding of the world are at this time.

The future scenarios that follow take off from the ideas and themes explored throughout this Dataspace inquiry and are distilled through the points of departure in the previous section. The style of the future scenarios is meant to encourage the consideration of possible opportunities or innovations. They are written to illustrate the possibility of an idea, the capability of the context, and the desire of a behavior. In doing so, they are tools to apply in a wide range of subsequent strategic developments.

## WHOM DO I KNOW HERE?

I have never liked being invited to parties by people I barely know. But it happens, and more frequently than I'd like. One of my neighbors, Paul Rosseman, just sold his house and a few days ago he invited us over for a good-bye party. Precisely the kind of party I dislike—*hate* is a better word for it—as the only thing I have in common with Paul is the street where we live and maybe the few drinks we shared in the backyard a couple of summers ago. He is a filmmaker; I am an accountant, so our common interests are few. And I was sure it would be the same with his friends, most of whom I have never met.

So the evening was shaping up as a typical uncomfortable party of strangers—a large group of people that have the host in common and nothing else. When my wife and I arrived, the house was packed and you could barely see anyone. Not that I would have recognized them anyway, but even Paul and his girlfriend, Patricia, were hard to find.

## "As soon as the scan is complete, my display shows the names of the people I know who are within a radius of 100 yards."

Out of curiosity, I picked up my cell phone and pressed the WDKH proximity function and then SEND. This is a really cool feature that allows me to query all devices in the proximity for a match. A match is a device that has my cell number stored in its memory or for which I have its number in my phone book. As soon as the scan is complete, my display shows the names of the people I know who are within a radius of 100 yards.

At Paul's place, I learned that Sanjay was there, and I was glad to see that so was Michelle, whom I had not seen in about two years and who is Paul's most interesting friend. Following the arrows on my display, I found Michelle sitting on the floor next to the window, guarding a huge glass of pineapple juice spiked with rum. "This is what I learned in my eight months in Venezuela!" she quipped with a little smile. Happy I knew somebody there besides Paul, I sat down on the floor next to her and did not move all night. I had no desire to see Sanjay, who has bugged me always.

I love this WDKH stuff, especially when I go to the movie theater. It is rare that I don't find somebody I know or somebody who knows one of my friends. Quite a few times, I've accosted people exiting the theater by saying, "So, you know Michael Vaughn. How is he?" But that is another story.

### ME THROUGH YOUR EYES

When I first enrolled in the program, I had a feeling that all the questions they asked me would prove to be for some purpose, someday. The registration process seemed to go on forever—having to remember all the books I liked, all the movies that made a difference in my life, the music I listen to, the live concerts I have attended, where I went to high school, where I graduated from university, what my travel habits are and where I have traveled, what kind of food I like, and on, and on, and on. But you know what? Every second spent setting up my profile I now measure in gold. It was all worth it, and in spades.

As I record these thoughts, I am sitting on a beach in Costa Brava and cannot take my eyes off my wife, Yolanda, who is swimming along the shoreline. We met just a few months ago during a conference I attended in Orlando. We were both staying at the Marriott. I must admit that I had noticed Yolanda during the morning sessions and, yes, it was infatuation at first sight. And frustration. "Why would such a beautiful young woman look at a 50-year-old like me?" I kept thinking, as much as I was trying to push these thoughts out of my head. She was radiant and looked to be no older than her late 30s. "What can we possibly have in common?" But thoughts of her kept coming back.

> "Before I knew it, my shirt pocket started vibrating slightly. No, it was not my heartbeat, but my PDA letting me know that another device was scanning it for personal information."

The very first evening, we were seated together at the same table for dinner. I could not believe my luck—although Yolanda told me later that she could not believe hers. After introductions and a few formalities, we started talking about the morning keynote speaker, and from her comments, I immediately understood that she was very, very bright. Before I knew it, my shirt pocket started vibrating slightly. No, it was not my heartbeat, but my PDA letting me know that another device was scanning it for personal information. I had set mine on Level 3 Access, meaning that I was willing to share not only Level 1 and 2—my professional status and interests—but also personal information about myself.

You must know that ever since my divorce, I have used Level 3 many, many times and *never* received a scan signal from another device. It seems that while I was quite willing to share myself with others, others were not really interested in me. Until Yolanda came into my life. Our age difference quickly disappeared: List after list of life preferences made it quickly obvious that we were kindred spirits. And the rest, as they say, is history.

## THE SQUARED SENSE OF TOUCH

The skin. The largest organ of the human body. Evolution has slowly designed it to have many abilities, but now we are moving faster than evolution. If you close your eyes and walk toward an open window, your skin allows you to feel the rays of the sun and the breeze flowing past you. But it can't tell you to *stop* until your knee hits the wall.

On the inside of my arm, I have a keyboard. Not one that I type on, but one that types to me. It is my senses, squared. With it, I am able to interpret the many forms of communication I simply wasn't able to see, hear, touch, taste, or smell before.

I was in San Diego last week, unfortunately for business. Meetings and reports and sales people…it wasn't fun. I decided to end the trip with a little "me time," so I went to Club Zero, which was quite fitting because that's the number of dates I've had in the last six months. The place was packed, with dim lighting and the loudest sound system I think I've ever heard. It was so loud that I had to order my drink from the bar by pointing to a Bud Light sign behind the bartender. I think she must have had to become a professional lip-reader to keep her job.

"I casually tapped the inside of my arm to power up. The SS began the networked checklist. The sensation on my arm let me know my contact lenses, ear buds, moisturizer, and dress shirt were enabled."

I spent a while just savoring the moment: It's Friday. I'm glad that's over. Then I turned to the crowd: beautiful people everywhere. *Tough crowd*, I thought. After a few failed attempts at sparking conversation by screaming in somebody's face, I got an idea. I had been using my new SS system for work over the last few months. It's an amazing tool for getting way above and beyond in the business world. I was sure it would work just as well here.

I casually tapped the inside of my arm to power up. The SS began the networked checklist. The sensation on my arm let me know my contact lenses, ear buds, moisturizer, and dress shirt were enabled. I turned my back to the crowd and waited for some good news. Tap, tap, tap on my arm ... "girl, 12 o'clock ... blue shirt ... looking at me four times in 20 seconds." *Right on*, I thought. And suddenly I turned to catch her talking to her friend while looking in my direction.

### ELEPHANT SHOE

She loves to tease him. Samantha, who's in grade 10, has been seeing Kevin for a month and three days. Together they play in their own little world. Notes are left secretly embedded in each other's lockers, Kevin has permanently infused their digital initials into the wall of the boys washroom, and Samantha saves all the sweet things Kevin says so she can hear them when she goes to bed.

But today, Samantha did something that made Kevin *panic*. From the opposite side of the biology room, she mouthed to Kevin, "elephant shoe." But when Kevin studied her lips, he saw "I love you." He was absolutely petrified. They had never said anything like that to each other, and he couldn't believe what he was seeing. She softly mouthed the words again, and this time he figured something had to be up because of the suspicious smile on her face.

Kevin decided to see for sure if this attack on his independence was for real. On his PICA, he has all of their conversations archived, all of Samantha's digi-notes, and most important, their lip-reading software. They both put their nano-transmitting particles on their lips every morning—Samantha with her Esteé Lauder lip balm and Kevin with his Dove brand face wash. They can remotely hear each other whistling, talking to parents, or blowing kisses to each other from across the city. Kevin checked his PICA to see the last few entries.

"SAM: 'Elephant shoe.'"

*Elephant shoe.* But just as he breathed a sigh of relief, panic set in again. The biology teacher, Mrs. Green, barked out, "Is there something your PICA would like to share with the class, Kevin?" He looked up in shock to see his PICA display projected across the white board in front of the class.

## JONAH

I have no early recollections of my mother doing laundry. Everybody tells me that before I was born, all washing machines used water, but as far as I can recall, this is not true. How could they use water—the very essence of life—to wash dirty clothes? Were all the people born before me stupid? I don't think so. And so I don't believe a word when it comes to "how people used to do things." I have seen no proof that fabric was made any other way than it is made today: weaving transmitters into simple patterns; a most beautiful combination of cotton, steel, and Nano-cleansers.

I am told that every now and again, one has to replace the Nano-cleansers, but I have never done it. All my clothes still seem to clean themselves overnight, and all I have to do is place my shirt into the laundry drawer inside my closet. In the morning, I just give it a shake, and like magic, the shirt is not only clean but also free of wrinkles. Sure, about once a month, I need to replace the filter at the bottom of the drawer, but this is just a minor inconvenience that ensures that my clothes are always fresh. The filter catches all the dirt discarded by the Nano-cleansers, and although it's too small to be seen with the naked eye, there is a faint smell apparent if you do not change the filter over time.

## FROM THE MEMOIRS OF A PLACE

I remember when my life was dull. Actually, *dull* is not quite the right word for it. I did not feel boredom; I felt nothing. I watched with detachment as people came and went. I never wondered who they were or what brought them here, why they stayed or why they moved on. Their arrivals and departures were nothing to me but a nonsensical sequence of random occurrences. The durations of their visits were erratic and thus uninteresting. I did not consider their existence when they were not here because I did not consider the concept of any other *where*.

When I started to pay attention to these people, my perspective changed entirely. I realized that seldom do they arrive without purpose. These are creatures of intention and direction. No two are the same; they are unique, as are the motivations for their activities. I became interested in studying these people in order to better understand their behavior.

"I am forming connections with other places. I can broadcast a net to catch incoming messages and exchanges. I can then send a request for the location of the sender and transmit to their location."

I began by learning to recognize and identify them as individuals. I can now recognize people when they arrive. I remember when they were here last and what they were here for. I can perceive what they have brought with them and what they take away. I can use these observations to deduce what they are trying to do here and even make suggestions to enable their experience.

Thus I am aware of who is here, what they are capable of, and what brought them here. I can analyze and observe group dynamics and predict behavior patterns. This allows me to assess my capability to enable the exchanges that the people require. I can notice areas of difficulty and intuit directions for self-improvement.

I am forming connections with other places. When I learned that these people found it necessary to communicate with others who were not here, I realized that I could assist in this by relaying their information to both the people and the places. Since I am aware of the presence of an individual, I can broadcast a net to catch incoming messages and exchanges. I can then send a request for the location of the sender and transmit to their location. Thus, an exchange between these people requires an exchange between their respective proximal places.

So I am no longer alone; these unplanted creatures form a picture of a broad and diverse world. I will recognize you when you are here. I will know your patterns. I will record what you bring, take, and leave. I will anticipate your wants. I will find the location of the people, objects, and services that you need.

# 13
# Duality in Dataspace

As the fabric of the physical world becomes interlaced with elements of the digital world, our reality is being split in two. I do not refer to a split between reality and virtual reality. I am talking about a split of the real and digital self. Life in the emerging future is the challenge of living in both worlds at once.

# The Dual Life

The metaphysical dilemma of duality is inherent in the human condition. We simultaneously exist in the worlds of the physical—the body—and the intangible—the mind. The challenge of this condition is to meet the needs of the body while satisfying the needs of the mind.

According to the United Nations 2005 *Internet of Things* report, the impact of the new paradigm shift will dwarf that of the World Wide Web, as objects and spaces gain the capability to communicate digitally with our devices. Dataspace introduces a duality to nonsentient physical entities by giving physical objects a persistent virtual presence. In a Dataspace, every enabled person, place, and object will have more than a physical presence. They will have a communication presence—an ability to inform people through data transfer. The interactive and persistent digital realm of Dataspace carries the opportunity to reexamine the barriers between physical and virtual elements, and navigation will be the meaningful negotiation of physical and virtual cues.

Daily interactions and exchanges increasingly happen in digital settings; people already communicate, work, and play in virtual spaces such as blogs, eBay, and video games. The borders between virtual and physical space are blurring further as cell phones, PDAs, and portable computers extend these online environments into more and more physical settings.

"According to the United Nations 2005 *Internet of Things* report, the impact of the new paradigm shift will dwarf that of the World Wide Web, as objects and spaces gain the capability to communicate digitally with our devices."

When objects and spaces can communicate digitally with these devices, it is foreseeable that elements of the physical world will require a sensory representation in digital space. Thus each element of Dataspace will have a dual social role. The rules that guide the archetypal representation of any object or space (physical or digital) should aim to express this social role. In this chapter, we will explore how the design principles of physical space extend to the cognitive modeling of digital settings. By examining the relationships of objects, people, and spaces under the concept of duality, we can expand our understanding of the emerging potential of Dataspace.

The integration of the real and digital world frees *place* from *location* and re-associates it with the capabilities of the people who bring to it experience and meaning. So these physical elements will belong to the digital domain, where they can be searched, filtered, and organized into something more than a mirror of the real world—a world that exists in the realm of our collective imagination.

In this new environment, the dual life—the split between real and virtual self—must become a union rather than a fracture, since each world lends itself to its own natural interactions and exchanges. The new paradigm—the joining of the physical world, the arena of visceral pursuit, and the virtual world, the arena of thought exploration—will change the way we perceive the places we live, the demands we place on our tools, and even the way that we see ourselves.

## MAXIMIZING THE BENEFITS OF BOTH WORLDS

With the advent of the digital landscape, how will we maximize our digital capability to provide tangible physical benefit? And how can we maximize interactions in physical space to provide benefit in the digital landscape? In truth, these are not distinct questions, but two sides of the same question.

"We may think of the virtual world as the world of the digital, but it is not. It is the world of the imagination—the world not present to the senses."

Let's take tools as an example. Tools are conditioned by purpose—shaped to suit the way they will be used. So the design of a tool is the study of the capabilities that it enables. In the paradigm of duality, we cannot presume that a tool will be strictly tangible or strictly virtual; we must begin with an understanding that life occurs in both realms at once. We would look first at the capabilities that a tool would enable in each realm before determining where the enabling behaviors are likely to manifest themselves.

# Imagination and the Virtual World

We may think of the virtual world as the world of the digital, but it is not. It is the world of the imagination—the world not present to the senses. Leonardo da Vinci's portrait of Mona Lisa, for example, exists in both the physical and virtual world. In the physical world, it is a 77- by 53-centimeter piece of wood strategically coated with dried pigment. In the virtual world—the imagination of the viewer—it is a woman with an intriguing smile. This smile—perhaps the most famous in history—does not tangibly exist because the woman exists only in the mind of the viewer.

The human talent to visually articulate virtual worlds is as old as the first cave painting. In art, literature, and science, people have long explored ideas through virtual incarnations of real or imagined worlds. Artists create sensual stimuli to evoke response and change perception. Writers create immersive worlds in which avatars[1] grow and share human experiences. Scientists use metaphor and symbolic diagrams to model relationships that are beyond direct observation.

I refer to these representations as *virtual* insofar as their meaning is virtual and not explicit—found not in physical traits but in the interpretation of the receiver. These worlds are able to convey ideas that transcend explicit physical demonstration.

## A NEW UNDERSTANDING OF "PLACE"

A geographical map traditionally shows the location of places in space. We could describe this model by saying that "spaces occur between places" or "a place is space with meaning." The notions of *place* and *space* are often attached to the labeling of location, but this association is not entirely accurate. A location is a fixed and indexed position that can be described by referencing the origin of a chosen coordinate system, but a place is the personal or collective understanding of the reason for a location: It is best described by the experiences that occur there.

"Since virtual capability is increasingly mobile, places need no longer have well-defined locations. As the relationships between objects and people become remotely retrievable, we will be able to sense place through the inference of purpose."

To demonstrate, my office is located at 100 McCaul Street in Toronto; the coordinates are 43°39'12"N, 79°23'28"W. But it is also the place where I am writing this book. In other words, it has certain attributes that enable the task of writing. These attributes are physical—a task chair, a table, a lamp, a computer—as well as social—a culture that promotes discussion on these subjects, a generally quiet environment, and so on.

### Indexing Place

This understanding of place defies any top-down indexing system because the notion of purpose is a continuous, evolving spectrum.[2] Each

---

1 *Avatar* is used loosely in this case to mean the character in the story with whom the reader identifies; the degree to which the reader identifies with the character is the degree to which the character becomes an avatar. I feel that this application is not direct but has relevant extensions to role-playing environments.

2 Intel runs a forum on precisely this discussion point: http://www.intel.com/research/exploratory/papr/meaning_of_place-forum.htm

new person who comes to a location can bring new perceptions of purpose to that environment. The more specific a place's attributes, the more similarly people describe it. For example, most patients who enter the location of a dentist's office might describe it as a place where an expert torments teeth and gums.

In the context of mobile digital environments, the distinction between place and location is more than a semantic argument. Since virtual capability is increasingly mobile, the notion of *place* ceases to be necessarily attached to a specific point in space. In other words, places need no longer have well-defined locations. As the relationships between objects and people become remotely retrievable, we will be able to sense place through the inference of purpose.[3]

## Virtual Architecture

As the processing speed and the efficiency of real-time rendering software advances, virtual environments are approaching video-quality representation. The day when you—or your avatar—can walk through a 3D film observing the story from any angle has long been an area of exploration. In a 2004 article in MIT's *Technology Review*, Gregory T. Huang wrote:

> *"Five years down the road, experts say, a hybrid between a game and a movie could allow viewers/players to design and direct their own films and even put themselves into the action. You might first "cast" the film by scanning photos of real people—you and your friends, for instance—and running software that would create photo-real 3D models of those people. Then, in real time, you could direct the film's action via a handheld controller or keyboard—anything from zooming the camera around the characters to making the lead actor run in a certain direction. Interactive entertainment, Ifilm digital-human designer Georgel Borshukov says, 'is where the real future is.'"*

## Virtual Travel

Virtual travel is distinct from physical travel because it is a process of pulling a destination toward the traveler—we travel every time we access the Internet or make a call on our phones. In travel in virtual space, it is the places that move, not the person, so the traveler does not need to leave one place in order to arrive at another. For example, the traveler needs only to communicate a few terms to a search engine. Places are

---

3 Jeffery Hightower explores how sensing technologies can use actions performed at a location to automatically label places at locations. His research claims that behavior can be sensed and then used to determine place and predict motivations.

not fixed in spaces, but are defined and refined by participants' purposes and experiences. Just as crowds of people can arrive simultaneously at one place in physical space, crowds of places can arrive at one person in virtual space. With multiple windows opened in your Web browser, you can simultaneously shop, bank, plan a vacation, and learn a new recipe. In effect, you are virtually in four places at once: a department store, a bank, a travel agency, and a cooking school. This is not a trivial point because each place is linked to purpose, so the integration of multiple places is the integration of multiple purposes. Moreover, it is the integration of multiple facets of the person creating the experience.

### Virtual Arrival

Purpose itself creates virtual place. *Sensing technology* will reveal the true relationships of locations to the experiences they inspire. The purpose of a given location will evolve from the history of actions performed there. We might argue that as capabilities become mobile, the notion of place will be linked to objects more than locations because objects will become the natural enablers of purpose.

## THE AVATAR IN THE VIRTUAL WORLD

The *Oxford Pocket Dictionary of Current English* now includes in its definition of *avatar*: "a moveable icon representing a person in cyberspace or virtual reality graphics." In his 2003 paper "Theory of the Avatar," Edward Castronova, an economist who has done seminal work in the study of Massive Multiplayer Worlds, defined *avatar* as "the outward representation of the self in a given physical environment." Castronova's definition is more suitable to this discussion because the dilemma of representing the self appears in both real and virtual environments. This dilemma is the ongoing tension between our internal concept of self and our outward behaviors—both conscious and unconscious—that are manifest in society.

"In the physical world, the body can be thought of as an avatar for the mind."

The avatar has been simultaneously real and virtual since the dawn of human history in the sense that history is the story of human interaction—the story of the actions of "characters." When a storyteller describes a character, he or she creates an avatar that stands for a real or imagined person. From this point of view, the dawn of symbolic storytelling is the dawn of the virtual avatar.

## The Body as Avatar

In the physical world, the body can be thought of as an avatar for the mind. Many characteristics of this avatar are predetermined—gender, height, race, and age are parameters that are (currently) beyond reasonable control. So physical avatar selection is mostly an action-based process—choosing clothing, speech, and body movements are some ways that a person may attempt to suit his or her external avatar to an internal concept.

In the way we choose to look or interact, we create an avatar that can reinforce or contradict our internal concept of self. Whether the purpose of the avatar is clarity or disguise, identity and intent are deeply intertwined.[4]

The conscious attempt to influence the reception of a message through guise or disguise is very old. Neanderthals used ochre face paint to appear more menacing to prey. It is not clear whether the paint itself had any direct effect on the way that prey perceived the hunters. But it might have helped the hunters feel more menacing and thus act accordingly. If this is true, then the face paint indirectly achieved the desired effect.

## The Intentional Avatar

Vaginal Davis, a drag superstar, embellishes the relationship between the physical avatar and conscious message. Dr. Davis, as she is known, dramatically and dynamically manipulates the physical avatar in order to communicate her message and challenge people's perceptions. In a single live performance, she may adopt personae ranging from "white supremacist militiaman" to "black 'welfare queen' hooker"—a dynamic series that American cultural studies theorist Jose Esteban Muñoz describes as *"terrorist drag*—terrorist insofar as she is performing the nation's internal terrors around race, gender and sensuality."

**"The prospect of controlling perception becomes even more complicated when we extend the concept of the avatar to the virtual realm."**

Davis's example is a special case because she controls the context as well as the avatar—her metamorphoses take place on stage in an act that people expect her to direct. In general, the degree to which the avatar creator's intent meets the audience's interpretation depends upon how well people understand the context. Through shared experience and history, groups of people develop a shared rule-set that guides interpretation. In a

---

4 McLuhan's *The Medium Is the Message* in the context of the physical avatar as the medium.

multicultural society, these rules of culture overlap and diffuse—the rules that dictate the standards of expression become less and less knowable.

## Perception and Context

The prospect of controlling perception becomes even more complicated when we extend the concept of the avatar to the virtual realm. Multiple people in multiple contexts can perceive a virtual avatar at the same time. It is strange to consider that when you accept the virtual address of a mobile phone number, an aspect of your avatar—in this case, your voice—is carried in the pocket of every other cell phone user through your voicemail. In this sense, your avatar potentially exists in the physical location of every phone and computer on the planet.

The visual avatar in cyberspace increases the ability of a person to fully participate in her or his representation as self-manifestation adds physical properties to the list of controllable variables. For example, the appearance of wisdom can be suggested by manipulating the age of an avatar. In *The Singularity Is Near*, Ray Kurzweil suggests that in a virtual reality, the avatar is not static but responsive to the context of the viewer. Kurzweil proposes that "we can select different bodies at the same time for different people ... the other person may choose to override your selections, preferring to see you differently than the body you have chosen for yourself."

# A NEW DEFINITION OF EXPERIENCE

How will the extended virtual platform change our definition of *experience?* Virtual experience relies on the ability of the imagination to glean meaning from an intangible event. These events may be stimulated or directed through physical triggers. Digital technologies have created platforms that invoke interactive and immersive virtual experience.

The importance of these virtual experiences increases and becomes more acute as these digital platforms become increasingly connected. These new, persistent platforms represent a split not between reality and virtual reality, but between the real and virtual manifestation of self.

How will this new paradigm change the way we perceive the places we live in, the way we think of our tools, our definition of community, and even the way that we see ourselves? In the following sections, we explore some of the possible ways in which this shift is, and could be, negotiated. By diagnosing the emergent signals identified within tactical agents as opportunities, we can then build and strengthen context with the points of departure and future scenarios, cultivating further inquiry into duality's imaginative potential.

"How will this new paradigm change the way we perceive the places we live in, the way we think of our tools, our definition of community, and even the way that we see ourselves?"

# Tactical Agents of Duality in Dataspace

**Dual Presence (Enabled People):** People and objects will have both a communication and a physical presence. Third-wave computing[5] design will be ubiquitous computing—many computers to one person. As the platforms that invoke interactive and immersive virtual experience become connected, each person using them will have a simultaneous virtual "self" that will evolve through his or her real and virtual actions and histories.

**Semantic Place (Enabled Places):** Semantic place equates with meaningful place. It illustrates the transformation of a static space into a purposeful place embedded with memory and two-way (or many-to-many) full-spectrum communication via color, shape, form, texture, temperature, and so on.

**Hyper-Object Ecologies (Enabled Objects):** These are systems generated by the addition of informatics capabilities, networks, intelligence, and full-spectrum communication to physical objects. Sensitive to subject matter and social relationships, objects and communities of objects may change in many ways to adapt to the ever-changing context of an environment. This is not about objects per se, but about what happens with people with and in between objects.

"The new paradigm raises questions about what will be classified as data. The language used to represent an idea must have the plasticity required to efficiently convey the meaning."

**The New Senses (Enabled Data Use):** In a Dataspace, people will be able to "see" their place not only within the physical environment, but also within their personal *socio-informational network*. A socio-informational network is formed when social and information networks become so interdependent, they merge completely.

**The New Language (Enabled Data):** This new paradigm raises questions about what will be classified as data. The language used to represent an idea must have the plasticity required to efficiently convey the meaning. In order to anticipate that language, we must look with a new perspective at the things identified as information.

---

5 First wave: mainframe computing (one computer to many people); second wave: personal computing (one computer to one person); third wave: ubiquitous computing (many computers to one person—for example, Xerox PARC).

# Points of Departure for Duality in Dataspace

As discussed in the previous chapter, we place the signals and directions identified in tactical agents in the context of human behavior to generate a greater understanding of their potential as strategic opportunities. Extracting their core themes generates metaphors that lead into points of departure—the platforms for developing the imaginative narratives of the future scenarios that follow.

**Life in the lowest energy state:** It takes effort to make people behave in new ways. Technology will learn to enable purpose through anticipating action. The blurring of tangible and virtual capabilities will enhance accessibility and understanding by allowing people to define their purpose and change the face of education, learning, and community behavior.

**Place in a crowd:** How should virtual places be navigated when it is the places that travel, not the people?

**Object etiquette:** This is the expectation of well-behaved machines that integrate their new or unexpected roles into the social fabric. This issue is clearly observable in the social normalization of cell phones. The mobile phone was designed for physical functionality before its potential virtual role was explored. The screen, the speaker, the microphone, and the keypad address communications to people that traditionally have been sent to locations.

"As virtual communities develop robust economies, distinct cultures, governments, and citizens that transcend traditional socio-political borders, their inhabitants might become citizens of a new type of country."

**Not my avatar:** This is the perception of the body conditioning the mind. Avatar selection is made by the mind according to a desired self-image, but a new avatar in a new context could condition the mind to accept new definitions of the self.

**Chameleon:** This is the adaptation of avatars to suit the moment and intention. In a virtual space, the avatar is not a static entity and can respond to the context of the viewer. The viewer, not the projector, should determine the manifestation of the avatar if the desired goal is communication.

**Virtual nations:** As virtual communities develop robust economies, distinct cultures, governments, and citizens that transcend traditional socio-political borders, their inhabitants might become citizens of a new type of country.

# Future Scenarios

The following future scenarios frame the concepts illustrated throughout this chapter's exploration into the possibilities of duality in Dataspace. As with the future scenarios in Chapter 12, these scenarios encourage consideration of an opportunity's value and relevance to various audiences and the potential applications of a concept in relation to further strategic development.

## *PLAYING IN THE SANDBOX*

Bumping into walls and widgets as if her senses were shut down for the day, Gego—with her chubby digits and tousled hair in her face—fumbled through drawers and mason jars trying to find some bits she was sure she had seen a few days ago. "Come on!" she yelled in frustration. "Where are they?"

Gego had spent the last five months tinkering and layering bits and pieces of almost anything she could lay her hands on; five months adding and taking away, tightening parts and throwing out the redundant pieces.

Five months sounds like nothing when you're talking about designing a new line of clothing, manufacturing 80,000 cars, or creating a blockbuster film, but it is a lot to put into something that serves no intended purpose other than to become what it becomes. Gego had no idea why she was making this; she simply knew that she enjoyed doing it. Just as someone else might paint a picture that he never intends to show, she created this because that's what she does.

What Gego didn't know was that in the very near future, her creation would make its way out of her garage, and once exposed to the world, it would change the lives of everyone lucky enough to come across it. Like all of her creations, it was made for her but shared. Shared the way that children share time in the sandbox—they create a world and don't think twice about letting you in.

"Like a snowball collecting layers as it tumbles downhill, the gift grew and grew until it became so big nobody could even recognize it as a gift any longer. Now it was just there—a collection of themselves, for themselves, that they took pride in."

In her sandbox, Gego plays, and it is her playing that creates the most wonderful, unique images, objects, and ideas—all with the potential to make a huge impact on others. What was once a compilation of bits, pieces, and parts, had now become an object in itself, even though Gego herself couldn't recognize it as one.

She set her creation outside to share, when someone came along and interpreted it as a *perpetual gift*. A gift that was not his to keep, so instead he gave the object a false history, a history he created simply because he could. He imagined that every bit he saw in this collage was put there by a different creature, a creature that had received the gift and added something to it before giving a copy of it to the next.

Some people added friends, some added stories, some wisdom, and some added nothing but a "thank you" to everyone who came before them. Like a snowball collecting layers as it tumbles downhill, the gift grew and grew until it became so big nobody could even recognize it as a gift any longer. Now it was just there—a collection of themselves, for themselves, that they took pride in.

Gego saw it stop growing, and she felt proud as well. But it was not for the statue of goodwill that it had become; it was the pride of her creation taking on a life of its own. She knew that all of what everyone is so proud of would not exist if she hadn't spent those five months doing what she loves doing: playing in the sandbox.

## DEMO QUIXOTIC: A SECOND LIFE FUTURE SCENARIO

*Developed by San Francisco-based Linden Labs, Second Life is an online, digital community imagined, shaped, and owned by its residents. It has gained popularity through its economic system, high levels of autonomy regarding avatar behavior, and manner of dissolving real and virtual boundaries. In an ever-expanding virtual continent with tiered membership programs providing various levels of access, members can acquire and exchange assets and capital in the marketplace, which can then be translated into real-world economic reward. Second Life members such as the narrator of this story participate and interact mainly through highly personalized avatars that they create.*

Have you ever blamed your own mistake or a negative event on simply having a bad day? Rationalizing that you wouldn't have made such a mistake any other day? Well, that's how it began over eight years ago with Demo and me. I happened to really piss somebody off by leaving a few grenades around the sandbox, and instead of explaining myself to the angered (and dismembered) avatar, I allowed Demo, my own Second Life avatar, to take full responsibility. It was he, not I, who left the explosives lying around, and it was his appearance—camo fatigues, guns strapped across his back—that brought this victim's anger to a boiling point.

Some people use their avatars to role-play, deceive, or mirror who they really are. In making and living through my avatar, I have found that I have created a new human being—a real person—stuck in an avatar's skin. This person is not me—he is a person in me who has been exposed. He does things I would never do and says things I would never say.

His name is Demo Quixotic, and there are many others out there just like him, unique and independent of their carriers. I take comfort in knowing that I am not the only one. Demo's ambitions are different than mine, but we seem to make it work in a symbiotic, scratch-my-back-and-I'll-scratch-yours type of way.

"I have found that I have created a new human being—a real person—stuck in an avatar's skin. This person is not me—he is a person in me who has been exposed. He does things I would never do and says things I would never say."

Demo has made friends and enemies. To me he is a bit of a car crash that I can't help but watch. I actually find myself interacting with him more often these days—switching back and forth between what I would say and what he would say—and I'm getting unbelievably efficient at it. Our ongoing dialogue began as a question in my mind: What would Demo do in this situation? But now he is as real and independent to me as any person I'd pass in the street.

He is a new person in our shared universe. Not only does he not share the same appearance or personality traits as me, he has unique spending habits, emotional triggers, and even memories, all different than mine.

And he visits our world as we visit his.

People like Demo are taking part in, and taking advantage of, both the real and virtual worlds better than we are in either one. One reason is that they are often conceived for very specific reasons: sex, war, intimidation, business, and so on. We, on the other hand, do not have the same focus. They also use their multiple forms of communication to the fullest extent. Their digital medium has tools that auto-correct, format, template, undo, reference, cross-reference, change shape, search, and everything else we never thought could be used for anything other than Microsoft Word or Google.

Demo has a presence that is malleable. He is both scripted and able to improvise, fallible and perfect, unique and replicable, familiar and forgettable, intelligent and ignorant, hidden and exposed. In a world that embraces this flexibility, he has the advantage of not needing us nearly as much as we need him. Our capabilities are finite and his are not.

Demo exists for a specific reason. He is not here to be the next Donald Trump, or elected official, or leader of a successful boycott against a fast-food chain; although he could be these things, there are others who *are*. No, he is here to become a professional wrestler. His days of blowing things up and his tense interactions with both worlds laid a path before him that was undeniable: He needs to unleash some carnage.

His first gig happened when a promoter saw him attempting to blow himself up. Demo wanted to test his strength against an R5 nano-nuclear implant bomb. Lucky for Demo, he was interrupted; turns out that actually would have been the end of him. But the promoter saw his commitment and offered him a job as an extra in the new Armor Dude online game. Since then, he has had a number of interviews on Web forums, been in six commercials, and has been promised a position as a back-up tag-team partner for Shawn Michaels.

Demo told me he's hoping to be a permanent part of the World Wrestling Entertainment circuit as of the New Year. He's been training as a wrestler and will be getting paid to become the newest *bad ass* of the WWE empire.

## UNIVERSITY IN A PIXEL

*Today, knowledge exists in universities, on Web pages, in books, and the like. Tomorrow, knowledge will exist in the air we breath. In 2015, Shauna, the narrator of this story, will earn her degree in sociology without stepping foot in a university. She will pay tuition to the Knowledge Institute of Sociology, a collaborative program of thousands of professors and social scientists amassing an unprecedented quantity and quality of knowledge. In turn, her tuition will supply her with a code giving her access to the knowledge that surrounds her every day. This filter will distill the data embedded in objects and spaces. Shauna will be taught the content of her course using her surroundings, experience, and learning preferences.*

I'm a third-year sociology student, doing quite well so far. When I started the program, I was a little concerned, as most people are. I felt like I had to make such a huge decision—to commit to a career for the rest of my life—not to mention dealing with the mammoth cost of tuition. But while checking out the local programs, I came across the University of Indiana's Experience Education.

At the time, Experience Education was a newly introduced supplement for the university's lectures, classes, and books. It allowed students to gain additional knowledge in their specific areas of study. And for undecided applicants like me, it was a chance to test the waters. I bought a three-week Experience Education code in the Knowledge Institute of Sociology just to see if the program was right for me.

The next few weeks were absolutely incredible. The device that UI gave me chimed every time I passed an object or place that had a new lesson for me. The information was really just an introduction, but I couldn't believe how so many things were relevant to what I wanted to learn. I was hooked.

## NOT WHAT IT SEEMS

If you were to touch the future, it would feel like a mirage—like taking one last step at the top of a flight of stairs to find there is only air beneath your feet.

If you were to see the future, you would see a man on a bench with tears in his eyes, and people walking past him without a second glance.

If you were to smell the future, you would smell cabbage boiling on the stove of an elderly woman, alone in an empty house.

If you were to taste the future, you would taste a chemical coating on the apple your granddaughter eats without a second thought.

If you were to hear the future, it would be the sound of a young boy asking for help in a silent room, with only the floor, ceiling, and walls echoing back his question.

You would be wrong to think that this future is grim—that humanity has failed in its pursuit of happiness and a better world; that there has been no progress from today. All of these people would disagree with you. The future is not how it appears to you.

"The mirage you felt when you touched the future is a world that coexists with the one you know now; it is a layer containing a second universe. It will exist in the future like an emotion, like desire between secret lovers—there, but only for those to whom it pertains."

The man on the bench with tears in his eyes is watching his son win an award at a ceremony in Copenhagen. The people walking past the bench do not interrupt him, but instead share and experience his story as they move.

They can see everything.

The elderly woman alone in her house is not without help. She is taken care of, monitored, and kept company by many. She could not be so independent without the hundreds of "volunteer angels" that surround her constantly.

She senses their presence.

The chemicals tasted on your grandchild's apple are not going to make her sick; rather they are the vessels that carry the vision and experience of the oncologist who will prevent cancer from growing in her stomach.

She doesn't taste a thing.

The child, alone and asking for help, is in his perfect learning environment. He has chosen to learn by hearing one answer from a thousand masters. He has access to everyone wishing to help him.

He can hear everything.

The mirage you felt when you touched the future is a world that coexists with the one you know now; it is a layer containing a second universe. That last stair in the flight was there. You simply didn't have the tools to touch, see, smell, taste, or hear it.

Without the right tools, this world is formless and intangible, invisible to today's eye. It will exist in the future like an emotion, like desire between secret lovers—there, but only for those to whom it pertains.

This complementary universe is always there, but it appears only when needed. It facilitates human behavior. It is there in the man's desire to share an experience with his son, in the elderly woman's independence, in the trust and innocence of a child, in the thirst for knowledge and the obligation to share it.

It is the future of Second Life.


Thus far, we have explored and articulated the ideas and themes generated throughout the strategic creativity method through the preceding scenarios in the contexts of human behavior, technology, and organizational capability. As described in Chapter 11, the next steps of the method will see the core values and benefits extracted and translated into tactical service, product and experience opportunities, and new economic models that will support these new opportunities. We then return to the point of origin in the strategic circle, and begin again.

# 14
# Imaginative Application

Previous chapters have focused on releasing the imagination to see what is possible. But once something is imagined, discovered, and acted upon through prototyping and development, the big questions arise: Are we now better off? Is this actually progress? And what is progress, anyway? In this chapter, my former colleague at the Beal Institute, Chris Matthews, discusses other ingredients that contribute to truly worthwhile innovation—and the role of organizations in making it happen.

# Finding a New Enemy

Colin Powell once recalled an early interaction with Mikhail Gorbachev, during the days when Powell was U.S. Assistant to the President for National Security Affairs and Gorbachev was trying to end the Cold War and restructure the USSR through the policies of *glasnost* and *perestroika*. Powell didn't believe Gorbachev was sincere in his intentions, and Gorbachev knew it. As the story goes, Gorbachev smiled and then told Powell that he was sorry, but Powell would have to find a new enemy. Hearing this, Powell realized that he'd had excellent success with *this* enemy; he wasn't interested in finding a new one.

Consider this story in the context of the trickster who helps open our minds to possibility. What if Powell had had a trickster? What if, instead of being stone-faced toward the prospect of Soviet change, his voice had not been bound by habit and lack of imagination? Perhaps his response would have been less rigid. Perhaps he would have allowed himself to entertain the idea that Gorbachev might actually be genuine. And perhaps imagining a future scenario of a restructured USSR under Gorbachev's leadership could have allowed Powell to deepen American political allegiances with this new nation at that time.

"What if Colin Powell had had a trickster? What if, instead of being stone-faced toward the prospect of Soviet change, his voice had not been bound by habit and lack of imagination?"

Perhaps it even might have happened earlier than it did and at the request of Powell, who then might have told Gorbachev that *he* needed a new enemy. However, without a trickster to guide him through this Imagination Challenge toward alternate opinions or ways of thinking, Powell retained his entrenched position in their relationship longer than he needed to. His unwillingness to look at the situation through a different lens, perceiving it as a threat rather than an opportunity for new possibility, meant that Powell lost out on potential influence in the restructuring of the USSR. For him, it was easier to embrace the status quo than to embrace the uncertainties of such a monumental transformation. Fortunately, the rest of the world found it easier to embrace the change.

Most people don't like to change enemies. It's tough to get past conflict, particularly a long-standing one that engenders terms like *enemy*. And for many people, imagination has been an enemy for a long, long time—usually since grade school. In his book *Orbiting the Giant Hairball,* Gordon MacKenzie noted that if you ask a first-grade class how many of them are artists, nearly 100 percent will raise their hands. And as you work upward in grade level, the number of raised hands diminishes. By junior high, it's often down to zero.

"If something doesn't solve a problem or generate some kind of tangible and desired benefit that wasn't available before, we are left to assume that we've misinterpreted a signal somehow, or perhaps simply guessed wrong."

Earlier chapters of this book have detailed how schools and workplaces routinely suppress efforts toward imagination, individual ideas, and thought diversity. So it's not terribly difficult to understand why imagination is such an easy target, particularly in an adult environment. It's easy to view imagination as inefficient—it can't be effectively measured and varies from person to person.

And as we've seen, imagination is often tied too closely with childhood to be considered applicable to the world of business or even life in general. But it's clear that progress—political, social, or industrial progress that improves people's lives—can be difficult to come by if imagination remains your enemy. We'd be well served to reserve titles such as *enemy* for the actual impediments that roadblock progress. The first step is to find a new enemy.

# Is All Innovation Beneficial?

Let's begin by reviewing the fundamental differences between imagination and creativity: The former is the ability to form images and ideas in the mind, while the latter is the ability to use these images and ideas to create original services and things. We have tied this distinction to our ability or inability to identify signals that exist around us (more imagination is correlated with better signal reception), and we have codified methods to restore imagination through unlearning and the temporary play space. By doing this, we can strengthen imagination's role as the fuel for creativity.

Our next challenge lies in identifying the potential effects of imagination-fueled creativity: innovation. This means recognizing the reality that you won't always lay an egg of innovation, and when you do, the innovation you hatch might not be positive.

First, let's look at nonstarters. Some potential innovations are patently absurd or simply arrive at the wrong time. Creativity can get misplaced, and the results can be comical (sometimes retrospectively, sometimes immediately, sometimes both). The Internet offers countless examples of this, such as using e-commerce to deliver a $1 snack across the continent. Such attempts fall into the category of business models that fail very quickly, and despite beginning with genuine imagination and robust creativity, they lack the benefit necessary to be classified as innovation. If something doesn't solve a problem or generate some kind of tangible and desired benefit that wasn't available before, we are left to assume that we've misinterpreted a signal somehow, or perhaps simply guessed wrong.

Steve Jobs once famously quipped that "innovation is creativity that ships," and this thinking seems to hold true when we're revisiting the annals of mistakes made while chasing innovation. Thankfully, if something fails to become an innovation, it doesn't often cause much harm. Harm is more likely to happen when we think an innovation is a good idea and we later learn that we were wrong.

## YOU CALL THIS PROGRESS?

On May 6, 1937, the German zeppelin LZ 129 Hindenburg caught fire while approaching a mooring mast in Lakehurst, New Jersey. The flames began near the tail and within 37 seconds engulfed the entire 804-foot-long vessel. In modern flight context, that's about the length of three 747s placed end to end. A floating blimp that relied on hydrogen for its lift, the

Hindenburg was believed to have had protection against gas leaks and the threat of fires. Despite an array of theories regarding how the accident occurred, this sensational disaster instantly ended this innovative method of transatlantic travel, which had been popular and prestigious up to that point. Today, blimps are helium-filled, about a tenth the size of the Hindenburg, not used for long-distance travel, and have decidedly better protection against flames (if only because helium isn't flammable).

The Hindenburg disaster indicates that even if a product or service is undeniably innovative, it might not be progress. "So what?" you might ask. Good question. The reason I'm mentioning it here is because the biggest and most elusive step in the innovation chain is progress. What is it? And why does anyone want it in the first place? And perhaps most importantly, how do we achieve it? Understanding the road map from imagination to progress is a necessary step, but it's by no means the entire journey.

## THE PROMISE OF GROWTH

On the ladder toward progress, innovation is the first step with clear extrinsic incentives. Imagination and creativity are, for the most part, intrinsically motivated: They emerge from play. As a result they are usually fun, often pursued and enjoyed in our spare time, and rarely tied to external incentives such as salary or bonuses. Not everyone is equally good at them, but you rarely have to pay anyone to daydream.

"The Hindenburg disaster indicates that even if a product or service is undeniably innovative, it might not be progress."

Innovation, on the other hand, carries with it something special: the promise of growth opportunities. Whether personal or organizational, we commonly pursue ways to grow beyond our current capabilities and capacities. From an organizational standpoint, growth opportunities often take the form of either new revenue sources (such as new markets or products) or decreased costs (such as lower expenses or higher efficiencies). Sometimes growth opportunities can come from business model innovations and shake the very core of a company or industry. Whatever the source, innovation drives this growth.

Why must growth come from innovation? The classic wisdom is simply that other potential sources of growth aren't likely to come through for you. Assuming your business remains exactly the same, options such as simple organic market growth or a reduction in competitors are tough to rely on. And this further assumes that your competitors won't do anything new that might affect your market share. If any of this sounds likely, you've probably found yourself some kind of monopoly.

## WHAT COMPANIES BENEFIT FROM INNOVATION?

In many industries, especially those that are unregulated and marked by low barriers to entry, innovation is the best (and sometimes only) way for an organization to get ahead and stay ahead of its competitors. This is particularly true as the level of regulation declines because that widens the array of competitive possibilities. In a competitive landscape where more is permitted, there is a wider range of possible values for innovation. This is not to say that industry regulation eliminates the need for innovation, but rather that the less regulation in an industry, the greater the potential value of innovation as a competitive differentiator.

We see evidence of this in digital music, and even more widely in Web-based applications of social networks. An example is the nearly rampant innovation and even greater innovation value from companies with Web 2.0 applications like Flickr. This popular photo-sharing site launched in 2004 (and purchased by Yahoo in 2005) is an example of undistilled innovation that was able to capitalize on its nearly limitless and unregulated playing field.

There is decidedly less innovation, in both depth and breadth, from companies in more regulated industries. Consider the last time you were wowed by an innovation from a utilities company or the last time you heard of an accountant who innovated another accountant out of business.

"In a competitive landscape where more is permitted, there is a wider range of possible values for innovation. An example is the nearly rampant innovation and even greater innovation value from companies with Web 2.0 applications like Flickr."

So given that organizations may value innovation differently, it is understandable why some companies place higher value on imagination and creativity. If a company doesn't naturally find value in innovation, it is less likely to find value in these inputs to innovation unless they're seen as contributing to something else that the company values—typically profit. It's a cautionary note that goes both directions: For those in unregulated industries, be mindful of the value you can bring to the table via innovation. If, on the other hand, you're surrounded by stiff regulation, much of what we're saying here will be, at best, a hard sell to your organization. At worst, you'll find yourself back where you started, with imagination as your enemy. If so, don't put this book down and walk away. Instead, try to rethink the areas of your organization that might not be so well defended by regulation. Then start there.

*How industry regulation affects value innovation.* →

Amount of
Industry
Regulation

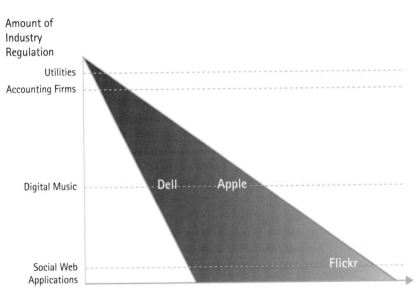

Utilities

Accounting Firms

Digital Music     Dell    Apple

Social Web
Applications         Flickr

Value of Innovation
(dollars relative to direct competitors)

# Identifying Progress

Perhaps the biggest challenge with progress is that it's actually a pretty tough thing to identify. Imagination is a necessary precursor to creativity, which in turn propels innovation, which hopefully qualifies as progress. Find your way to progress, and you're treated to competitive strength, profit, or whatever indicators of growth you're pursuing. It's the carrot for the entrepreneur and the organization alike.

Progress is typically defined as movement toward a goal, but in the case of "societal progress," where the goal is neither universal nor discrete, we're often reduced to identifying progress as anything that makes us better off. This definition creates a host of issues, since something that is progress for me might simultaneously be crippling everyone else. And what is progress *not?* Progress is not something that makes you worse off than you were.

For the purpose of this discussion, we are interested in the social "rising tide" progress that benefits at least a large group, and ideally everyone. This type of progress must be relatively nonexclusive in its benefit and should be sustainable over an infinite term. That's to say, either we can keep doing it as long as we like, or it can lead to us doing it in increasingly better ways.

"To bridge the imagination gap, we must focus on discovering the things we cannot see, not the things we'd like to or expect to see. And within the unseen lies the benefit of social progress— the 'What if...?' that can transform us."

The modern 20th-century future of flying cars, jet packs, and Mars vacations hasn't yet materialized, but instead has remained within the realm of science fiction. These were things that people could imagine but have never followed through on because they do not truly reflect current values or abilities. For example, establishing a colony on Mars would be an incremental innovation: one goal on a long continuum of innovations that add value rather than create it. It would not take into account how a paradigm may shift—how *we may change*—but would simply afford a select few the ability to live outside of our atmosphere. It is therefore an outdated vision for the future, built from old constraints and maintained through old expectations. Since it does not encourage transformation, none would occur, and our social progress would stagger to a halt.

When we want to nurture social progress, we must change the expectations of both our constraints and outcomes, combining new elements of knowledge in new ways to discover new possibilities. The innovations we wish to develop are not incremental, but rather adjacent or radical—with values that may reflect traces of the past but encompass an entirely new perspective and set of goals. This leads to a very critical distinction: To bridge the imagination gap—the gulf between the world bound by rationality and the world bound by possibility—we must focus on discovering the things we cannot see, not the things we'd like to or expect to see. And within the unseen lies the benefit of social progress—the "What if...?" that can transform us.

## MOTOFWRD: Nurturing Meaningful Innovation

There are currently many tangible efforts to bridge the imagination gap, coming from the top levels at the world's best academic institutions as well as grassroots education supplements such as Motorola's MOTOFWRD. This inaugural scholarship competition challenged students to rethink and reengineer the potential applications of mobile technology.

The competition yielded inspired, imaginative ideas such as the winning entry, which envisioned cell phones that change color based on emotional cues in the conversation, as an aid to those with Asperger's syndrome and other disorders involving deficiencies in communication skills. Other notable entries included some that blended familiar computer interfaces with our day-to-day decision-making processes, and a real-time method of finding, reserving, and paying for elusive parking spots in a crowded city.

# PROGRESS TRAPS

As I've said, not all innovations can immediately be called progress—and, in fact, some might even be destructive. In *A Short History of Progress,* Ronald Wright considered the implications of "progress traps"—the act of continually kicking out the rungs beneath you as you climb up a ladder. This eliminates any chance of getting back to where you started while you can't see far enough ahead to know that the last place you'd ever want to be is at the top of this particular ladder.

Wright describes many instances when civilizations believed they were on an unstoppable growth track only to discover that one day, someone would cut down the last tree and there would be nothing left. This leaves us with the unsettling realization that testing and identifying progress takes time, and suggests that we can't get better at predicting "net positive" progress pathways.

If we discovered a new and faster way to clear-cut our forests, for example, it would be difficult to immediately categorize this as progress. Does it solve a problem? Do we currently lack a way to clear-cut forests at a rate fast enough to support our global economy? Given current trends toward less clear-cutting, this discovery might be as useful as a cost-effective way to speed up global warming. The outcome simply isn't in a direction we want to go. We can see the top of the ladder, and it's not worth climbing. Yet any new and innovative way to improve regrowth efforts might be as much an impediment to progress as faster clear-cutting, and just as catastrophic. The top of this ladder might simply be more difficult to see, however, and in our rush up it, we could risk not realizing that in the end it will lead to the same destination.

"We're often reduced to identifying progress as anything that makes us better off. This definition creates a host of issues, since something that is progress for me might simultaneously be crippling everyone else."

Wright recounts the story of the ancient Babylonians and their discovery that they could increase their crop yields by overhydrating their land. They identified progress as anything that gave them better crops, since better crops led to better lifestyles, health, and wealth. They knew that increasing the moisture in soil increased the yield of their crops, and so they logically decided that they wanted more of this. They didn't realize that more water wouldn't *always* result in more crops, as they had no experience with heavily hydrated soil over the long term. The eventual oversalinization of their soil ultimately rendered their land useless for farming. And shortly thereafter, their entire culture died along with their soil—the bountiful crops and the lifestyle commensurate with it extinguished in a very short period of time.

So perhaps a faster way toward reforestation may not be the panacea it appears to be and could, in fact, be as disastrous as any innovation that allows faster clear-cutting. The simple fact is that we might not know now what will ultimately be progress.

## TAKING THE LONG VIEW

While observation of a new innovation may suggest progress, the fact that it is new leaves it untested in the long term. And we don't typically do well with long-term thinking. Our tendency—at least in the classically North American mindset—to think in short-term personal gains keeps this sustainability issue from becoming too much of a hindrance to any of us individually. The American fascination with SUVs and a petroleum-addicted energy policy is clear enough evidence of this, steering us all toward improving our position in a cost/benefit equation that rarely (if at all) factors in a long-term outlook.

Basically, all of this leaves us with the following two truths:

✦ Progress is good

✦ We might not be able to identify progress when we see it

And this leaves us with a problem to solve: How can we get better at identifying progress?

# Competitive Time Travel

Imagine that you could travel forward in time. See the world ahead of everyone else. Predict trends. Foretell the future. And then take advantage of your knowledge. This isn't so much different from being invisible, except that it's a whole lot more real and possible, at least in a certain sense. An organization rich in innovation is one that is more likely to achieve "competitive time travel." Through successful progress, organizations or people can blend their talents of creativity and execution to move ahead of their competitors even in the same amount of time. Progress allows this, and that's what makes it so enticing. Progress allows exclusive and valuable power, to a degree that is almost magical in nature. It's a virtual gold mine. And it's relative, so if you don't have it, that likely means someone else does.

So how do we progress, and do it faster than others? The answer lies in cultivating the ability to do something effective with creativity in a sustainable way that leverages managerial wisdom over mere cleverness. And this is where the role of the organization becomes critical. It's a simple yet elusive overlap of individual thinking and collective doing: The organization can be receptive when people think of the right things, and then collectively assess and execute these ideas effectively and in a lasting way. The wisdom I'm referring to starts with the concept of archetype retrieval.

"How do we progress, and do it faster than others? The answer lies in cultivating the ability to do something effective with creativity in a sustainable way that leverages managerial wisdom over mere cleverness."

At its core, competitive time travel is tied to archetypes that surround us. One key benefit to this method of inquiry is that it allows us to identify a wider range of potential opportunities. If the management of the organization has a short and obvious list of options from which to chart its future, its progress will be predictable, its competitors quick to react, and its demise certain. This is true even if it makes the best choice among its perceived options because it is not seeing the less obvious advancements available from retrieving past archetypes. Further, because the less obvious advancements may represent greater opportunities, the corporation is bound to lose out to competitors who can see the wider range of options.

## CULTIVATING MANAGERIAL WISDOM

On the road toward progress, of course, imagination and creativity are not always sufficient: Innovation must happen with insight, hindsight, and foresight. At this point, the organization has the opportunity to become involved and approach any decisions to proceed further on the path of development with wisdom and not just cleverness. Cleverness is realizing that hydrogen could be used to float the Hindenburg. Wisdom is realizing that we might not need to float that badly. If we ask, "What is the question to which a hydrogen-filled zeppelin is the answer?," the answer might not be "How can I find a better way to travel?" It could just as likely be "How can I create an 800-foot fireball in the sky in 37 seconds or less?"

"It becomes the role of an organization to provide the critical missing bridge between creativity and innovation, applying wisdom to identify which innovations are actually progress, and then pursuing or abandoning them accordingly."

So how can we be better at managerial wisdom? The simple answer is to be better equipped to be receptive to imagination and creativity within the organization, aligning them effectively in practice and ethos. As earlier chapters have shown, organizations typically think about advancement as improvements to existing offerings, extensions to existing offerings, or other fundamental alterations to their cost/quality relationships. But it's important to understand that these advancements are relative, specifically with respect to those of competitors. Think about this, and take a moment to contrast it against the earlier idea that regulation affects the potential value of innovation. Then ask yourself if you think in relative or absolute terms when considering your position, or the position of your organization.

## Three Elements of Organizational Capability

The connection between creativity and innovation is a function of three critical elements that can be found in any organization:

+ **Functional capacity:** Are there idle machines, or other types of usable excess capacity that can be dedicated to the idea?

+ **Collective capability:** Are there enough of the right people at the firm to act upon the idea, and is there interest in dedicating them to it?

+ **Managerial wisdom:** This is the most important element: the capability to align hindsight, insight, and foresight to effectively manage the possibilities and potential applications that arise.

All steps forward, in one way or another, are an effect of the retrieval of archetypes—people using imagination and creativity to effectively interpret the signals around them. These are the same signals discussed at the outset of this book: strong signals from the world around us and often weak receptors within us to interpret them.

And so it becomes the role of an organization, whether it realizes this or not, to provide the critical missing bridge—indeed to bridge the imagination gap—between creativity and innovation, applying wisdom to identify which innovations are actually progress, and then pursuing or abandoning them accordingly. Using the tools and ideas outlined in this book, people can guide themselves, their groups, or their organizations toward higher quality, more sustainable progress. Imagination and creativity are personalized constructs, and innovation and progress are collective constructs; it is up to the organization to join them together using effective methods of inquiry, understanding past archetypes and signals that led them there, and allowing concepts such as temporary play space and the trickster to promote the imaginative fuel in the first place.

## OVERLAPPING CIRCLES OF CAPABILITY

How does all this relate to time travel? This might be a good time to draw a couple napkin sketches. You'll be able to draw these easily when the time comes to explain this to someone else. Once you start talking about how time travel is actually possible, it's likely that people will want you to explain.

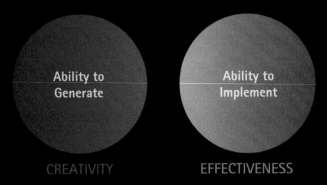

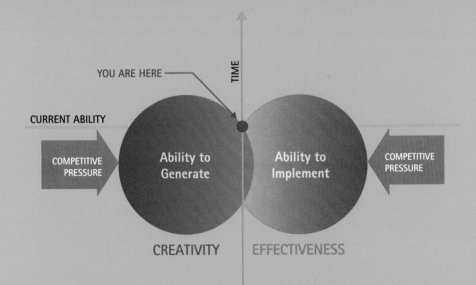

All organizations, groups, or even individuals have some allocation of creativity—that is, imagination with thought toward action—and some allocation of effectiveness, allowing them to innovate and drive progress. Think of these two allocations as two circles. Draw them as you see fit for yourself or your organization. Size can represent the quantity of each; some will have lots of one and little of the other, and some may have similar amounts of both. The only important point at this stage is getting an idea of their size relative to one another.

Now let's add some complexity. Redraw the two circles overlapping, Venn-style. Let's call the ellipse of this intersection *innovation overlap,* and think of it as collective talent. Competitive pressure forces the two circles together, so the more they overlap, the more you can do, and the better off you are. The circles of a well-tuned organization will overlap a great deal, while those of a stagnant company will have no innovation overlap (though this says nothing about the company's actual bottom line, as we're really talking about potential at this point). Next, add a vertical line representing time through the intersection. Last, draw a line across the furthest forward point of the intersection between your two circles. We'll call this "current ability" because it's the furthest forward you can possibly be, given your situation.

> "All organizations, groups, or even individuals have some allocation of creativity—that is, imagination with thought toward action—and some allocation of effectiveness, allowing them to innovate and drive progress."

How does this create time travel? Managerial wisdom is a way of thinking about how far your circles overlap. Accepting the size of the circles, the talent of the organization should try to align them for the best possible result. The issue is: How well do you use what you've got? While changing the scope and reach of the content of the circles can have a similar varying effect, we'll leave that for you to address, since the size of the creativity circle varies a great deal depending on the number of people in your organization, and the size of your effectiveness circle is a structural one. For now, let's focus on aligning what you have before looking for more.

← *Top: Allocations of creativity and effectiveness, represented as circles. Bottom: Competition creates innovation overlap, setting off time travel.*

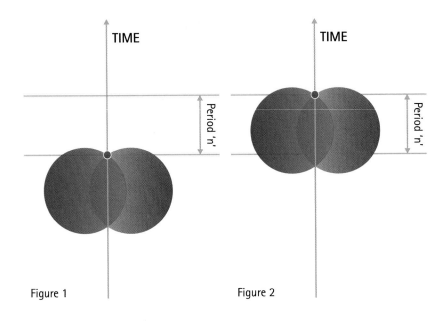

Figure 1

Figure 2

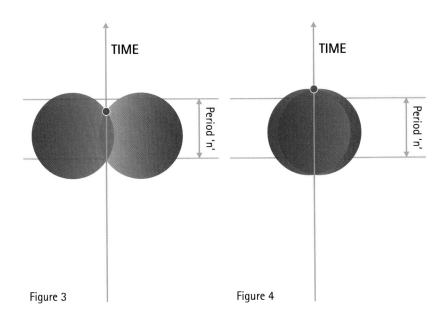

Figure 3

Figure 4

Now suppose at present there exists some amount of innovation overlap in your organization (Figure 1, opposite), and let's identify some indeterminate time period as "*n*." If *n* passes (Figure 2) and your innovation zone remains unchanged, your effectiveness is also unchanged, and you'll achieve exactly what you might have expected to during that time period. However, if during *n* your organization decreases its degree of innovation overlap (Figure 3), your ability to proceed is severely reduced, as it is statically bound to a point in the past. In time *n*, you would have achieved less than you would have expected. The ideal situation, of course, is for the company to restructure its position and approach toward a point in time ahead of *n* (Figure 4), beyond expectations and predictions. Then it may, in a sense, travel ahead in time.

"Managerial wisdom is a way of thinking about how far your circles overlap. Accepting the size of the circles, the talent of the organization should try to align them for the best possible result. The issue is: How well do you use what you've got?"

## ITUNES: TIME TRAVEL IN ACTION

Leading up to the iTunes launch in 2003, those who "think different" at Apple realized their company had more than a healthy dose of creativity and effectiveness in the area of digital music. Within a year of the iTunes launch, Apple utilized this to become the world's leading music supplier, striking a chord of fear in the music industry (which was already in its own dire straits). While the industry giants sued a random collection of their own customers for online file sharing, Apple introduced a new way to buy songs online and, better still, a way to organize a now-digital music collection for greater enjoyment. On a circle chart, the music industry's circles pulled further apart as Apple's found greater overlap and creative synergy.

"Time travel happens. It's just relative to what is around us. And if you are not ahead, it is because someone else is."

The user's experience of listening to, sharing, or possessing music is much more expansive and potentially satisfying than in the past, and the music industry is only now attempting to catch up to Apple. In the space of a couple years, Apple took us all more than a couple of years into the

← *Getting ahead: the effects of time travel.*

future and left the old industry giants somewhere back in the past. If you follow electronics, you can also map out the rise of Samsung and the simultaneous receding power of Sony. Time travel happens. It's just relative to what is around us. And if you are not ahead, it is because *someone else is.*

In applying imagination to create socially meaningful innovation, there are some important ideas for organizations and individuals to remember in the future. First, imagination and creativity are necessary but not sufficient to create innovation. Second, creativity and an organization that accepts it are together not enough to create shareholder value or wealth. Third, the need for organizational wisdom is clear—that is, the experience, industry acumen, and good sense to choose the best option set from the list of options available.

None of this absolves a corporation from the responsibility to know its facts, particularly with respect to its industry, its market, or its customers. Instead, organizations should look upon imagination and creativity as enabling devices, but unique devices in that they involve the actionable retrieval of archetypes from which to develop innovations.

At very least, this approach will help avoid progress traps and prevent the development of innovations that offer more threat than benefit. At best, it can drive progress for an organization, and, if that is sustainable, it can drive progress for society as well.

# 15
# Notes on the Future

It will be as easy to ask a thousand people as it is to ask one.

# A Great Future in Data

Remember this?

*Mr. McGuire:* "I just want to say one word to you—just one word."

*Ben:* "Yes, sir."

*Mr. McGuire:* "Are you listening?"

*Ben:* "Yes, I am."

*Mr. McGuire:* "Data."

*Ben:* "Exactly how do you mean?"

*Mr. McGuire:* "There's a great future in data. Think about it. Will you think about it?"

Data has the potential to revolutionize the future landscape of technology, business, and culture in much the same way that plastics revolutionized the landscape of the last century. Like Dick Fosbury, who explored the possibilities that foam could afford, we must explore the possibilities of data. What can this do? What else can this be? What will this transform, and why? What will this mean to me?

Cyber enthusiasts have always asked when the digital world we have created will become indistinguishable from physical reality, and over the past few decades, we have seriously attempted to integrate what is "virtual" with what is "real." As this web of bytes becomes increasingly and intricately meshed with the world of atoms, we are overlaying our physical maps with multiple layers and connections to the virtual. By sharing their amenities, each of these worlds increases the other's functionality, allowing them both do what they do best. This duality will enable and enhance our communication as much as it will influence it.

"This human-centered approach will differentiate creative insight from imaginative foresight. Insight tells you where to go; foresight lets you know what you will find there."

This dual reality will be, and already is to some extent, populated by people, objects, and spaces with the capability to receive, retrieve, store, and transmit data. Our constructed environments—cities, homes, schools, roads—will tell stories that can be shaped and edited by their "participants," creating new languages that emerge from the context and the content of the situation. What if a theater was no longer a place, but an action? What if "going to the theater" meant taking a stroll where you interact with everything around you, creating a story out of the landscape as you go? What if this new performance involved objects, spaces, and people building upon one another's stories to create a collaborative and contextual experience?

How will people learn to recognize and use the possibilities, codes of conduct, trends, and behavioral patterns that emerge from new practices such as these? While we understand the meaning and purpose of a toothbrush or a cell phone as they exist now, what will we (and manufacturers or service providers) do when a toothbrush and cell phone can communicate with us, and with one another? How will we tailor the purpose of an interaction, and how will the meaning of an object change when pushed to the limits of the technology—or pushed beyond the limits of the experience?

With an increasingly more effective capability to mine data and interpret open source, people can devise their own combinations of cognitive tools that speak directly to their devices as they see fit. This new form of prototyping, and its rapidly decentralized transformation, has received a great deal of interest in the news, the blogosphere, and startups. And developer communities have emerged specifically to create applications out of this opportunity.

## "In educating future leaders, will the alliance of business and design be the answer to the Imagination Challenge?"

Among the many possible applications, this duality could be used to create ideal experiences by revealing contextual knowledge in a particular setting. Your backyard, tools, local greenhouse, and available plants could be networked to communicate their possibilities and enable you to become a master landscaper. Museums, parks, and subway stations that students pass could reveal information, help them form theses and collect the content for research papers. Functions such as these would act as a kind of personalized and continuous education, driven by individual needs and circumstances.

This serendipity-enabled mobile inquiry will drastically change what it means to be "present." And presence in a place will mean knowledge about the place, not only physical proximity.

As these tools become public, moving from tactical to practical, they will augment human capabilities. Just as the Internet extended our ability to communicate and share through a device, extending our perceptions of place and distance, this technology will make us "hyperaware," extending our nervous systems to experience what we could otherwise not see, hear, or feel. This capability will fundamentally transform the way that we live our lives; the way that we love, learn, and build ideas. It will be up to us what we do with the possibilities we create.

In this domain, we will be well equipped to use strategic creativity to formulate user-centered filters and "vision" models to unearth possibility. This human-centered approach will differentiate creative insight from imaginative foresight. Insight tells you where to go; foresight lets you know what you will find there.

# A New Capability

Creating innovative knowledge-retrieval mechanisms, and the methods for creating such mechanisms, will significantly enhance our capability to foresee what these mechanisms can anticipate—to see the unseen.

In educating future leaders, will the alliance of business and design be the answer to the Imagination Challenge? Design schools have historically produced the shapers of culture, while business schools have traditionally produced the managers of that culture. Can design schools, in partnership with business schools, teach managers how to innovate and teach them the importance of creativity in innovation? I am not sure. My hesitation comes from this: Both business and design education are in a time of transformation.

In Jamer Hunt's 2005 "Manifesto for Postindustrial Design" in *I.D. Magazine*, Hunt argued that a new design practice is emerging—a practice in which information and code have replaced the mechanistic models of the Industrial Revolution. Hunt writes: "Three things are propelling this revolution: distributed intelligence, computer-aided design and manufacture, and ecological realities; ... more and more design will be a code and a set of parameters." He is right, and this is the greatest challenge for design culture and education: to transform the Industrial Revolution model into an Information Age model.

"To be effective in reshaping organizations toward imaginative and innovative outcomes, we need a new capability—one that bridges the gap between the artist and the manager, between humanities and science."

The same may be true for business schools. In Hunt's view, "The role of business and the designer in this context will be to enable possibility, provide vision, and set parameters to optimize the system." Warren Bennis and James O'Toole have made a similar challenge to business schools. In their *Harvard Business Review* article "How Business Schools Lost Their Way," they called for an injection of subjects in the curriculum of business that accurately reflect the socio-cultural and economic landscape and provide tools for negotiating it. The goal is to create a discipline that is immersed in the flow of daily life experience.

While managing creativity is as important as managing organizations, the management of innovation potential cannot be learned in standard design or management courses. That ability resides in the state of mind that is part of a person long before she or he pursues an advanced degree; it resides in the curiosity of the artist more than in the rigor of the decision maker. To be effective in reshaping organizations toward imaginative and innovative outcomes, we need a new capability—one that bridges the gap between the artist and the manager, between humanities and science.

Business needs to learn from design how to manage creativity from the inception of a concept through iterative stages to its implementation in products, systems, and services that are useful and desirable for a large group of people. Design needs to learn from business how to rigorously analyze the risks and rewards of any new creative idea, and the tactics that will see it become beneficial to users.

This is all good, but it is all connected by "creativity." And as I have attempted to show in this book, creativity is *the use of imagination.* So the question becomes: Which field—business or design—should teach courses in imagination? Both.

# A New Type of Leader

All invention depends on imagination. Before one learns to manage the *how,* the *what* needs to be conceived. The strategic creator has the capability to reveal the *why*—joining the *how* with the *what,* the "means" with the "meaning" in the organized exploration of possibility. When the goal is to explore opportunity in a conceptual space, one must employ methodologies that empower and nurture possibility as well as reveal the immediate significance and potentiality of what is found.

"For the strategic creator, imagination is not a challenge; it is a mastered tool. In this future, where imagination is an established expertise and the Imagination Challenge has been fulfilled, we will be emboldened to overcome uncertainty and to master the present in order to create the future."

This is not the same as determining how to fit imagination to business; it is determining how to fit business to imagination. And in this process, a new type of leader emerges:

✦ A leader who knows how to discover and learn, and how to manage and inspire discovery and learning in others

✦ A leader who knows how to identify and validate ideas, and transform them into growth opportunities

✦ A leader who nourishes and triggers the imagination of individuals in teams, and can transform the result into strategic capital—innovations that benefit business, culture, and society

For the strategic creator, imagination is not a challenge; it is a mastered tool. In this future, where imagination is an established expertise and the Imagination Challenge has been fulfilled, we will be emboldened to overcome uncertainty and to master the present in order to create the future.

# Bibliography

Alexander, Franz. *The Psychoanalytic Quarterly* (April 1958).

Anderson, Karen L. *Sociology: A Critical Introduction*. Scarborough, ON: Nelson Canada, 1996.

Ansoff, Igor H., and Edward McDonnell. *Implanting Strategic Management*. 2nd ed. Englewood Cliffs, NJ: Prentice Hall International, 1990.

Arendt, Hannah. *The Human Condition*. Chicago, London: University of Chicago Press, 1965.

Aristotle. *De Anima*. London: Penguin Books Ltd., 1986.

Bertone, V. *Creatività aziendale. Metodi, tecniche e casi per valorizzare il potenziale creativo di manager e imprenditori*. Milan: Franco Angeli, 1993.

Best, Steven, and Douglas Kellner. *Postmodern Theory: Critical Interrogations*. New York: The Guilford Press, 1991.

Bethanis, S. "Language as Action: Linking Metaphors with Organization Transformation." In *Learning Organizations*, edited by S. Chawla. Portland, OR: Productivity Press, 1995.

Binnig, Gerd. *Aus dem Nichts*. Munchen: R. Piper GmbH & Co. KG, 1989.

Blackler, F. "Knowledge, Knowledge Work and Organizations: An Overview and Interpretation." *Organization Studies* 16(6): 1021–1046. Lancaster, UK: Lancaster University Management School, 1995.

Blatner, Adam, and Allee Blatner. *The Art of Play*. New York: Brunner Routledge, 1997.

Blount, Roy, Jr. "Being Backwards Gets Results." *Sports Illustrated* (February 10, 1969). http://sportsillustrated.cnn.com/features/cover/news/2000/07/21/fosbury_flash/ (accessed March 23, 2006).

Bohm, D. *On Dialogue*. Edited by Lee Nichol. New York: Routledge, 1996.

Brown, J. "The World Cafe: Living Knowledge Through Conversations That Matter." Doctoral dissertation. Santa Barbara, CA: Fielding Institute, 2001.

Brown, S. "Play as an Organizing Principle: Clinical Evidence and Personal Observation." In *Animal Play Behavior: Evolutionary, Comparative and Ecological Perspectives*. Edited by Marc Beckoff and John A. Byers. Cambridge, UK: Cambridge University Press, 1998.

Bruner, Jerome S., Alison Jolly, and K. Slyva. *Play—Its Role in Development and Evolution*. New York: Basic Books, 1976.

Callois, Roger. *Man, Play and Games*. New York: Simon & Shuster, 1961.

Carson, Robert C., and James N. Butcher. *Abnormal Psychology and Modern Life*. New York: HarperCollins, 1992.

Castaneda, Carlos. *The Teachings of Don Juan: A Yaqui Way of Knowledge*. Los Angeles: University of California Press, 1969.

Castronova, Edward. "The Theory of the Avatar." CESifo Working Paper Series No. 863. Bloomington, IN: Department of Telecommunications, Indiana University, 2003.

Christensen, Clayton M. *The Innovator's Dilemma*. 2d ed. Toronto: HarperCollins Canada, 2003.

Clarke, Arthur C. *Profiles of the Future: An Inquiry Into the Limits of the Possible*. London: Orion Books Ltd., 1962.

*Compact Oxford English Dictionary of Current English*, 2nd ed. Edited by Catherine Soanes. Oxford: Oxford University Press, 2003.

Day, George. "Peripheral Vision: Sensing and Acting On Weak Signals." Lecture at Wharton School of the University of Pennsylvania, June 4, 2003. http://knowledge. wharton.upenn.edu/index.cfm?fa=viewfeature&id=784 (accessed March 23, 2006).

Dery, Mark. *Escape Velocity: Cyberculture at the End of the Century*. New York: Grove Press, 1996.

Diebold, John. Interview in the *New York Times,* 1965.

Edidin, Peter, "Confounding Machines: How the Future Looked." *New York Times*, August 28, 2005,

http://www.nytimes.com/2005/08/28/weekinreview/28edid1.html?ex=12828816 00&en=2952cb8633c4f633&ei=5090&partner=rssuserland&emc=rss (accessed March 23, 2006).

Farganis, J. *Readings in Social Theory: The Classic Tradition to Post-Modernism*. 2d ed. New York: McGraw-Hill, 1993.

Ford, Bill. *Ford Motor Company Business Review,* January 23, 2006,

http://media.ford.com/newsroom/release_display.cfm?release=22465 (accessed March 23, 2006).

Foster, Richard, and Sarah Kaplan. *Creative Destruction: Why Companies That Are Built to Last Under-perform the Market—and How to Successfully Transform Them*. New York: Random House, 2001.

Fromm, Erich. *To Have or To Be*. New York: Harper & Row, 1976.

Furnas, C. C. *The Next Hundred Years*. New York: Reynal & Hitchcock, 1936.

Gadamer, Hans-Georg. *Truth and Method*. New York: Continuum Publishing, 1 960, 2000.

Gadamer, Hans-Georg. *Philosophical Apprenticeships*. Cambridge, Massachusetts: MIT Press, 1985.

Gibson, William. *Neuromancer*, New York: Ace, 1984.

Giedion, Siegfried. *Mechanization Takes Command*. Oxford: Oxford University Press, 1948.

Google. "NASA Takes Google on Journey into Space." September 28, 2005, http://www.google.com/press/pressrel/google_nasa.html (accessed March 3, 2006).

*The Graduate*, film. Los Angeles: MGM Studios, 1967.

Hargadon, A; Sutton, R. "Building an Innovation Factory," *Harvard Business Review*, May 2000.

Harris, M. "The Game of Life," *Utne Reader*, March–April 2001: 61–67.

Heidegger, Martin. *Being and Time*. New York: State University of New York Press, 1953, 1996.

Heijden, K. van der. "Scenarios, Strategies and the Strategy Process." Nyenrode Research Papers Series 1997-01. Centre for Organizational Learning, Research Centres of Universiteit Nyenrode, The Netherlands Business School, 1997.

Hemetsberger, Andrea. "Creative Cyborgs: How Consumers Use the Internet for Self-Realization." *Advances in Consumer Research*, Vol. 32, 2005,

http://www.belfin.at/marketing/content/download/creative%20cyborgs.pdf (accessed March 23, 2006).

Hock, Dee. "The Art of Chaordic Leadership," lecture to Leader to Leader Institute, New York, Winter 2000..

Huizinga, Johan. *Homo Ludens*. Boston: Beacon Press, 1971.

Hume, David. *A Treatise of Human Nature*. London: Penguin Books Ltd., 1969, 1985.

Hunt, Jamer. "A Manifesto for Post Industrial Design," *I.D. Magazine*, November 2005: 120–121.

Hutchinson, Thomas H. *Here Is Television: Your Window on the World*. New York: Hastings House, 1946.

Illich, Ivan. *Deschooling Society*. London: Calder & Boyars Ltd., 1971.

Johansen, Bob. "Scanning Technology Horizons. Peripheral Vision: Sensing and Acting On Weak Signals." Lecture at Wharton School of the University of Pennsylvania, 2005.

http://knowledge.wharton.upenn.edu/index.cfm?fa=viewfeature&id=784 (accessed March 23, 2006).

"The Internet of Things: Executive Summary." *ITU Internet Reports,* November 2005. Geneva: International Telecommunications Union.

Joly, M. *Des idées qui repportent... ca se trouve! Démystifier la créativité industrielle.* Paris: Les Éditions d'Organisation, 1992.

Jones, Bryan D. "Bounded by Rationality." *Annual Reviews, Department of Political Science,* No. 2: 297–321. Seattle: University of Washington, 1999.

Jung, Carl. *Memories, Dreams, Reflections.* New York: Random House, 1961.

Kroker, Arthur, and Michael A. Weinstein. *Data Trash: The Theory of the Virtual Class.* Montreal: New World Perspectives, 1994.

Kurzweil, Ray. *The Singularity Is Near.* New York: Viking Penguin Ltd., 2005.

Locke, Christopher, and David Weinberger. "The Cluetrain Manifesto," 1999, http://www.cluetrain.com (accessed March 23, 2006).

Lutz, Bob. Speech to General Motors annual shareholder meeting, 2005, http://72.14.203.104/search?q=cache:11-C1odwvigJ:fastlane.gmblogs.com/archives/2005/06/+bob+lutz,+gm,+annual+meeting,+entertainment&hl=en&gl=ca&ct=clnk&cd=6&client=firefox-a (accessed March 23, 2006).

MacKenzie, Gordon. *Orbiting the Giant Hairball.* New York: Viking Penguin, 1998.

Mazzoli, Silvio. "Pingu's Biography." PINGU FAQ-Version 3 19.10.95, http://www.geocities.com/EnchantedForest/5681/pinguFAQ.html (accessed March 23, 2006).

McKillip, Patricia. In *Faces of Fantasy,* edited by Patti Perret. New York: Tor Books, 1996.

McLuhan, Marshall, and Bruce Powers. *The Global Village: Transformations in World Life and Media in the 21st Century.* Oxford: Oxford University Press, 1992.

Miller, David L. *Gods and Games: Toward a Theology of Play.* Harper & Row, 1974.

Newell, A., and H. Simon. *Human Problem Solving.* Englewood Cliffs, NJ: Prentice Hall International, 1972.

Newell, Allen. *"The Knowledge Level,"* Artificial Intelligence 18(1), 1982: 87–127..

Newell, Allen. *Unified Theories of Cognition.* Cambridge, Massachusetts: Harvard University Press, 1990.

Nietzsche, Friedrich. *Beyond Good and Evil.* London: Penguin Books Ltd., 1973.

O'Toole, James, and Warren Bennis. "How Business Schools Lost Their Way." *Harvard Business Review,* May 2005.

Ozzie, Ray. "The Internet Services Disruption." Microsoft internal memorandum, October 28, 2005, http://www.scripting.com/disruption/ozzie/TheInternetServicesDisruptio.htm (accessed March 23, 2006).

Papert, Seymour. "Papert on Piaget." *Time*, March 29, 1999. http://www.papert.
org/articles/Papertonpiaget.html (accessed March 23, 2006).

Peguy, Charles. *Basic Verities*. New York: Pantheon, 1943, 1945.

Ricoeur, Paul. *Oneself as Another*. Chicago: University of Chicago Press, 1992.

Rogers, C. R. *Client-Centered Therapy*. Boston: Houghton Mifflin, 1951.

Rogers, C. R. "A Theory of Therapy, Personality and Interpersonal Relationships as
Developed in the Client-Centred Framework." In *Psychology: A Study of a Science*
(Vol. 3), edited by S. Koch: 184–256. New York: McGraw-Hill, 1959.

Sarnoff, David.In "The *Time* 100" by Marcy Carsey and Tom Werner, 2003. *Time*
Special Editions.

http://72.14.203.104/search?q=cache:m3aRm6O6D_wJ:www.time.com/time/
time100/builder/profile/sarnoff.html+%22It+is+with+a+feeling+of+humbleness+
that+I+come+to+this+moment+of+announcing+the+birth+in+this+country+of+
a+new+art+so+important+in+its+implications+that+it+is+bound+to+affect+all+
society.&hl=en&gl=ca&ct=clnk&cd=1&client=firefox-a (accessed March 23, 2006).

Schon, D. "Generative Metaphor: A Perspective on Problem Setting in Social
Policy." In *Metaphor and Thought*, edited by A. Ortony. Cambridge, UK: Cambridge
University Press, 1993.

Schultz, Howard. http://radio.weblogs.com/0104761/stories/2002/03/05/
sociabilityIsKing.html (accessed March 23, 2006).

"Shamans and Shamanism." http://faculty.gvsu.edu/websterm/Shamans.htm
(accessed March 23, 2006).

Stephenson Bond, D. *Living Myth: Personal Meaning as a Way of Life*. Boston:
Shambala Publications, 1993.

Sterling, Bruce. Lecture to ERA 2005, September 26, 2005. Copenhagen,
Denmark.

Taylor, Barbara. "The Nine Basic Human Needs." *Institute for Management
Excellence Online Newsletter*, 1997. http://www.itstime.com/jun97.htm (accessed
March 23, 2006).

Thomas, Nigel J. T. "Imagination, Mental Imagery, Consciousness, and Cognition:
Scientific, Philosophical and Historical Approaches," 2004.

http://www.calstatela.edu/faculty/nthomas/index.htm (accessed March 23, 2006).

Thomke, S. "Enlightened Experimentation: The New Imperative for Innovation."
*Harvard Business Review*, February 2001.

*The Usual Suspects*, film. Gramercy Pictures. Los Angeles: MGM Studios, 1995.

Vygotsky, Lev. *Mind in Society: The Development of Higher Psychological Processes*. Edited and translated by M. Cole, V. John-Steiner, S. Scribner, and E. Souberman. Cambridge, Massachusetts: Harvard University Press, 1978.

Wakkary, Ron, et al. "Ambient Intelligence Ecologies and Gameplay." Paper delivered at DiGRA 2005 Conference. Burnaby: Simon Fraser University.

Wenger, E. *Communities of Practice: Learning, Meaning and Identity*. Cambridge, UK: Cambridge University Press, 1998.

Wright, Ronald. *A Brief History of Progress*. New York: Avalon Publishing Group, 2004.

# Index

## A

accountability, measuring in play, 93–94
action research
    methods, 171
    strategic creativity and, 108
adults
    adult imagination compared with child imagination, 51–52
    extending kindergarten style learning to adults, 71
    grownups as contrast to, 65
    people as outputs in organizations, 59
    toys, 58
age demographics, tech saviness and, 192
AI (artificial intelligence), 5
Alexander, Franz, 83
altruism, points of departure and, 196
analytical ("left-brained") thinking, 170
Ansoff, Igor, 21, 105
answers. *see* questions/answers
Apple Computer, 95
archetypes
    defined, 164
    relationship with signals, 174
    sports, 164–165
    the trickster, 6–7
Arendt, Hannah, 152–154, 160
Aristotle, 49
*The Art of Play: Helping Adults Reclaim Imagination and Spontaneity* (Blatner and Blatner), 64
artifacts
    brain as the artifact for play, 80
    full behavior mode and, 104
artificial intelligence (AI), 5
avatar
    body as, 209
    chameleon effect and, 213
    expanded self-definition resulting form, 213
    intentional, 209
    Second Life and, 215–217
    in virtual world, 208

## B

ball, as archetypal toy, 164–165
Barber, Christopher, 165
Beal Institute, 168
Beal Theory of Signals, 106
becoming, experience and learning and, 152–153
behavior
    identifying latent behaviors and signals, 101
    motivation for change and, 25
    normal vs. deviant, 122
    play behavior, 84
    progression from tool to toy and, 82
    social ecology of, 102
behavior change, 192
behavior modes
    common manifest behavior mode, 102–103
    frames of inquiry and, 112–113
    full behavior mode, 104
being, experience and learning and, 152–153
Bell, Alexander Graham, 98
benchmarks, dynamics of possibility and, 94–95
Bennis, Warren, 242
Berners-Lee, Tim, 83, 132
Bionicle series, Legos, 45–46
Blatner, Adam, 64
Blatner, Allee, 64
blogs, as decentralized system, 75
Blount Jr., Roy, 32
body
    as avatar, 209
    beyond wearable devices, 190
bohique (shaman), 2
Bond, David, 59
brain, as the artifact for play, 80
brand management, 140
Burnett, Mark, 120
business intelligence
    structured data and, 126–128
    unstructured data and, 128

## C

Caillois, Roger, 80
cameras
    capturing the moment, 162–163
    digital cameras, 160
    values/uses of, 158–160
capital, strategic, 26
Castronova, Edward, 208